JOHN
gospel for a new age

LEONARD DOOHAN

WIPF & STOCK · Eugene, Oregon

Acknowledgements

I thank my wife, Helen, and my daughter, Eve-Anne, for their constant support. I also express my thanks to Ms. Karla Huffine for her help in preparing the manuscript.

Wipf and Stock Publishers
199 W 8th Ave, Suite 3
Eugene, OR 97401

John
A Daring Vision of Faith
By Doohan, Leonard
Copyright©1988 by Doohan, Leonard
ISBN 13: 978-1-5326-0657-1
Publication date 8/31/2016
Previously published by Bear & Company Publishing , 1988

SERIES PREFACE

This biblical theology and spirituality series is designed for personal and community enrichment. The series explores how Scripture's timeless message continues to inspire and motivate us in our contemporary lives. Scripture is the primary source of inspiration, edification, and challenge, an inspired vision of what discipleship can be, a measuring rod of authentic teachings and practices. This series' reflections on how Scripture can motivate us in the twenty-first century comprise a dialogue between the unchanging Word of God and the constantly changing situations of our times. It offers a call to new life.

The commentaries explore a biblical book's audience, purpose, key themes, understanding of church, sense of mission and ministry. The series can be used as the basis for personal study and enrichment, for parish adult education programs and Scripture study groups, for retreats, and for personal theological and spiritual renewal.

CONTENTS

Introduction
AN INDEPENDENT CHURCH'S VISION OF FAITH 1
    A different understanding of the good news . 1
    A local church's interpretation of faith 3
    Dedication to the essentials of religion 4
    Gospel for a new age 6

Chapter One
THE WORLD OF JOHN'S GOSPEL 9
The Beginnings of Christianity 10
    The Jesus of history 10
    Jesus of faith 12
The Jewish Roots of Christianity 14
    Judaism 14
    The religious parties of Judaism 16
Hellenistic Setting of Early Christianity .. 19
    The Hellenistic world 19
    The diaspora Jews 21
History of Early Christianity 23
    Missionary expansion 23
    The organization of the early Church 24
The Setting of John's Gospel 26
    Influences on John's expression of faith 26
    Membership of John's community 28
    The history of John's community 30
    Location of John's community 31

Chapter Two
THE AUTHOR OF THE FOURTH GOSPEL 33
John in Tradition 34
    Some unique features of the Fourth Gospel . 34
    Early testimonies concerning the author ... 35
    The Beloved Disciple 37
    John the evangelist 39
John the Author 41
    The Fourth Gospel's style 41
    Some specific stylistic features 42
    Symbolism in the Fourth Gospel 44
    His readers 45
John and the Synoptics 46
    The tradition behind John 46
    John's sources 47
    John's relationship to the Synoptics 49
    The redaction of John 50
The Johannine School 52
    A community tradition 52
    Other Johannine writings 53
    A regional church 54

Chapter Three
PROCLAMATION FOR A NEW AGE 57
John's Understanding of History 58
    A new age made known in history 58
    John's concept of history 60
    Reinterpretation of tradition 62
Eschatology in the Fourth Gospel 63
    Eschatology 63
    Realized eschatology 64
    Judgment 66
Dualistic Concepts 67
    Light or darkness 68
    Truth or falsehood 69
    The other world or this world 70
    Spirit or flesh 71

Vision of a New Age 72
   The Prologue 72
   The Baptist's testimony 74
   A new order replaces the old 75
   John: evangelist and interpreter 76

Chapter Four
THE PURPOSE OF JOHN 79

Aims of the Fourth Evangelist 80
   Influences on the purpose of John 80
   Recent studies of John's gospel 81
   Pastoral concerns and interests 83
   Structure of John 84

The Gift of Life 88
   Life in Christ 88
   Conditions for receiving life 90
   Fullness of life 91

The Signs 93
   Nature of Johannine signs 93
   Structure and number of the signs 95
   Teaching of the signs 97

The Discourses 99
   John's use of the discourses 99
   The teachings of the discourses 100

Chapter Five
PORTRAITS OF GOD 105

The Father 105
   "The Father possesses life in himself" 105
   God's love for the world 107
   The Father and Jesus 108

Jesus 110
   "We saw his glory" 111
      The preexistent Lord 111
      The Word 113
      The Son 114
      Savior of the world 116

"The Word became Flesh" 119
    The ministry 119
    The Last Supper 121
    The Passion 122
    The Resurrection 125
The Holy Spirit 127
    "God ... does not ration his gift of the Spirit." 127
    The Paraclete 128

Chapter Six
DISCIPLESHIP IN JOHN 131
Nature of Discipleship in John 132
    Disciples are Jesus' own 132
    Discipleship — a transforming gift 133
    Active responses 134
    Abide in me 135
Disciples in John 136
    The first disciples 136
    Other models of discipleship 138
    Women disciples in John 139
Rejection of the Sinful World 140
    "Do you also want to leave?" 140
    Prove the world wrong about sin 142
Commitment to Believe 144
    Journeys to faith 144
    Nature of belief in John 147
Life in God 150
    Love of God 150
    Love of others 151

Chapter Seven
CHURCH IN JOHN 155
Nature of the Church in John 156
    Church in the Fourth Gospel 156
    Models of Church in John 158

Living as Church 161
    A sharing Church 161
    Baptism 162
    Eucharist 164
    Other Johannine rituals 165
Authority in the Church 166
    Ministerial leadership 166
    Institutionalized authority 167
    Mary the mother of Jesus 170
Mission in John's Community 171
    Mission and ministry 171
    Witnessing 172
    Building unity 174

A CONCLUDING WORD FROM THE JOHANNINE JESUS 177

    Notes 179
    Bibliography 193
    Index of Subjects 199
    Index of Authors 205
    Index of Scripture References 207

Introduction
AN INDEPENDENT CHURCH'S VISION OF FAITH

A different understanding of the good news. The Fourth Gospel is different from other New Testament writings. As a foundational document for Christian faith, it is both challenging and refreshing: challenging insofar as it calls to a mature faith, and refreshing insofar as it avoids the clutter of petty laws and power struggles so typical of inauthentic religion. The modern reader of the Synoptics is often distracted, knowing that several episodes and passages are used and abused, in season and out of season, by politically minded religious administrators to support their interpretations of faith or to justify their unwillingness to share the power they have come to love. John offers such insecure ministers little help in their venture. Although John appears only a few years later than the Synoptics, he presents a different tradition, one that focuses on the essentials of faith and one that shows how his community learns through its own pain to distance itself from the all-too-human aspects of organized religion.

The gospel draws its readers into a lyrical, frequently poetical, but very moving confession of faith. The portrait of Christ is awesome and commanding, but at the same time warm and loving. While not neglecting the humanity of Jesus, the Fourth Gospel emphasizes the preexistence and present glory of the Lord. Insight into who Jesus is, and faithful commitment to remain dedicated to him in obedience and love, are the challenges of every page of this proclamation. In fact, John's good news, particularly his christology, and his understanding of the nature of the Church, morality, discipleship, mission, and ministry, all flow from his faith in Jesus. The Synoptics give us descriptions of the people Jesus met; the Fourth Gospel simply tells us of the Jesus people met.

The Fourth Gospel gives the impression that it comes from the fruits of reflection and deep prayer; it can hardly be appreciated without a mystical recollection; and it provokes a sense of union between readers and their Lord. Yet it is not an example of religious escapism into a devotionalism unconnected with the real problems of struggling humanity.

We begin our study of the Fourth Gospel by considering the world of John. This gospel makes a remarkable contribution to the beginnings of Christianity in its faith-filled appreciation of Jesus the Lord, coming at a turning point in Christianity's development, and establishing the future direction of all the Church. The gospel, rooted in Judaism, presents the challenge of faith to the Hellenistic world. John's community is unique in early Christian history partly because of influences upon it and partly because of its diverse membership.

This unique contribution to early Christianity claims to be the vision of the Beloved Disciple. Chapter 2 examines the author, his style and use of symbolism, and the ways he challenges his readers. The tradition at the source of this gospel is independent of the Synoptics, and may well come from a school of thought that influences churches within a large region.

The Fourth Gospel presents the arrival of a new age in Jesus and interprets his teachings for believers in changing times (Chapter 3). This new age is the beginning of the final times and already evidences the universal judgment of humankind, dividing people into the world of Christ that is truth, light, spirit, and life, and the dark, false, shadowy existence of the evil prince of this world.

John stresses how authentic religion leads to enrichment and fullness of life. He states this purpose explicitly and also through Jesus' signs and discourses (Chapter 4).

Chapter 5 shows how John's portraits of God center on Jesus. The Father loves the world and offers it life through Jesus. The Holy Spirit is sent by Jesus to continue Jesus' work and to make his teaching present again in ever new ways. Jesus is preexistent Lord, the Word and Son of God, the Savior of the World, and the Son of Man. Throughout his life and ministry, Jesus is always shown as the exalted Lord in control of all the events, the center of the gospel, of the disciples' lives, and of world history.

Discipleship flows from one's vision of Jesus (Chapter 6). Disciples of Jesus are his own friends whose active response to the Lord's call produces a transformation of life that is preserved by abiding in Jesus in faith and love. This commitment has communal implications in building up the community in love through sharing life within the community and reaching out to witness to the world concerning the love of God (Chapter 7).

A local church's interpretation of faith. When John wrote his gospel, there were already signs of a uniform approach to Christianity. The decrees of the Council of Jerusalem, and Paul's claims to authority over several churches, were the beginnings of common impositions on churches with different foundational experiences. John's church preserved patterns of belief and practice which are quite different from the churches founded by the Twelve and their disciples, based upon the Synoptics and their tradition. The universal Church seems to have been reluctant to accept the Fourth Gospel as an authentic formulation of faith. In fact, John's vision of Christianity receives its initial support from heretical groups, a reaction that John will struggle to put behind him. The Johannine community develops in a parallel way to the Great Mother Church and finds little reason to establish unity with it until after the death of the Beloved Disciple. By that time the Johannine communities have their own religious emphases: a portrait of Christ as preexistent Lord, a view of discipleship as abiding in Jesus, and a reluctance towards accepting institutionalized aspects of religion. Their traditions contained little reference to structures, discipline, or ethics. Yet they were convinced that their interpretation was valid, traceable to a Beloved Disciple, and a vision from which the rest of the Church could learn. When the occasion and need for unity with the rest of the Church came, the Johannine community sacrificed some of its interpretations but kept most, enriching the universal Church with its vision.

For about four decades, John's community had struggled

to formulate its understanding of faith so as to give room to a variety of groups. The theological vision that emerged was eventually accepted by the universal Church, even though the Great Church absorbed the Johannine community into its own structures. John's gospel remains as a warning to anyone who would like to stamp out different interpretations of our common faith. Authoritarian imposition of uniform interpretations of faith damages the Church's ability to grow and limits the maturing of faith, as well as showing the immaturity of those who need it for their own comfort and security. Only totalitarian regimes see uniformity and the stunting of creativity as desirable. Faith can never be authentic when imposed, nor does it grow as a result of authorities' control and imposition. In the 1980s, several Christian groups and churches have demonstrated an immature authoritarian approach to faith, thus damaging the credibility of Christianity as a movement that leads to integral growth. John's formulation of faith challenged the world Church by being different while insisting that its interpretation was valid. So, too, contemporary regional and local churches throughout the world should learn from John to preserve their own approaches and to enrich the Church with their differences. When local churches run in the company of Peter, they may well arrive at vision before him; and although they respectfully let him enter first, they may well be more mature in their faith than Peter (20:3-8).

The growth of contemporary Christianity does not take place at the level of the universal Church but at the level of the local church. Vision and growth do not filter down to the people, but percolate up. John's spirit of independence within ecclesial union is an excellent model for local churches in the 1980s and 1990s.

Dedication to the essentials of religion. John's gospel has no lists of laws, no detailed handbook on discipleship, no recommended attitudes for vigilantly awaiting the end, no emphasis on discipline, no focus on ethics. He gives no church structure and does not refer to human channels of authority; in fact he excludes even a list of the Twelve.

Present-day religion in America and elsewhere seems overconcerned with structures, authority, power, and money.

INTRODUCTION

It shows arrogant, exclusive claims to orthodoxy for one minority or another's interpretation of faith; treats opposition with spite and nastiness; has not addressed the rectification of organized injustice against women; and will not change laws that could be changed. Many outspoken "religious" statements are on issues that were present in Jesus' life but which he never chose to address.

John challenges the quality of religious commitment. There is no clutter of laws, power, and money, such as we see in much contemporary religion. He calls for a faith that is unflinching, as he draws out the implications of early Christian beliefs and firmly expresses the absolute centrality of the preexistent Lord. This gospel challenges disciples to believe in Jesus and his teachings, and to convincingly confess that he is the center of history, their God, their all.

The Johannine Jesus, while rejecting the powerful centers of religion of his day, calls all to worship in spirit and in truth. Disciples find that John removes the comfortable supports of traditional religious practices, community devotions, priestly guidance, and moral and ritual legalism. He calls for an abiding union with Jesus, convinced that all other issues will take care of themselves.

John's only command to prove one's dedication is love of God and love of neighbor. This love is a participation in the life and love of God. Given the differences among members of his community, John might well have given in to prescriptive religion and established laws and directives for community discipline and uniformity. Instead he chose to stress love, without which the laws serve little purpose except to give power to the law-givers.

John, convinced that authentic religion is a way of seeing the world, presents an integrated approach to life that leads to growth. The believer lives in truth, knows the light of life, wants to see the true way, is nourished by the vision of Jesus, and satisfies a thirst for answers to life's problems. The genuine believer is willing to go public with faith, to take risks, and to pay the price of convictions.

Authentic religion is not sexist. John presents women in key roles of faith and witness. Men are as dependent on women as sources of testimony as women are on men. No authority is based on sex; men do nothing women do not do. John's presentation avoids the early exclusion of women, a trend that itself postdates Christ, rationalizing inauthentic expressions of religion up to our own day.

Gospel for a new age. Amidst all the problems of contemporary religion, some churches are facing up to their deficiencies and strengthening their vision. Men and women are abandoning expressions of religion that fall short of their human hopes. In some cases, they leave pastors who are out-of-date with their church and world, going across town to another parish. In other cases, people change a religious tradition their family may have held for generations. People who yearn for God and authentic forms of religious living now find some of their hopes satisfied as they integrate religion with their deep loves and hopes of life.

Many well-educated Christians, dedicated to their families and country, value freedom and independence as they direct their lives to God. Expecting religion to be relevant to themselves, and not an imported commodity parallel to their national, cultural, and family values, they carefully examine past experiences, knowing many of them are good and play a meaningful part in the religious direction of their lives.

John's different gospel holds particular appeal in our changing times. A maverick, he holds firm to his independent expression of Christianity and gives little value to many expressions of religion in which our contemporaries also see little worth. John sees unity with the Mother Church as a value, but also knows other churches can learn from his community's expressions of faith. A universal vision of Church is built up from the contributions of local churches; it does not filter down from high in the structures.

Churches, such as the Roman Catholic Church, are experiencing a decrease in vocations to the institutionalized priesthood, but an increase in vocations to ministry among the laity, as rank and file members respond to God's call to service of others. As the latter take over many positions of ministry, we see new images of Church developing, and John's discipleship model again gives encouragement, direction, and hope.

The goods news of Jesus was expressed in varied ways by the different communities of the four evangelists; sometimes one, and sometimes another, seem to call and challenge us with increased relevance. John's daring expression of faith is particularly special as the following pages will show.

Chapter One
THE WORLD OF JOHN'S GOSPEL

*The true light, which enlightens everyone,
was coming into the world. He was in the world,
the world came to be through him, but
the world did not know him. (Jn 1:9-10)*

The Fourth Gospel presents the extraordinary dedication of a community whose faith had taken on different formulations than other Christian communities. Differing notably from Matthew, Mark, and Luke, John's bold proclamation is shaped by conflict with several Jewish groups, by hostility from the surrounding world, and by tension with the developing Mother Church of Christianity. John's distinctive form of Christian belief and practice survives alongside that of the Synoptics and eventually enriches the maturing faith of the expanding Church.

Better than any other New Testament work, John's gospel demonstrates the importance of a local, independent expression of faith and how that faith can grow through dedicated struggle. It shows a community's successful integration of sub-groups and potential opponents while avoiding a superficial religious eclecticism. It portrays courageous independence without allowing itself to become exclusive or sectarian. Admittedly, the community has weaknesses, some of which grow into serious heresies. Nevertheless, its creative struggle enriches Christianity in the first century, as it continues to do now. Its painful efforts to gain recognition from the wider community of Christians resemble the struggles of contemporary Christian churches whose expression of faith is conditioned by regional values and culture.

John's gospel makes unyielding claim to be based on the testimony of an early eyewitness of Jesus' life, deeds, and teachings, even insisting that this trustworthy account comes from a disciple who was more faithful to Jesus than the founders of the early mainline churches. Although claiming to be rooted in history, John's is the gospel that, more than any other, portrays the Jesus of faith in its high christology.

Although strongly influenced by Judaism, John's gospel probably was not written in Palestine. John's community, part of a large cosmopolitan city, experienced most of the social and religious challenges of first-century Christianity. This community interacted with the followers of John the Baptist; was aware of issues important to the various Jewish religious groups, such as the Essenes and the Pharisees; dialogued with the Samaritans; and was sensitive to the religious values and convictions of the Hellenistic world.

John's gospel brings an interesting perspective to the history of the missionary expansion of the Christian movement, its search for unity and orthodoxy, and its struggle with persecution. Since John's community exemplifies growth patterns, structures, creed, and discipleship different from other churches, it helps us appreciate the pluralism of early Christianity. Since John's gospel is the expression of a community that is molded, challenged, and oppressed by its environment, this first chapter focuses on the world of John's gospel.

The Beginnings of Christianity

The Jesus of history. Around the year 27 CE, during a period of religious revival, the prophet John the Baptist preached repentance and baptized the converted. He preached along the river Jordan, the location of other renewal movements besides his own, and the gospels attest that John baptized Jesus (Mk 1:9; Mt 3:13). Shortly after this encounter, Jesus began his own ministry which lasted between one and three years, depending on the evangelists' varied presentations. According to John, the early ministry of Jesus coincided with the forty-sixth year of the rebuilding of the Temple, which would be 27 or 28 CE (Jn 2:20).

Jesus was a Galilean, and his early ministry began in the open-minded northern regions of the country. Jesus, who was in his thirties when he began his work (Lk 3:23), spoke Aramaic, as did his disciples, although Greek was also spoken in several of the places he visited. The Jewish historian Josephus and several rabbis, in addition to his own followers, affirm that Jesus exorcised demons and healed the sick, practices also known among other charismatic figures of the times. His teaching, often presented in parables, stressed the coming of God's reign and probably implied that the end of the world would be coming soon. Crowds appreciated his teaching and respectfully addressed Jesus as "rabbi." He was bold in challenging Jewish leaders' interpretations of the Law and gained a reputation for breaking the Law by his Sabbath healings and his attitudes to ritual prescriptions and rabbinical practices. A non-conformist, Jesus gained a substantial following among the masses, and this did not endear him to religious authorities who checked on his orthodoxy even when he preached in Galilee (Mk 2:24; 3:22).

Probably sometime in the year 30 CE, Jesus made his final journey to Jerusalem. The Jewish religious authorities clearly wanted to be rid of him, and the betrayal of Jesus by one of his own close followers provided them with an opportunity. Jesus, who consistently preached about the reign of God and spoke about it as an end-time banquet, celebrated a special meal with his disciples the evening before his arrest. After the meal he went with his disciples to Gethsemane, a garden on the lower slopes of the Mount of Olives where, no doubt, they intended to spend the night sleeping in the open, planning to return to the city the next day for the national feast. However, Jesus was taken prisoner. He was interrogated by the High Priest, Caiaphas, son-in-law of the religious power broker and real authority, Annas; was questioned by Herod Antipas, the ruler of Galilee, who was visiting Jerusalem at the time of the Passover feast; and was eventually tried and condemned by the Roman procurator, Pontius Pilate. Since Jesus was not stoned to death, the penalty for blasphemy, there can be no reason to doubt that he was executed by the Romans for political reasons; the charges may have been trumped-up and misrepresented by some of the High Priest's court and supporters. Jesus' crucifixion occurred around 30 CE.

The Jewish historian, Flavius Josephus (37-100? CE) who had collaborated with the Romans when they invaded Palestine in 67-70 CE, offers limited information about Jesus' ministry, his miracle-working activity, and his passion. In *Antiquities of the Jews*, he refers to Jesus by name and gives a brief description of his ministry.[1]

Interpretations of the Law by authoritative rabbis of the first and second centuries CE are collected in the Mishnah. One of these rabbis, Eliezer, a disciple of Rabbi Johanan ben Zakkai — the founder of the Jamnian school, and a contemporary of Jesus — speaks slightingly of Jesus in a passage that implies Jesus' miraculous activity, and suggests something unusual about his birth. The same rabbi Eliezer was later arrested and falsely accused of holding Christian beliefs. His trial scene documents the historical fact of Jesus' life and ministry, the support Christianity received in Galilee, and the Jews' desire to stamp out the teachings of Jesus. While Jewish sources give no new information about Jesus and are generally polemical, they confirm the success of his healing and teaching ministry, his challenge to authorities, and his crucifixion.[2]

For believers and non-believers alike, Jesus is one of the greatest figures of history. Yet his public life lasted at the most three years, and little is known of the precise events. Nothing is known of his early life. Since the prophets foretold the Messiah's davidic ancestry, early Christians presumed Jesus was born in David's city of Bethlehem. The date of his birth is unknown and is arrived at by calculating backwards for thirty years (Lk 3:23), giving an approximate date of 5-6 BCE.[3] The traditional date of December 25th is a Christian adaptation of the birthday of the Sun, following the winter solstice which occurs about December 21st.

Jesus of faith. Paul's first letter to the Corinthians, written in the early 50s CE, affirms that Jesus "was raised on the third day in accordance with the scriptures" (1 Cor 15:4). A little later, in his letter to the Romans, he claims that Jesus was "established as Son of God in power according to the spirit of holiness, through resurrection from the dead" (Rm 1:4). In the same letter he proclaims: "We know that Christ, raised from the dead, dies no more; death no longer has power over him" (Rm 6:9). Elsewhere he states that "if Christ has not been raised, then empty [too] is our preaching; empty, too, your faith" (1 Cor 15:14). All these Pauline credal statements come from the 50s and are based on earlier formulations from missionary preaching.

Luke's Acts of the Apostles, written between 85 and 95 CE, again tells us "God raised him [Jesus] from the dead; of this we are his witnesses" (Acts 3:15; 4:10). "God raised this Jesus; of this we are all witnesses. ... Therefore let the whole house of Israel know for certain that God has made him both Lord and Messiah, this Jesus whom you crucified" (Acts 2:32, 36). Peter tells the Gentile Cornelius about Jesus' resurrection: "This man God raised [on] the third day and granted that he be visible, not to all the people, but to us, the witnesses chosen by God in advance, who ate and drank with him after he rose from the dead. He commissioned us to preach to the people and testify that he is the one appointed by God as judge of the living and the dead. To him all the prophets bear witness, that everyone who believes in him will receive forgiveness of sins through his name" (Acts 10: 40-43).

Like all religions, Christianity begins in the middle of the founder's life when people, moved by his charismatic qualities or by the purity of his teaching, become aware of the leader's salvific power and dedicate themselves as followers. This communal intuition that the leader can save them from life's sin is the central experience that gives birth to faith which when shared becomes a religion. For Christians, this central communal religious experience is the resurrection. The followers know only a little of their founder's recent life, and they now move forward as disciples to spread the message. As they move forward in time to express their faith through missionary expansion, they also move backwards in time expressing their faith through the reconstruction of their founder's unknown earlier life. Luke does this, telling us about Jesus when he was twelve years old (Lk 2:41-52), and both Matthew and Luke give us the narratives of the birth of Jesus and even events surrounding his conception. As disciples enthusiastically dedicate their lives to the Lord, new questions arise about the founder, the source of his power, his relationship to the Father, and his own nature.

Since very little is known of Jesus before his appearance along the river Jordan, the answers to disciples' questions are expressions of faith more than historical information. Thus the infancy narratives of Matthew tell us what the Old Testament expected the Messiah to be, more than what Jesus' early life was like. Luke's infancy narratives are more a pre-ministry understanding of who Jesus will later be recognized as rather than who he was.

John's gospel was composed later than other gospels, even though possibly based on earlier traditions. Although further away from actual historical events, the evangelist makes claims that his knowledge of the Jesus of history is completely reliable. At the same time, this gospel presents the Jesus of faith in a more profound and conclusive way than any other New Testament writing. John draws out the implications of earlier traditions and in doing so stands apart from the Synoptics in his higher christology. His message is profound but easily exploited by heretics. The Mother Church will integrate the insights and benefit from them but will also have to warn against exaggerations and confront heretical deviations.

The Jewish Roots of Christianity

Judaism. John's gospel presumes knowledge of Judaism: its history, religion, sects, feasts, and laws. The Jews traced their ancestry to Abraham, a semi-nomad from upper-Mesopotamia, who migrated to the land of Canaan in the early part of the second millenium (c. 1800 BCE). Abraham's descendants, Isaac and Jacob, lived in the hill country of Canaan until a famine drove the sons of Jacob, the twelve patriarchs, to migrate to Egypt in search of food. The Hebrews remained in "the land of Goshen," a fertile area in the east of the Nile delta, first welcomed, then enslaved, until early in the reign of Pharaoh Ramases II (c. 1290-1224 BCE). Ramases' father, Seti I, moved his capital city from Thebes to Avaris and enslaved the Hebrews to construct the cities of Avaris, later renamed Ramases, and Pithom, which was in the heart of the region where the patriarchs had settled.

A Hebrew leader arose called Moses, who is unknown outside the Bible. His name is Egyptian and thus the Bible's suggestion that he was brought up in the court of the Pharaoh could well be authentic. He identified strongly with the Hebrews and, after a religious experience of the God of his people, he confidently dedicated himself to serve this God, Yahweh, who claimed to have watched over his people's history and to have plans for their future. Under Moses' leadership, the Israelites left the slavery of Egypt and journeyed to Sinai. There they established a treaty or covenant with Yahweh, who had saved them and made them into his nation. Around 1220 BCE to 1200 BCE, the semi-nomadic Israelites began the conquest of Canaan, which was a slow and complicated undertaking. The tribal system took shape, and some groups already inhabiting Canaan were incorporated into the confederation at a ceremony in Shechem. Tribal warlords, called judges, led specific campaigns in times of crisis, but individual tribes still retained local government. Early attempts to centralize government failed, but Samuel, the last of the judges and the first of the prophets, set up a unified kingdom, first under Saul, then eventually under David. During the reigns of David, the ideal king (c. 1000-970 BCE), and his successor, Solomon (c. 970-931 BCE), literature and culture flourished in their courts, and the great religious epics which form the early part of the Hebrew Bible were written, giving religious explanations of the origin of their nation and faith.

After the death of Solomon, national unity ended and the kingdom was divided between the northern kingdom of Israel (922-721 BCE) and the southern kingdom of Judah (922-586 BCE). The Assyrian Empire, centered in Nineveh, which frequently threatened the northern kingdom, fell in 612 BCE. The Babylonian Empire conquered Jerusalem in 587 BCE, and the nation's leaders were taken into exile (587-538 BCE). When Cyrus the Persian conquered Babylon in 539 BCE, the Jews were allowed to return to their homeland, rebuilding their nation and temple (520-515 BCE). A period of political and religious reforms followed under the direction of Nehemiah and Ezra which lasted until about 400 BCE.

Little is known of the history of the nation in the period immediately following Ezra. Alexander the Great conquered the Persians in 333 BCE, and Palestine fell under his control. Ten years later, at the age of 33, Alexander died in Babylon. After seven years of struggle, his empire was divided among his generals, Seleucus (Syria), Ptolomey (Egypt), and Cassandra (Macedonia).

The Ptolomies ruled Palestine until 198 BCE, when Antiochus III (223-187 BCE) annexed it to his Seleucid Empire, but his expansionist policies left the empire in disarray. Seleucus IV (187-175 BCE) was eventually succeeded by Antiochus IV Epiphanes (175-163 BCE), who tried to hellenize Judea and destroy its religion. When he imposed the worship of Zeus, Mattatias, a priest of Modein, a village northwest of Jerusalem, opposed him. His family under the leadership of his son, Judas Maccabeus, began a guerrilla war and won a surprising victory against Antiochus IV, rededicating the Temple in 165 BCE. The Maccabean resistance assured a century of independence until successors of the Maccabees, the Hasmonean dynasty, fought among themselves. The Roman general, Pompey, intervened and after a three-month siege took Jerusalem in 63 BCE. Rome then governed the entire region from Syria. For the next 35 years, fighting between Pompey and Caesar influenced Palestine, whose leaders changed sides as they felt it appropriate. In 37 BCE, Antigonus, the last of the Hasmoneans, was beheaded in Antioch at the request of Herod, who then ruled Palestine until 4 BCE. At his death, Rome divided his kingdom between his sons, but Archelaus, who governed Judea, was exiled to Gaul in 6 CE. Rome then governed directly through procurators until 66 CE, except for the brief reign of Agrippa I (41-44 CE). Open rebellion against Rome began in 66 CE, lasting until the destruction of Jerusalem in 70 CE. There were pockets of resistance in the years that followed, with the final attack on Masada in 73 or 74 CE. Thus we come to the end of an era.[4]

The religious parties of Judaism. Several religious parties existed within first-century Judaism, all responses to attempts to hellenize the Jews, and each played a significant role in the ministry of Jesus or the life of the Johannine community.[5]

The *Sadduccees* were a conservative, priestly aristocracy, who considered the high priesthood, the Temple, and ritual worship the central religious values of Judaism. They were mentioned for the first time during the reign of John Hyrcanus (135-104 BCE), when they supported this king's decision to be high priest. Although their name is traceable to Zadok (1 Kings 2:35) and suggests interest in legitimate priestly succession, they tended to give their support based on what was politically appropriate rather than what was religiously legitimate. Sadduccees accepted only the first five books of the Bible, thus valuing its stress on priesthood and ritual and rejecting later teachings, such as belief in the resurrection, with which the Pentateuch did not explicitly deal. They were fundamentalist, both in their use of scripture and in their approach to ritual. They showed little interest in the religious needs of the people and totally ignored the dispersion Jews. They showed little concern for Jesus until his teaching threatened their status quo, at which time they were willing to have an innocent man put to death rather than risk loss of their own position and suffer Roman intervention (11:48).

During their exile in Babylon, the Jews became accustomed to the loss of the Temple and its rituals, and instead focused their piety on the Law. Even though the restoration under Ezra renewed the priestly hierarchy and its teaching authority together with the Temple, fidelity to the Law became the principal element in post-exilic Jewish life. During the Maccabean resistance the hasidim, or pious ones, formed an assembly of loyalists to the covenant and the Law, and it is out of this group that most contemporary scholars believe the *Pharisees* emerged. The Pharisees were liberal laity, rigorously dedicated to the Law. They accepted oral tradition and eventually all the books of the Hebrew Bible. During Jesus' ministry the Pharisees evaluated his orthodoxy, questioned his interpretations of the Law, and condemned his disciples' lax observance and his disregard of Sabbath restrictions.

The Pharisees offered a detailed program of life to all faithful Jews, eventually developing a plethora of secondary restrictions to safeguard fidelity to God's Law. Although Jesus criticized their obsession with the "traditions of the elders," many Pharisees mutually supported each other's fidelity but contrasted themselves with those who were not so meticulous (9:24-34), even referring to them deprecatingly as "the people of the land." Originally a movement highly respected by the people, Pharisaism separated itself from the people, thereby losing some of its support.

In the time of Jesus, the Pharisee party, consisting of over 25,000 members and associates, was the most influential group. After the fall of Jerusalem and the disappearance of the Sadduccees, the Pharisees consolidated their control and established their center in the rabbinical school of Jamnia. Under the leadership of Rabbi Johann ben Zakkai, Jamnian Pharisaism challenged early Christianity and set the stage for a period of open confrontation. John's gospel reflects the post-Jamnian period when the Pharisees were in charge.

In 152 BCE, Jonathan, who had succeeded his brother Judas in 160, was proclaimed high priest by the Seleucid pretender, Alexander Balas. Although a Levite, Jonathan was not of aaronic descent, as established in the genealogy of Zadok, and is considered by some to be the wicked priest of the *Essenes'* documents found at Qumran in 1947. The actual high priest who was expelled to make way for Jonathan is considered to be the Teacher of Righteousness, who gathered together some Essenes and founded a community at Qumran. Prior to their organization at Qumran and other towns along the Dead Sea, the Essenes, whose name is a Greek form of "hasidim," had chosen to withdraw from society rather than obey an unacceptable high priest. When the Teacher of Righteousness organized this amorphous group of ascetics, not all of them joined his community, and these rebels were seen as traitors and their leader as "the man of lies."[6]

Documents discovered at Qumran describe the Essenes as dedicated to prayer, asceticism, and study. They practiced celibacy, poverty, and rigorous community discipline, as they awaited the apocalyptic end of the world. Some commentators see connections between John the Baptist and the Essene community and suggest parallels between their teachings and those of the fourth evangelist. The center at Qumran was destroyed in 68 CE, and the remaining Essenes were wiped out by the Romans in the early 70s.

The Essenes are never explicitly mentioned in the gospels, but the *Zealots* are. This latter group was composed of patriotic fighters who again traced their remote origins to the armed resistance at the time of the Hasmoneans, but more proximately were likely to have been a radical group within the Pharisees who came to the fore around 6 CE with Judas the Galilean, who uncompromisingly rejected Roman presence. His revolutionary movement, a holy war, ended in disunity at the time of the attack on Jerusalem. A few escaped to Masada where they resisted until 74 CE.

In 722 BCE the Assyrian king, Sargon, defeated the northern kingdom. He exiled a good number of the inhabitants, and his successors sent foreigners to colonize the region. Although the *Samaritans* claimed ancestry from Ephraim and Manasseh, the Jews considered them heretical schismatics of mixed descent. The Samaritans opposed the reforms of Nehemiah and Ezra, and the break between Jews and Samaritans was complete when the latter built their own temple to Yahweh on Mount Gerizim. During the Maccabean Wars, the Samaritans sided with the Seleucids and in 128 BCE John Hyrcanus destroyed their temple.

Samaritans are mentioned in the ministry of Jesus, and John's gospel and the Acts of the Apostles refer to Christianity's spread among the Samaritans. They accepted only the Pentateuch, believed that the true temple was on Mount Gerizim, and that a great prophet would come at the end as Taheb, or Restorer, of the centrality of Mount Gerizim.

Hellenistic Setting of Early Christianity

The Hellenistic world. Alexander succeeded his father, Philip of Macedon, in 334 BCE, and two years later he set out to conquer the Persian Empire which had been threatening Greece for years. His military conquests were remarkable, as he pushed his empire to the borders of India, but far more significant was his cultural impact. A student of the philosopher Aristotle, Alexander the Great established a common language and civilization in the world he conquered. A mixture of Greek and Oriental features, this Hellenistic civilization survived even as Alexander's divided empire successively fell to Rome: Macedonia in 146 BCE, Syria in 64 BCE, and Egypt in 30 BCE.

Alexander gave the Mediterranean world language, culture, and civilization, but Rome gave it political stability, common government, favorable transportation, and nearly two hundred years of "the peace of Rome" (*Pax Romana*). From Octavian's rise to power in 27 BCE to the death of Marcus Aurelius in 180 CE, Rome maintained reasonably favorable conditions for the expansion of Christianity. There were periods of local and imperial persecution, but in general the new religion benefitted from the protection of Rome. Life in the empire depended on one's social class. Wealth was in the hands of a few who maintained their standard of living with large numbers of slaves.

Greek religion saw the gods and goddesses as the embodiment of social and political values: order, love, justice, and beauty. Prior to expansion and conquest Roman religion was based in the family, with national celebrations extending this sense of religious unity. As the empire grew, national deities of conquered lands were seen as the same Roman gods with different names or were drawn into the ever-growing pantheon.

This ever-increasing number of deities, together with some of the exaggerated myths that tried to justify belief, led people to begin looking in other directions for answers to the problems of life. Some chose the rationalistic approaches of philosophy, while the less educated, feeling helpless before the uncontrollable forces of Fate, tried to anticipate the future through astrology or placate Fate through magic.

Both religious philosophies and popular attempts to control Fate proved inadequate responses to the skepticism provoked by the breakdown of belief in the Roman pantheon. Both philosophy and magic distanced the people from religious experiences for which they yearned. Many filled this need by participation in the mystery religions that claimed to offer access to the secrets of life. Through re-enactment of religious dramas, the devotees believed they shared in the life of the gods, received the pledge of immortality, and found support in the community of believers.[7]

Alexander offered the world a common culture, and Augustus offered a common political system. Philosophies offered supportive moral standards to their world views, but variety again led to eclecticism and decline. The popular mystery religions, some of which lasted into the third and fourth centuries CE, assured salvation to those who participated in the rituals, but offered neither challenges to change their lives, nor directions for moral living. Thus, they too gave no adequate response to human life and its yearnings.

The two hundred years before the birth of Jesus Christ were years of profound and at times restless human search. Efforts to establish a common culture, language, and political system were painful but successful. Four centuries of war and peace, in which generals and emperors had been called "savior," "redeemer," and "bringer of peace," bore fruit in regional stability. Hellenism made common ideas accessible through the same imperial language. The struggles of philosophy and religion exemplified the people's yearning for a vision of life and an experience of the mystery beyond them. At Jesus Christ's birth the world was ready for his message of hope, peace, community, moral integrity, and encounter with God.

The diaspora Jews. From the time of Alexander and the succeeding Seleucid kings, Palestine was greatly affected by Hellenism, although reluctant to accept it. Jews outside of Palestine, however, had integrated Hellenistic values into their cultural and religious view of life, leading to new approaches and interpretations of traditional faith. Conquests by Assyria and Babylon led to the exile of Jews, who eventually established their families in the cities of their exile. Other Jews had taken up residence in Egypt to escape famine or war. In the first century CE there were over a million Jews in each of three regions: in Mesopotamia, especially in Babylon; in Egypt, especially in Alexandria; and in Asia Minor. About a hundred thousand lived in Italy, especially in Rome, and in Northern Africa, especially in Cyrene, and many others were scattered throughout the Mediterranean world. The dispersion reached such proportions that twice as many Jews lived outside of Palestine as lived within their homeland.

Dispersion Jews spoke Greek, and their scriptures were read in Greek and interpreted in terms of Hellenistic philosophy and religious devotion. Synagogues provided a focal point for public worship and Jewish identity. After 70 CE, the Academy of Jamnia became the main influence on the interpretation of the Law. Scholars trained there emigrated and became guides for communities in the dispersion. Other academies were established in Rome and Babylon, the latter becoming the major center of Jewish scholarship by 200 CE. It was difficult to maintain the purity of Palestinian Judaism's interpretation of the Law. Philo of Alexandria, a contemporary of Jesus, is an example of a Jewish leader who was both dedicated to the Law and appreciative of its universal application through its integration with Greek philosophy.

Many Jews were given rights of citzenship in cities like Alexandria and Antioch, but these privileges were not extended to all. Emperors such as Claudius (c. 41 CE), affirmed the Jews' rights to religious freedom and accepted their quasi-autonomous organizations within cities of the empire. From time to time anti-Jewish sentiment flared up, as it did in Alexandria in 38 CE, in Rome in 41 CE, and in Northern Africa in 72 CE. Jews insurrected locally in support of their Palestinian nation at the time of the attack on Jerusalem. Dispersion Jews in Egypt, Cyprus, and Cyrene revolted against Trajan in 117 CE, while others revolted against Hadrian's ban on circumcision in 135 CE.

Jews in dispersion throughout the empire formed an excellent starting point for Christian missionary activity. Paul's method in ministry is well known: he systematically visited the synagogue to first proclaim his message. The Jews' knowledge of the Old Testament, use of the Septuagint, and distance from the centrality of the Temple made them a natural, immediate audience for the Christian proclamation, if not always an accepting one.

John's gospel was possibly written in the Ephesian region, and Ephesus, the Roman government's provincial capital, had a well-developed Jewish community that had maintained good relationships with other groups in the city. Their religious freedom was guaranteed; they held high positions in city government, and some were numbered among the wealthiest and most successful people of the region.

The social and religious setting of Christianity was predominantly Hellenistic, but an initial missionary contact was diaspora Judaism, itself already greatly influenced by Hellenism. John's gospel, located outside of Palestine, still has a very strong Jewish flavor to it and cannot be understood without a knowledge of Judaism.

History of Early Christianity

Missionary expansion. According to the detailed presentation of the Acts of the Apostles, the early Christians initially lived in Jerusalem as a sect within Judaism. Little is mentioned about the Twelve. Peter continued to act as spokesman but left Jerusalem after imprisonment (Acts 12:17), returning briefly for the Council in 47-48 (Acts 15:6-29), at which time James was in charge. The Twelve, who symbolized a new community, did not see themselves as a permanent authority group and neither exercised extended authority nor maintained their own permanence through succession. Initially the Twelve (Acts 6:2; 15:6) and then the college of elders (Acts 11:30; 15:6) made important decisions, but soon James, a relative of Jesus, assumed leadership in Jerusalem and throughout the region (Acts 12:17; Gal 1:19). His very firm pro-Judaism stance made him a welcome transitional leader, but he ultimately failed both to channel Christianity to the Gentiles and to maintain his welcome within Judaism. He was martyred in 62, stoned to death by the authority of Ananus, the High Priest.

Even in the first decade after Jesus' ascension, the Church in Jerusalem was not uniform. Alongside James' pro-Judaism group, the Hellenists, with their own leaders, developed a radical theology of rejection of the Temple and Law. This led to Stephen's martyrdom and to persecution of a section of the Church (Acts 8:1-5), even though the pro-Temple group and the Twelve remained unaffected (Acts 8:14; 9:26). The persecuted Hellenists became the first missionaries, taking the message not only throughout Palestine, but to Samaria (Acts 8:5) and to the Greek-speaking coastal cities, too (Acts 8:26-40). The attack on Jerusalem in 70 CE further dispersed the Christians, some of whom went to Pella in the Decapolis under the leadership of Symeon, another relative of Jesus.

Non-Palestinian centers of Christianity soon developed, notably in Antioch; and Paul, in the course of three missionary journeys, 47-48, 50-53, and 54-58 CE, set up communities throughout Asia Minor and Macedonia. He wrote to the

Thessalonians in 49; to the Corinthians, Galatians, and Philemon, between 54-58; to the Romans in 58-59; and to the Philippians sometime between 61 and 64. Thus, within thirty years of the death of Jesus, Christian communities were flourishing in all these cities. Paul journeyed to Rome in 60 and tradition believes Peter arrived there in 63-65. Both found Christianity already flourishing. However, by the end of the 60s, James, Peter, and Paul had all been martyred.

Missionary expansion continued in the 70s, and in the years following, through the preaching of the disciples of the great apostles. These were also years of persecution: Nero's local persecution in Rome in 64-65, and Domitian's religious trials in 93-96. After the latter's murder in 96, Nerva maintained two years of peace for the Church; this came to an end under Trajan, who vigorously promoted the emperor cult. Early Christianity increasingly focused on the Gentiles, decided that there would be no immediate return of the Lord, and organized for institutional permanence. During this time the various strands of oral traditions concerning Jesus interracted with each other in preaching, catechetics, worship, and Church discipline. Local churches collected and wrote down the teachings; first Mark around 65-70 for the Roman church, Matthew in 80-90 for the Antiochene church, and Luke in 85-95 for an unknown Gentile church.[8]

The organization of the early Church. Some Christians in Jerusalem, especially those inspired by James' leadership, lived in close union with Judaism, attending the Temple and observing the Law (Acts 15:5; 21:21). James' view was strongly felt at the apostolic council (Acts 15:6-29), and his authority extended to Antioch (Gal 2:11-14). However, early missionary endeavors among Gentiles, requiring a transition from a Palestinian-based message to interpretations suitable for the Hellenistic world, made the Church more aware of its growing independence from Judaism. The Jerusalem church was originally modelled on Judaism with its twelve patriarchs and Sanhedrin government. The seven deacons, leaders of the Hellenists, were a temporary parallel structure that disappeared after persecution. Peter's departure left James as the main authority, and his government was similar to that of the high priesthood.

In the early decades "church" was a local concept: "the church of Corinth," or "the church of Rome." Outside of Jerusalem, a variety of local church structures developed. Leadership was respected (1 Th 5:12), but was very fluid: Mark challenged the established authorities of Jerusalem and the Twelve;[9] Matthew stressed the importance of prophets and teachers;[10] Luke established the first links in an apostolic succession of offices;[11] and Paul developed a variety of local leadership structures, although controlling each of them himself.[12] Whatever the local structure, there was a commitment to shared responsibility; several people exercised ministry even though not holding a specific office of authority (1 Cor 16:15). In fact, ministry was often not defined at all (Col 4:17). Several local churches showed their sense of responsibility for other churches, giving clarifications of teachings (Acts 15:22-29); collecting for financially struggling communities (Acts 11:27-30; 2 Cor 8:1-15); and sending and supporting missionaries (Acts 13:1-3; Ph 4:10-20).

Each community developed forms of sharing their faith in prayer, worship, poverty, hospitality, and friendship.[13] They focused on the teachings of the apostles and delighted in learning of the Lord's life. Early common confessions of faith and a common approach to baptism were complemented with the community prayer of the celebration of the Lord's Supper on the first day of the week (1 Cor 16:2). Local churches were not isolated but demonstrated an awareness that faith leads to the ministry of evangelization. Thus, they spread the word through their missionary efforts.

First-century communities were independent, expressing their local organization, worship, prayer, and formulation of the Gospel, in varied and complementary ways. Terms such as overseer (Acts 20:28; Ph 1:1; 1 Tm 3:1; Tt 1:7), elder (Acts 20:17), teacher, priest, prophet (Eph 2:20), deacon (Ph 1:1), and deaconess can be found but cannot be understood as equivalent to the same concepts today. The first century was a time of pluralism, but also of a striving for unity in organization, ritual, and orthodoxy.

When we read Paul today we see that he fosters a sense of unity among his churches, shows respect for the leaders of the Jerusalem church when he visits (Acts 21:18), and feels co-responsible for the development of the Roman church even though he neither founded nor visited it (Rm 1:8-15). Matthew and Luke build their expressions of the Good News on the previous formulations of Mark and Q.

Efforts towards unity go hand in hand with the painful break from Judaism. Some communities are reluctant to make the break (Letter to the Hebrews), others stress their links and roots (Matthew's gospel), some make a clear break, and others oppose their Jewish roots (Stephen's speech in Acts 7:1-54).

Christology is an issue that demonstrates both differences and efforts for unity. Mark rejects a divine-man approach and shows traditions of a low christology, as does Acts in its first four chapters. Paul's Lord and Christ is an earlier stage in understanding than Ephesian's or Colossian's cosmic ruler (Col 1:15-20; Eph 1:15-23). As the early churches struggled to express their faith, the distinction between orthodoxy and heresy was not all that clear. In fact, there seems to have been very little standardization of faith in the first century, a fact confirmed by the variety of second-century heresies that would be difficult to understand had there been any notable solidarity among first-century churches.

John's community experienced both the growth and the struggles of first-century Christianity. As a result, the Fourth Gospel epitomizes better than any other New Testament writing the development of doctrine, the struggle for orthodoxy, the strains of working for unity, and attempts to redefine and reinterpret the message of Jesus in and for a new era.

The Setting of John's Gospel

Influences on John's expression of faith. John's community claims to base its tradition about Jesus on the testimony of a reliable witness to the events of Jesus' life. Not only do they claim to know what happened, but the gospel also presents the community's faith-filled understanding of these historical events. Itself an expression of the missionary expansion of early Christianity, John's community is rooted in Judaism but located in the Hellenistic world. The Johannine community produced the most complicated writings in the New Testament in which readers and scholars have found many influences from Oriental, Hellenistic, and Jewish milieux.

The dualism and anti-Baptist emphases of the Fourth Gospel suggest Iranian philosophical-religious thought, as found originally in Zoroastrianism, but more proximately in Mandeanism. The latter, a dualistic mythical explanation of the world, honored John the Baptist as its founder. According to Bultmann, John's gospel is a Christian revision of the Mandean myth that presents Jesus as the divine messenger and savior.[14] There are similarities between the Fourth Gospel and Mandean literature: the portrait of savior is similar, dualism is in both, and the Son of Man is close to the anthropos of Poimandres.[15] However, the Mandeans only compiled their scriptures at the time of the Moslem conquests, and it is unlikely that Mandeanism had any formative influence on John. The Qumran documents, which are closer to the Palestinian milieu, also evidence a moderate dualism.

John's dualistic language, portrait of the savior, understanding of the incarnation, and presentation of God's activity in history suggest a relationship with Gnostic thought.[16] We have no Gnostic writings that predate the second century, and those we have document Christian Gnosticism. It is again presumed that the Gnostic movement goes back to a pre-Christian period. It was dualistic and contrasted a higher spiritual world with a negative material world.[17] Its system was synthesized in a myth that explained the creation of the world, its need of redemption, and the task of the redeemer. John's prologue has several similarities with this myth, suggesting dependency to some. However, it is more likely that "the gospel was written in terms and ideas ... that later found expression in the writings of the Gnostics."[18] Several commentators see affinities with popular Platonism in John's use of real vine, or true light; parallels to Stoicism in his use of "the word;" connections with Hellenism's wisdom literature; and possible knowledge of the writings of the first-century Alexandrian Jewish philosopher, Philo.[19] Thus some writers see John's gospel as a missionary document, intertwining Hellenistic and Jewish ideas, and written to appeal to the Hellenistic world. Others, including myself, see no more Hellenistic influences than were current throughout the world at that time,[20] or as required to present his message in a pastorally relevant way.

Although John has few Old Testament quotes, — and those he has are free translations including inaccuracies — he deals with the major issues current in Judaism more than any other New Testament writer. He presents Christ "as offering in reality that which Judaism meant to offer, but failed to provide."[21] Sometimes he makes explicit claims, other times just subtle allusions, to issues important in Judaism. While there may be some slight indirect influence from Oriental philosophy and Hellenism, Judaism's influence is formative and suggests we are dealing with a Christian-Jewish dialogue or confrontation. At times, John's gospel is the New Testament's most Jewish writing, at other times the most anti-Jewish.[22] Not all John's conceptual world can be explained by mainline Palestinian Judaism, even accepting its amorphous character, and its syncretistic, heterodox milieu.[23] John evidences knowledge of mainline Judaism and its rabbinic interpretations, as well as extra-biblical Jewish thought, notably the theology of Qumran,[24] and even Samaritan interpretations.[25] Kysar concludes, "The fourth evangelist seems to be at home in a Jewish tradition which is not unaffected by rabbinic, pharisaic influences but it is similarly well-endowed with less orthodox forms of Jewish thought."[26]

No matter what the influences, the author of the Fourth Gospel has transformed these ideas into his distinctive understanding of Jesus. In fact, the greatest influence on John is his understanding of Christianity.

Membership of John's community. John's community was in its earliest stages of development around the 50s or 60s. It was influenced both by contemporary Judaism and by its Hellenistic environment. The gospel also shows influence resulting from the various groups that formed the membership of the community, and other groups with whom the community was struggling. The gospel displays a polemical tone towards Jews, followers of John the Baptist, and early heretical tendencies that later developed into Docetism and Gnosticism. There are signs of a schism among the hearers (7:43; 10:19-21), or indications of a struggle "between two groups of Johannine disciples who are interpreting the Gospel in opposite ways."[27]

A substantial group of John's community were converts from Judaism. These were the true Israelites in whom "there is no duplicity" (1:47). However, Christianity was now distinct from Judaism, and John speaks critically of "the Jews" (13:33) and "their Law" (15:25). So many rejected Jesus that John uses "the Jews" about 70 times as a symbolic expression of rejection.[28] Even some original converts recant and go back to the synagogue, finding John's christology hard to accept (6:60). Some Jews wanted to believe but were afraid of expulsion from the synagogue (9:22; 12:42-43); others confessed Jesus secretly, out of fear of losing their status in Judaism (2:23-25; 3:2; 9:16; 12:42-43); and still others confessed even though their faith was weak (6:60-66; 7:3-5).

Those Jews who converted to Christ and joined John's community were eventually excommunicated from the synagogue (9:22; 12:42; 16:2). The Jewish groups in John's community received much of the attention, either to strengthen their faith or to call them to conversion, (7:35) hinting that they might be diaspora Jews to whom the proclamation is addressed.

The Fourth Gospel gives tangible evidence of opposition to followers of John the Baptist. The Acts of the Apostles and non-Christian writings document a following of John the Baptist, some of whom in Ephesus receive his baptism (Acts 19:3) and even believe he is the Messiah. Thus, the rivalry we witness is understandable. Yet this rivalry, which leads to a deliberate presentation of John as merely witness to Jesus and a disclaimer that he is the Messiah (1:8, 15, 20), does not lead to a very negative portrait. Rather, John the Baptist is used to lead others to Jesus, suggesting that we are dealing with a group within John's community who were formerly disciples of the Baptist.

Chapter 4 shows considerable interest in Samaritans. In fact, they become early non-Jewish believers. Also several words used by John are of Samaritan interest and offer signs of a Samaritan ministry. Later the Jews criticize Jesus, accusing him of being a Samaritan (8:48). Brown points out that "The Johannine Jesus ... undergoes the harassment suffered historically by the Johannine community."[29] Thus the accusation is probably to be regarded as a criticism of one of the groups who formed part of John's community.

The history of John's community. Several authors have tried to reconstruct the history of John's community.[30] J. Louis Martyn divides the historical development into three parts: 1. An early period (60s-80s) when a Jew preached Jesus to other Jews, forming a community within the synagogue; 2. A middle period (late 80s) when the community divided after excommunication, some going back to Judaism and others becoming Christians; 3. A late undated period of growing self-identification for the community in relation to Jewish Christians and the Great Church. Georg Richter sees: 1. The beginning of John's community among Jews who accepted Jesus as the messianic mosaic prophet; 2. Some of these developed a higher christology, seeing Jesus as Son of God. This alienated part of the group who returned to Judaism; 3. Some of the "Son of God" Christians became Docetist, denying the real humanity of Jesus; 4. An anti-Docetic group revised the previous tendencies.

Some writers identify sub-groups within the community, thus implying a historical development. Others direct their attention to the redactional history of the gospel, but thereby suggest stages of community history too.

Raymond E. Brown offers the most detailed reconstruction of the history of John's community. 1. Phase One (mid 50s to late 80s): an originating group of Palestinian Jews who accepted Jesus as davidic Messiah were joined by anti-temple Jews who had made converts in Samaria and looked for a mosaic Messiah. The interactions of these two led to a high preexistence christology and provoked their excommunication from the synagogue. 2. Phase Two (c. 90s): acknowledging their independence from Judaism and welcoming Gentile converts, the community moved to the diaspora. Persecution from the Jews, and non-acceptance of their higher christology by Christians of Jewish origin, isolated the community and provoked division. 3. Phase Three (c. 100): the community divided, part going into Docetism and part refocusing their christology in a non-Docetic way in the teachings of the letters of John. 4. Phase Four (2nd century): the Docetists drifted into Gnosticism, the Johannine community joined the Great Church.

The outstanding contributions of the above scholars have been praised and criticized. Their suggested reconstructions lead to a series of conclusions. John's gospel is the result of interactions in a community with a long history. There are clear signs of varied groups with their differences and resulting polarization. Non-believers are detectable, as are groups that abandon Jesus. Furthermore, debates between Christians regarding their interpretations of christology and ecclesiology are readily identifiable. Hostility from without in the form of persecution and excommunication complements divisiveness from within. This leads to an emphasis on the ethical challenges of love within the community that even seems provincial at times. There are also indications of a sense of exclusiveness, a sharp break from the world, isolation, and defensiveness. "Threatened by opponents, socially disrupted, and still in the process of maturing theologically, they understandably found a dualistic distinction between 'us' and 'them' appealing."[31] At the same time the Johannine church's struggle for identification and recognition produced a synthesis of the gospel that is distinctive and a christology that became dominant in the universal Church.

John's gospel is a window through which we can catch a glimpse of the history of an early Christian community struggling for identification. It is also a mirror that reflects its challenges to us today as we struggle for community identification locally and internationally.[32]

Location of John's community. The beginnings of Christianity exemplify a religion's desire to root itself in history while offering theological reflections on its prehistory. John's gospel emphasizes the historical reliability of Christianity's roots while pursuing the pre-history of Jesus to preexistence. The synthesis cannot be understood without both a thorough grasp of Judaism and an appreciation of its various groups and theological currents. John, preferably to be located outside of Palestine in a diaspora community, since the writer presumes the readers are unfamiliar with specific places, is noticeably influenced by Hellenism. As the early missionaries moved out to the great centers of Syria and

Asia Minor, John's community seems to have established itself in a cosmopolitan area and, as the Johannine letters evidence, to have had several churches dependent upon the same tradition. The community was organized outside the structures of the increasingly unified Great Church, or Mother Church, that traced its origin along the synoptic lines to Peter and the Twelve. In a time of increasing organizational unity, John's gospel also stands out for its unique christology. Facing many problems, the community seems to have been energized by its struggles for acceptance, orthodoxy, unity, and relevant interpretations of the Gospel message.

While some writers suggest the community lived in Syria,[33] and a few offer Alexandria,[34] the majority of ancients and moderns consider John's community to be located in the Ephesian region. A Hellenistic city, known to have had a strong Jewish community, to have had followers of the Baptist, and to have been a seedbed of Gnosticism and Docetism, Ephesus fits well into the situation presumed by John's gospel. The influences identified in the gospel, and the groups that make it up, all find a home in this governmental capital of Roman Asia Minor.

Chapter 2, considering the author, will further clarify the location of his gospel and relate it to his other writings and the problems they portray in surrounding churches of the region.

Chapter Two
THE AUTHOR OF THE FOURTH GOSPEL

*An eyewitness has testified,
and his testimony is true; he knows
that he is speaking the truth, so that you may
also [come to] believe. (Jn 19:35)*

Christian art has traditionally represented the fourth evangelist as the eagle before the throne of God (Rev 4:7), for he soars to the heights of heaven, and his penetrating vision brings us insights into faith offered by no one else. He is "the theologian," the "spiritual evangelist," the "Beloved Disciple," whose originality, genius, and discernment lead to a maturity in faith unheard of in the rest of the New Testament. The gospel is appreciated by all Christian traditions, but this was not always the case. Like the other gospels it first circulated as an anonymous work until the gospels were gathered together, at which time "according to John" was used to distinguish the Fourth Gospel. No John is identified as its author in any of the twenty-one chapters, and its slow acceptance and relative disuse in the second century militate against an unquestioned apostolic authorship. Nevertheless, by the end of the second century many church fathers presumed that the author was John the apostle, the son of Zebedee.

In considering the author, "we must keep before us the broad context of the ancient conception of authorship, ... Sometimes the 'author' of a book is simply a designation for the authority behind it."[1] In this chapter we will consider the identity of John, the author of the Fourth Gospel, what authority he had in the early Church, and how his tradition relates to the Synoptic proclamation.

The name "John" means "Yahweh grants grace or favor,"

or "the Lord shows goodness and mercy." This work of grace and mercy is a penetrating vision of the goodness of God for us in Christ. Even if the author remains unknown to us, his "anonymity in no way prevents the splendour of his work from shining out . . . his genius shines perennially."[2] However, if we can know a little more about him, his interests, sources, companions, and community, we can catch glimpses of early Christian history and a new interpretation of faith that can help us face contemporary critical issues with similar originality and faithfulness.

John in Tradition

Some unique features of the Fourth Gospel. No other book in the New Testament is like John's gospel. It has a style and "sound" all its own, presents a "different" Jesus, whose ministry, based in Jerusalem rather than Galilee, is two or three times as long as the Synoptics' ministry. From the first line of the prologue, Jesus is the incarnate Word; full of confidence, authority, and glory, he fills his audience with awe, and is worshipped by believers and enemies alike. He lives in constant union with his Father, and controls all the events of his ministry, including the passion. The story is told with strength of conviction, maturity of faith, enthusiasm, and passion. Karl Barth suggested that everywhere we hear "the fiery and stormy soul of the son of thunder." John's work bears an original christological focus, transforming the Synoptics' interest in the establishing of the kingdom into a very personal portrait of Jesus.

The Fourth Gospel's convincing and inspiring presentation is the work of "a powerful and independent mind," who has "masterfully controlled" both his sources and whatever influences may have affected him.[3] Chapter 21, added at an early date, confirms the explicit claims of the gospel to have been written by an authoritative witness (19:35). Chapter 21, which explains the death of an elderly and revered founder of the community, insists that this Beloved Disciple is a reliable witness. Some commentators believe Peter, Andrew, Philip, Thomas, and Nathaniel are introduced as the author's well-known colleagues or friends and are portrayed in unforgettable detail. Many passages have all the indications of eye-witness accounts as "again and again John has little extra details which read like the memories of one who was there."[4] The life-like details are complemented with firsthand knowledge of Jewish life and practices (1:21; 4:25; 6:14-15; 7:40-44; 12:34) and a clear appreciation of life in and around Jerusalem at the time of Jesus.[5]

Although having a strong semitic coloring, and many indications of the primitive traditions of an eye-witness, the gospel was written in Greek, and its style, language, and symbolism, hardly suggest a Galilean fisherman. Rather, "the more highly organized state of much of the presentation, and also some vagueness and inconsistency at times, indicate a long process of tradition."[6] The theological maturity, together with the implied theological debate, again indicates the possibility of an extended period of formation and community struggle. The gospel gives both history and interpretation, and "The result is not a biography; it is impressionistic rather than photographically accurate in detail."[7]

The author is presented with the grandiose title "the disciple whom Jesus loved." The gospel never mentions the sons of Zebedee and it refers to the Baptist simply as "John," since there is no possibility of confusion with any other John, unlike in the Synoptics. This absence of such a significant figure from the ministry reinforces some people's conviction that the unmentioned apostle, John, is the author. The authority behind this work is not afraid to compare his tradition of Jesus with Peter's, to insist on his beloved status above Peter's, and to "correct" the Synoptic tradition.

Early testimonies concerning the author. Paul visited Ephesus around 58 (Acts 20:18-38), and wrote to the Ephesians around 63 but makes no mention of the apostle John. Bishop Ignatius wrote to the Ephesians and refers to Paul's ministry there, but not to John's. Polycarp's biography says nothing of his having been a disciple of John, even though Irenaeus later claims he was. Papias, Bishop of Hieropolis, who preferred oral tradition to the written word, mentions a John as author of the Fourth Gospel, but he does not make the short journey to Ephesus to find him. In fact, Papias claimed that John the apostle was martyred with his brother James, thereby implying that the author was another John.[8]

Clement of Rome's first letter (c. 96), three of Ignatius' letters (c. 110), Justin's Dialogue with Trypho (c. 135), and the homilies of Melito of Sardis (c. 160-170), all show similarities to the Fourth Gospel.[9] The first exact quotation of John is found in Tatian (c. 170), and the first quotation, together with the claim that it is written by John, comes from Theophilus of Antioch in 180, although not even he claims that John is an apostle.[10]

Justin, in Ephesus in 135, refers to John the apostle as having resided there,[11] but the earliest explicit witness to John as the author of the Fourth Gospel is Irenaeus who wrote around 180.[12] He claims the author is the same John who sat next to Jesus at the Last Supper, and though Irenaeus does not identify John with the son of Zebedee, this could be presumed. In a letter sent to Pope Victor c. 190, Polycrates, Bishop of Ephesus, claims John the apostle lived and died in Ephesus.[13]

By the end of the second century the tradition of apostolic authorship of the Fourth Gospel is clearly sketched: John the apostle goes to Ephesus in the late 60s after Paul's departure from the scene; he is exiled to Patmos during Domitian's persecution (81-96), returning to Ephesus when Nerva becomes emperor; and he dies in Ephesus in the seventh year of Trajan (98-117), that is, around 105. It has been suggested that this tradition developed late because of the early misuse of the Fourth Gospel by heretics. Origen vigorously refuted Heracleon, a disciple of Valentinus, whose commentary on John was probably the first. Gaius, a Roman presbyter, in his debates with the Montanists, claimed John was written by the Gnostic, Cerinthus.

The key figure, then, in the claim of apostolic authorship is Irenaeus who, writing towards the end of the second century, uses the Fourth Gospel in his struggles against Gnosticism. Irenaeus states that John, while living in Ephesus, wrote the Fourth Gospel against the Gnostic Cerinthus, but that the Gnostics then misused it to support their own views. Irenaeus then "struggles to recover it for orthodox Christian faith,"[14] and "it is due to him above all that John was launched on its triumphal march in the Church."[15] Irenaeus' view finds support in the Muratorian canon (c. 170-200), the

Anti-Marcionite Prologue (c. 200), Clement of Alexandria (c. 150-215), and Tatian in his Diatessaron (c. 170).

Papias in 130, the fourth-century Apostolic Constitutions, Eusebius in his history, and Dionysius of Alexandria, suggest that there were two Johns in Ephesus,[16] information which has been used to propose that Irenaeus and others may have been referring to a lesser known John rather than the apostle, or to the presbyter who wrote the second and third letters of John.

Did Irenaeus successfully draw together the threads of early tradition, or was his insistence on apostolic authorship a means to legitimize his charges against the Gnostics? Dodd claims "His evidence is formidable," and insists "it is reasonable to accept [that] Irenaeus' testimony is on strong ground."[17]

The Beloved Disciple. The Fourth Gospel's appendix, written soon after the rest of the gospel since it is an authentic part of all manuscripts, implies the death of the revered source of the Johannine tradition. This reliable witness is referred to as the Beloved Disciple. If this designation "was conferred on him by others, it is a lovely title; if it was conferred on him by himself, it comes perilously near to an almost incredible self-conceit."[18] The title, used on five occasions, refers to the disciple at the Last Supper who leaned against Jesus' chest (13:23-26), stood near the cross with Mary, the mother of Jesus (19:25-27), ran to the tomb with Peter (20:2), and walked with Jesus and Peter along the shore of Tiberias after the resurrection (21:7, 20). He is identified with "the other disciple" (20:2, 8) who could also be the one mentioned as having access to the high priest's house (18:15-16) and as being one of the first disciples (1:40). Some scholars, impressed with the gospel's astonishing silence concerning John, the son of Zebedee, are convinced that he was the witness of this tradition and referred to himself anonymously as the other disciple, whereas his followers referred to him as the Beloved Disciple. Certainly, these authors insist, the Beloved Disciple would seem to be an apostle, present at the last supper, close to Peter, and entrusted with Mary.

Other writers point out that the mention of the sons of Zebedee in 21:2 speaks against the identification of the

Beloved Disciple as Zebedee's son: access to the high priest's court seems unlikely for a Galilean fisherman: and the fact that all references to the Beloved Disciple are in Jerusalem is again unusual if he were a Galilean. The suggestion that he was close to the cross goes against the known Roman practice of forbidding this. The proposal that Jesus entrusted Mary to the Beloved Disciple is contradicted by the information in Acts that Mary is with the brothers of Jesus (Acts 1:14). Moreover, his vague introduction in 13:23 as "One of his disciples, the one whom Jesus loved," and the evangelist's need to inform readers that this disciple was the source of the tradition (21:24), give the impression he was not as well-known as Zebedee's son would have been.

Various proposals have been made to identify the Beloved Disciple. Impressed by the fact that all references occur after the resurrection of Lazarus, who was introduced as "the one you love" (11:3), some authors are persuaded that Lazarus was the Beloved Disciple.[19] Another suggestion is John Mark.[20] A frequently supported position is that the Beloved Disciple is a paradigm of discipleship, "a symbolic figure probably invented by the evangelist or his community to contemporize the ancient traditions of Jesus of Nazareth."[21] This view is given some credence by the fact that the Beloved Disciple, although important, is never named. While entrusting Mary to the Beloved Disciple could be viewed as an idealized entrusting of the Church community to the ideal disciple, other episodes in which he appears are quite mundane: being informed of treachery (13:23-26) and going fishing (21:7). Moreover, 21:20-23 reports the death of the Beloved Disciple.

Tradition identifies the Beloved Disciple with John, the son of Zebedee. One of the inner three, Peter, James, or John, is considered to be quite likely, and since Peter is explicitly mentioned, and James dies, John alone remains. Moreover, the close association of the Beloved Disciple with Peter fits John from what we know of the two friends, from the Synoptics, and from Acts. Brown and Schackenburg supported this view, but both changed their minds.[22] Most of the arguments in favor of the Beloved Disciple being John the son of Zebedee are from silence: John, the son of Zebedee, was very important in the early Church, and yet he is not mentioned in this gospel; therefore he must be the author, who, with a presumed sense of humility, does not refer to himself.

The Beloved Disciple, the real founder of the Johannine community, is contrasted with Peter and the mainline churches. He represented the source of the community's theology. The Fourth Gospel's editor used the Beloved Disciple as the implied author, whose position of special stature close to Jesus became adequate defense of the community's peculiar understanding of the Gospel. It is likely that the Beloved Disciple was a real person, but probably not one of the twelve.

John the evangelist. The Fourth Gospel's unique features, and particularly its presentation of the Beloved Disciple, suggest it was written by an eyewitness. This view is thought to be confirmed by a growing agreement among early church witnesses and historians. Commentators, ancient and modern, find that the gospel offers a strong Jewish identity, eyewitness testimony, and direct evidence of authority; that it is the work of one close to Jesus, present at the Last Supper, the crucifixion, and the empty tomb; and that it interprets the tradition with an authority close to Peter's. This author of stature is considered to be John, the son of Zebedee. As Bruce Vawter expresses it, "There seems to be no doubt that John, the son of Zebedee, is meant: No other figure in John or the Synoptic tradition corresponds to what the evidence requires, whereas John does."[23] This view is considered to be supported by internal evidence on the silence concerning John, a silence thought to be unlikely if we were dealing with a disciple of John. Crossan insists that "it seems sheer hypercriticism not to accept the candidate for authorship which the earliest tradition has always offered us, i.e., the apostle John himself."[24]

Admittedly, this is the only ancient opinion that merits serious consideration. Suggestions that the author was John Mark, or Lazarus, or John the elder, mentioned by Papias, have little to commend them. Moreover, the view that the implied author is exclusively the idealization of the community is largely rejected, even though some contemporary writers continue that very process of idealization, making the one who leaned on Jesus' chest an intimate friend, mystic, and visionary whose understanding of the Lord's message replaces all others.[25]

There are a number of difficulties in identifying the author with the son of Zebedee. The seemingly overwhelming evidence is actually very unsatisfactory. Acts 4:13 claims that John was uneducated, thus hardly our author. The author is no longer the John we know from the Synoptics, but rather a person whose "life and death are completely woven about with legend."[26] Moreover, the internal evidence of the gospel is confusing. It claims eyewitness authority while "it seems impossible to vindicate the historical credibility" of some passages.[27] It is at once Jewish, non-Jewish, and anti-Jewish. It shows detailed knowledge of Palestine, while seemingly coming from the diaspora. It is at pains to legitimize its teachings in Judaism, while giving the impression it is an interpretation for the Gentiles. It claims authority from one of the Twelve, yet challenges the authority of Peter. It is rooted in tradition, yet is a very free rewriting. The eyewitness source of the tradition differs from the Synoptics' eyewitness claims. These variations and internal discrepancies together with the confusing early links in tradition have led to new proposals concerning authorship. While it is tempting to identify John, the apostle, as the author, Robert Kysar concluded "such a theory cannot be supported with evidence, only desirability."[28]

Biblical criticism, having shown that the Fourth Gospel comprises several strata of tradition arising in different circumstances and at different times, concluded that the apostle John was not the final author of the gospel. Thus, various theories of composite production have arisen. Some commentators distinguish between John the author, apostle, and Beloved Disciple, and the writer whose name is unknown.[29] Others, believing the work is more complex, identify the early tradition, the work of the evangelist, and later redaction to interpret or correct the tradition. Brown, and others, are convinced that the problems dealt with in the Johannine letters are integral to one's appreciation of the development of the gospel, and they posit the Beloved Disciple, the evangelist, the presbyter-author of the letters, and the final redactor of the gospel.[30]

The final redactor in Chapter 21 distinguishes between himself and the superior source of the tradition. The latter was more the Beloved Disciple of the community than of the historical Jesus. He was clearly a person of notable stature who bore witness to the Johannine community's theology, and implicitly challenged the Petrine tradition behind the Synoptics. Unfortunately, there is no unequivocal reference to his identity. The early church offers other examples of challenges to apostolic tradition in Antioch and Corinth, and in neither case are we dealing with a confrontation between apostles.[31] Here, too, the author is unidentifiable, but the community's conviction that their's is a faithful interpretation of Jesus' message is presented through a process of legitimization: their understanding of faith is formulated by one of their beloved prophets who gradually becomes Jesus' Beloved Disciple, seen to have an authoritative interpretation, comparable to Peter's. He is seen as one of the chosen three, with the only possible designation being John. The anonymous author is a person of stature in the community and an authoritative source for the traditions of Jesus.[32]

John The Author

The Fourth Gospel's style. Jesus and his disciples spoke Aramaic, and the earliest stages in the oral tradition were in that language. Much of this Aramaic, or Semitic, flavor in both language and style can be found in the Fourth Gospel. Nevertheless, there can be little doubt that John's gospel was originally written in Greek; it is not a translation. The language is simple and generally correct. His vocabulary is small and his expression hardly elegant, certainly not good classical Greek. The gospel originates in a Greek-speaking region outside of Palestine.

As we saw in Chapter 1, this gospel is influenced by several philosophical and spiritual movements of Judaism and Hellenism and has absorbed some of their characteristic forms of expression. Nevertheless, the gospel has a uniform style which is present throughout, and is the same no matter which character is speaking. Moreover, "The language of the Fourth Gospel is so clearly that of a particular faith community that we may not even be sure it would be properly understood by first-century outsiders."[33]

John's thought develops in spirals. His presentation alternates between signs and discourses, the latter often starting out as a dialogue, then merging into a monologue. He uses short sentences, frequently linked with "and." Much of his narrative retains the semitic flavor of its oral sources in its parallelism (5:19-29; 11:38-44), balance of narratives, rabbinical exegetical methods (1:51; 8:56), and Hebrew poetic techniques. John frequently punctuates his narrative with details of time and place with a precision not found in the Synoptics (1:39; 4:6, 52; 18:28; 19:14, 20). He deemphasizes some of the Synoptics' prominent terms, such as "kingdom of heaven," and elsewhere modifies ideas also found in the Synoptics, as when he doubles the Synoptic's "Amen," making it into a unique and solemn pause in an argument (5:19; 6:32; 8:51; 12:24).[34]

John's gospel demonstrates a good knowledge of the Old Testament. His quotes, which come principally from the psalms and the prophets, do not seem to follow any known Greek version, and are considerably fewer than in the Synoptics. Although there are eighteen direct quotes,[35] he often simply alludes to Old Testament themes or imagery (1:45; 2:22; 5:39, 46; 17:12; 20:9). He is deeply rooted in the Old Testament's theology and stresses the general witness to Christ by these scriptures when taken in their totality (1:17; 5:46-47; 8:33-59; 12:40-41).

One unusual feature in John is the presence of a series of breaks in the narrative: unusual transitions between chapters 4, 5, and 6, or the two endings in the last discourse. These seams, or "aporias," cannot easily be explained, especially by commentators who propose one person as author-writer. These breaks have led to several theories of displacement of sections of the text.

Some specific stylistic features. A common stylistic feature used throughout John's gospel is *parallelism* (3:16-18 // 12:46-48; 1:49-51 // 3:9-15; 5:28-29 // 11:24). In inverted parallelism, or *chiasm*, units are arranged ABCB'A', so that the first and last are parallel, the second and the penultimate, and so on. This feature not only illumines the structure of a section but focuses attention on John's theological emphases: Jesus' union with the Father (5:19-30), the kingship of Jesus (18:28 — 19:16), and the birth of the Church (19:19-37). *Inclusion* is also a form of parallelism in which a similar idea opens and closes a section of narrative, like brackets that set limits to a passage. At times the similar idea brackets a large block of material (1:28 and 10:40; 18:1-27 and 19:17-42), at times a small section (2:1-11; 4:43-54; 9:1-41).

John punctuates his narrative with *rhetorical questions* which are left unanswered in the text but which challenge readers to express their faith: "Can anything good come from Nazareth?" (1:46) "Are you greater than our father Jacob, who gave this cistern and drank from it himself with his children and his flocks?" (4:12) "Surely we are not also blind, are we?" (9:40) "What is truth?" (18:38) By these questions characters often unconsciously indicate a profound truth.[36]

Some words or phrases are given a *double meaning*; born from above and born again (3:3), lifted up on the cross and exalted in glory (3:14), giving water in a bucket and living water (4:10), going up to Jerusalem and ascending to the Father (7:8). Often the double meaning provokes *misunderstanding* and Jesus must explain the episode's deeper meaning for faith: the nature of the temple that will be destroyed (2:19-22), new birth (3:3-8), living water (4:10-15), real food (6:32-35), Christian freedom (8:31-38), the vision of the Father (14:7-9). At times, instead of causing misunderstanding and responding to it, John interjects *explanatory notes*, or short parentheses, then gives information gained after the resurrection in order to understand the deeper meanings of early events in the ministry.[37] Some of the explanatory notes are presented as a refrain which reminds the readers that they will understand later (2:22; 7:39; 12:16; 13:7; 14:26; 16:4).

John uses *repetitive devices*, echoing key words in a section (1:1-5, 9-12), or repeating ideas after inserting a new section of narrative.[38] He uses *concentric thinking*, moving around one central idea, and *spiral thinking* as he moves the reader closer to a key concept. Sometimes the author presents episodes in pairs, and he often uses symbolic numbers, especially sevenfold presentations of events.[39]

"By his use of *irony* the evangelist paints a profile of

himself as a person with a keen sense of incongruity, humor, and pathos."[40] There is irony in the entire account in which Jesus is rejected by the very people awaiting his coming. There is irony in individual sections: the Gentile centurion accepts Jesus but the Jews do not (4:43-54), the blind man sees who Jesus is and the watchful Pharisees do not (9:1-41). There is irony in short phrases: "Can anything good come from Nazareth?" (1:46) Jesus cannot be greater than Jacob (4:12) or Abraham (8:53), "Then, you are a king?" (18:37) "Behold, the man!" (19:5)

These stylistic features are skillfully used by John; they enrich his presentation, and focus the readers' attention on the power of the message.

Symbolism in the Fourth Gospel. Since earliest times John has been referred to as "the spiritual gospel." It contains more symbolism than any other part of the New Testament except the book of Revelation. His dramatic use of language evokes a response from his readers, calling them to appreciate the deeper spiritual call of his gospel. Thus, when Jesus goes to Jerusalem for the feast of Dedication, the Jews do not receive him well, and we are told "It was winter" (10:22). When Judas leaves the upper room to betray Jesus, John adds "It was night" (13:30). Not only is John's language suggestive and evocative but he can reuse Old Testament symbols, giving them a deeper meaning: thus, Jesus becomes the healing serpent (3:14; Numbers 21:9), the Good Shepherd (10:11-18; Ezekiel ch. 34), the humble Messiah (12:12-15; Zechariah 9:9). John's presentation of events draws the reader "to grasp insights into the symbolic meaning of what he says," and "peer between the lines at what he is presupposing and implying."[41] There are several levels in his thought and challenge which both the pious and the scholar can spend a lifetime searching and researching. Routine events offer a deeper meaning: when the first disciples are urged to "Come, and you will see" Jesus, it is no longer hospitality but an invitation to faith (1:39). Mary's suggestion to the wedding waiters to "Do whatever he tells you," becomes a fundamental challenge to the Church (2:5). The blind man is told to wash in a pool called "sent," as Christians are challenged to baptism in the name of the one sent from the Father (9:7).

"Symbolism obliges the thought to move and develop on two planes: that of the symbol itself and that of the superior reality designated by the symbol and of which it is a reflection and an image."[42] John's symbolism is primarily christological. Jesus is light, word, water, food, way, truth, shepherd, sheepgate, and vine. His miracles become signs which focus and deepen faith. The Johannine miracle, which "is conceptually close to the prophetic symbolic action,"[43] replaces the Synoptic parables and instructs the reader regarding faith in Jesus.

John also uses numbers, time, and dualistic language, symbolically.[44] His whole presentation can be read on at least two levels, and what is said of Jesus can be viewed as contemporary events in the life of the Johannine Christian. John's presentation is intuitive, suggestive, and evocative. "He is a witness to the pure apostolic faith, who describes heaven and earth, time and eternity, in the same breath."[45]

His readers. Several of the specific Johannine stylistic characteristics we have seen presume a very close relationship between the evangelist and his readers. He addresses them in the first person singular (21:25) or plural (1:14, 16; 21:24). He is a contemplative who does not explain but enthusiastically bears witness as "he sets his reader directly in front of Christ," convinced that the evidence of events and the awesomeness of the Lord will attract them to faith.[46]

Sometimes a dialogue, like that between Jesus and Nicodemus (3:1-21), or between Jesus and the Samaritan woman (4:4-42), imperceptibly becomes a conversation between Jesus and the reader. In fact, "This 'fading out' of the audience, to leave the speaker addressing the reader in isolation, is typical of Johannine style."[47]

John's use of irony, misunderstanding, and explanatory notes presumes a close rapport between writer and reader. The intended reader is presumed to know a lot about what went on in Jesus' time and what is going on in John's time. "The implied author smiles, winks, and raises his eyebrows as the story is told. The reader who sees as well as hears understands that the narrator means more than he says."[48] This "silent communication" between the two can be detected throughout the narrative, and present-day readers need to enter the climate of the work, experience the writer's enthusiasm for the message, and participate in the dialogue. The reader must grasp the real level of meaning that the writer intends, so that the impact of the message can be truly felt.

John and the Synoptics

The tradition behind John. The Fourth Gospel differs significantly from the Synoptics, and anyone who has previously read the latter gets the impression of entering a different world in John. If this book comes from eyewitness accounts why is it so different from the Synoptics? If its author is the apostle John and its tradition primitive, why is it so Hellenistic? If the Fourth Gospel depends on the others, questions arise regarding their relationship. If it does not, further questions arise regarding the independent development of the gospel form of writing simultaneously in Mark and John.

John's outline of Jesus' ministry is different from the Synoptics'; the former is based in Jerusalem, the latter in Galilee (4:43-45). In John, post-resurrection faith is read back into the earliest stages of the ministry, where Jesus is already Messiah (1:41), and Peter the Rock (1:42). John's chronology of the ministry is different; thus the cleansing of the Temple is at the beginning instead of the end (2:13-22), the anointing is moved (12:1-8), and the events of the passion occur on different days. The Synoptic Jesus, surrounded by the poor, sick, outcasts, and sinners, is replaced with the Word, Light, and Bread of Life, fully conscious of his messiahship (4:26). The Synoptic Jesus demonstrates the kingdom's power in his miracles; the Johannine Jesus reveals who he is through the signs: miracle stories that are not important as demonstrations of power, but are significant because they manifest Jesus' glory; they are signs pointing to the preexistent Lord. The Synoptic exorcisms disappear in John's gospel, and the many compassionate healings of the sick and distressed are replaced with two symbolic cures.

The Synoptic Jesus announces the arrival of the Kingdom, speaks in parables, lays down foundations of ethical living, and warns of apocalyptic events; the Johannine Lord has a different way of thinking and speaking. Important Synoptic episodes are omitted: Jesus' birth, infancy, baptism, confession at Caesarea Philippi, transfiguration, institution of the Eucharist, agony in Gethsemane, and the final apostolic commission. The Johannine Jesus alternates between revelatory signs and discourses; only two of the seven signs are found in the Synoptics (4:43-54; 6:1-15) and none of the discourses. In fact, John even omits the Sermon on the Mount and the eschatological discourse.

The Fourth Gospel gives considerable emphasis to events never referred to in the Synoptics: the wedding at Cana (2:1-12), Jesus' discussion with Nicodemus (3:1-15), Jesus' baptizing ministry (3:22), the encounter with the Samaritan woman (4:4-42), the raising of Lazarus (11:1-44), the meeting with some Greeks (12:20-36), the washing of the disciples' feet (13:1-20), the teachings of the Paraclete (Chs. 14-17).

Synoptic emphases on the kingdom, mission, authority of the Twelve, suffering of Jesus, and salvation of the Gentiles, are absent from John. Several brief sayings in John show verbal similarities to the Synoptics and have been called "Synoptic logia," but most of the Synoptic sayings of Jesus are not found in John.

Like the Synoptics, John uses the Old Testament, but less frequently, less accurately, rarely as proof texts, and with only five parallels to the Synoptics. He views the Old Testament as scripture, but omits reference to some writings, like Daniel, considered important by the Synoptics.

There are also many similarities: the ministry of John the Baptist, the cleansing of the Temple, the healing of the official's son, the multiplication of loaves, the anointing, triumphant entry, passion, and resurrection. Several isolated sayings are similar in John and the Synoptics. There are some common tendencies, such as an anti-Jewish polemic. However, the overriding differences are theological.

John's sources. When John uses material similar to the Synoptics, is he dependent on them as sources? When he presents an alternative version of the same event, as he does in describing Jesus' meeting with John the Baptist, or the trial scene, does he have a parallel source? When he gives extensive information in discourses or signs, where does it come from? Is it possible to identify sources that may underlie the Fourth Gospel?

This gospel is written in Greek, but some commentators suggest that the prologue and sections of the discourses were originally written in Aramaic. They also consider that the present Greek, confused in places, betrays a mistranslation of original Aramaic sections. Since the gospel as a whole never existed in Aramaic, were parts of it originally in Jesus' and the apostles' own language which our author found and translated? Those who believe the author is the son of Zebedee acknowledge that he would be bilingual, probably thinking in Aramaic even though writing in Greek. I think it most unlikely that we are dealing with Aramaic sources, and the original Palestinian traditions are enough to explain the present Aramaic traces in John.

Bultmann was convinced he had identified three sources in John: a sign source, a discourse or revelation source, and a non-Synoptic source for the passion account. It is suggested that the so-called sign source represents views of a miracle-working Jesus, which are pre-Johannine. Fortna considers the sign source to be a pre-Johannine gospel made up of Synoptic-like material and to be John's most extensive contact with synoptic traditions.[49] Some passages occur in the same order in John and in Mark and contain many verbal similarities (6:1 — 7:1). At times John parallels Mark and uses some of Mark's own expressions. Sometimes a seemingly respectful use of Marcan material cannot be explained on the basis of a pre-Marcan tradition since it is thought to include Mark's redaction. It is suggested that this is the case with the Sanhedrin trial, Peter's denial, and the passion. Several commentators now refer to John's use of Mark, or his knowledge of Mark, or at least the fact that he must have read Mark.[50] Those who deny a link with Mark must explain John's independent origin of the gospel genre. Nevertheless, the evidence falls short of proof, and the gospel genre existed in several communities before Mark wrote it down.

Commentators have shown particular interest in the relationship between John and Luke. Not only are there similar theological emphases and a series of common characters — Martha, Mary, Lazarus, Judas, and Annas — but there are several passages that suggest a dependence (12:2-8 and Lk 7:36-50; chs. 13-17 and Lk 22:14-38; 18:1-12 and Lk 22:39-53;

18:29 — 19:16 and Lk 23:1-25; 19:19-42 and Lk 23:25-56; ch. 20 and Lk 24). The relationship generates particular interest when John and Luke agree against both Matthew and Mark. However, the similarities are not strong enough to suggest John's dependence on Luke. In fact, a majority of authors explain the relationship by suggesting Luke is dependent on an early stage of the developing Johannine tradition, or that both of them used some similar sources.[51]

The links between John and Matthew are very few and weak, and hardly any contemporary author supports John's dependence on or knowledge of Matthew.[52]

I remain unpersuaded by the arguments for John's dependence on written sources. The reconstruction of non-Synoptic sources is unnecessary, and the meager material common to John and the Synoptics, about eight percent, is inadequate to justify dependence. If John had known the Synoptics, why did he not make greater use of them? Similarities can be explained even if John did not know the Synoptics, but divergences cannot be explained if indeed he did know them.[53] Moreover, the present text of John is a unity, and its stylistic characteristics identifiable throughout.

John's relationship to the Synoptics. John's relationship to the Synoptics can be adequately explained without presuming they were sources. In fact commentaries rarely presume such dependence. Several theories have appeared that propose various levels of relationship between the gospels.

An early tradition among Church Fathers, with supporters throughout successive generations, concludes that John wrote to supplement the Synoptics. This explains why he does not repeat their material, but rather presumes his readers know it. It is suggested that he begins where the Synoptics end. He fills in gaps in their narrative, offering explanations where they do not; thus, he tells us how Peter got into the high priest's residence (18:15-17). In places he makes explicit what is only implicit in the Synoptics: thus Jesus formally claims he is the Messiah (4:26). Since John is written later than the Synoptics and after more extensive community reflection, he can make a different choice of more relevant material and give new interpretations to it. Since the Synoptics emphasize a Galilean ministry, John can pass over it and expand Jesus'

Jerusalem ministry. This proposal presumes readers know the Synoptics and can appreciate allusions to their teachings. However, John does repeat some common traditions which would seem to undermine the idea that he is supplementing. In fact, differences are in places so strong, they suggest more a replacement than a supplementing.

Another theory considers that John and the Synoptics shared common traditions and any similarities can be explained by cross-influence of oral traditions. This opinion considers that John was acquainted with the community tradition represented in the Synoptics or that John's sources were influenced by the traditions behind the Synoptics. Theories of source analysis have not shown literary dependence and yet there are similarities which are now more commonly explained by theories of a common tradition.

John's gospel is very different from the other gospels. He shows no consistent identification with any of them, and where he shows similarities these are probably due to common oral traditions or the result of nothing more than a common outline of Jesus' life and message. Theories of dependence leave more problems than solutions: why did he omit valuable parts; why did he not relate to the Synoptics when he could have; why leave small differences which could have been smoothed over to parallel the Synoptics? The inevitable conclusion is that John is independent of the Synoptics and represents a distinct tradition. In some places his tradition parallels the Synoptics; in others it may well be more accurate in chronological and locational details. While both traditions are theological reflections on the events of Jesus' life and ministry, John's shows the kind of reflection that goes on at a distance from the events, and it is unlikely that it derives from an original apostolic witness.

The redaction of John. The Fourth Gospel, while portraying a sense of unity, has several signs of inserted passages, breaks, and seams. Some unusual changes of scene give the impression that events may be in the wrong order; thus Chapters 4, 5, 6 would read more logically as 4, 6, 5. Authors studying the history of the Fourth Gospel's composition think that some sections are now inaccurately located; thus 10:19-39 could belong with Chapters 7 and 8. The continuity of some discourses is broken (10:1-18 is continued in 26). Some sections solemnly end, only to begin again immediately (14:31 and 15:1). Some authors consider that several passages have been displaced, either accidentally or by the addition of new material, and they seek to rearrange the parts into a more accurate consecutive order. While authors such as C. K. Barrett, believing the book makes sense as it stands, insist it should not be rearranged, others, including Brown, consider "an unqualified acceptance of the present arrangement of the Gospel as truly chronological is not possible."[54] Some writers see the many breaks and seams as indicative that one author did not do all the work at the same time.

Those who see much of the displacement as the result of additions view the gospel as undergoing a series of expansions to respond to new community needs. These developmental theories of composition suggest several editions of John. Wilkens sees: (1) A basic gospel, (2) expanded by discourses, (3) finalized in a passover edition of John. Lindars offers five stages: (1) Traditions and sources, (2) Homilies, (3) First edition of the gospel, (4) Second edition of the gospel, (5) Post-Johannine additions. Brown's five stages are: (1) Oral traditions, (2) Traditions developed into Johannine patterns, (3) First edition of the gospel, (4) Second edition of the gospel, (5) Additions of a disciple-redactor.[55] While Brown considers his five stages minimal, others consider his hypothesis complicated, speculative, unsuccessful in separating material introduced at each stage, and motivated by excessive concern to protect apostolic authority for the tradition.[56] Nevertheless, analysis of the stages in editing is more successful than theories of source criticism in explaining the present form of John: its general unity in style and content, its many breaks, changes in theological emphasis, and insertions. Such analysis also clarifies how parts of the text can be very early, and others late, theological interpretations. The complex process can start with a Beloved Disciple's tradition and end in an entire community's refocusing of their faith. Yet if this is done within a closely-knit group of disciples who share the same approach to faith, the final outcome can remain uniform even though there may have been several contributing editors.

John's is a rich tradition. Part of his teaching is similar to the Synoptics but not because he depends on them. His complex presentation has developed slowly through several stages, and the community facing new problems found creative solutions in new interpretations of their tradition.

The Johannine School

A community tradition. The Fourth Gospel evidences both several stages of editing and also a sense of authorial unity. Although expanded and adapted to respond to new community needs, the gospel is clearly the work of a closely-knit group of disciples. While "our knowledge goes to show that it is great individuals, not communities, that are creative,"[57] experience also shows that many creative and charismatic figures need others to help them articulate and institutionalize their vision. The Fourth Gospel not only refers to the Beloved Disciple as the founding figure, whose authoritative testimony is the basis of the work, but it also mentions others who say: "we saw his glory" (1:14), "from his fullness we have all received, grace in place of grace" (1:16), "we know that his testimony is true" (21:24). The first two references could be to the Johannine community, or Christians in general, but the third is a statement of the final redactor of the appendix, one of the group responsible for the final form of John. The origins of John are complex, and it is hardly the work of one person. It is "very clearly and definitely the product, not of one man, but of a group and a community"; it is "the cumulative product of a distinctive Christian tradition that developed within an ongoing community"; "There are, in fact, good reasons for suggesting that John emerged from a school or circle of early Christianity."[58] Although the Muratorian Canon attributed this gospel to John, it insisted that the contents were revealed to the group of apostles. Even Clement of Alexandria, writing before the end of the second century, says that John "urged on by his disciples ... composed a spiritual gospel."[59]

The gospel in its present form is hardly the work of a Galilean fisherman, and yet it claims to be rooted in an authority that demands a hearing. Whether it is merely attributed to a foundational authority, or actually authored by such, is difficult to determine. The group is very dedicated to its founder, who acknowledges his own stature, and deals with his traditions with more freedom than other New Testament writers. The group endorses his testimony (21:24) and draws on his teachings as it expands its message. Thus, even later additions to the original proclamation bear the stamp of the founding author's thought.

Internal and external evidence supports the conclusion that the Fourth Gospel is the work of a school, not in so far as it is a compromise document from a committee, but rather that it comes from a small group of enthusiastic followers who are deeply committed to the shared vision of their Beloved Disciple. As new circumstances develop the followers are able to draw on the authority of the community's founder, giving applications and interpretations of his tradition concerning Jesus.

Other Johannine writings. The Johannine writings have traditionally included the Fourth Gospel, the three letters of John, and the book of Revelation. The gospel does not name its author, but tradition has always attributed it to someone called John. The first letter does not name its author, but he is a revered figure. The second and third letters are sent by an unnamed elder (2 Jn 1:1; 3 Jn 1). The book of Revelation names its author as John (Rev 1:1, 4, 9; 22:8). The second and third letters are short and are examples of a simple form of correspondence. Some similarities of style and vocabulary suggest that the second letter was authored by the same person who wrote the third. The first is not strictly a letter but rather a theological commentary and interpretation of the Fourth Gospel. Nevertheless, some similarities of language and style between the second letter and the first lead to the conclusion that the same person authored all three letters. At the same time the first letter follows the structure of the final form of the Fourth Gospel and is a commentary on it, thereby indicating a close connection between the author of the letters and the final editor of the gospel. Early traditions regarding Revelation are mixed. The majority, knowing it comes from John who was exiled to the island of Patmos (Rev 1:9), saw this John as the apostle and Beloved Disciple. They linked the authorship of the writings as follows: John the Beloved Disciple while on Patmos wrote the book of

Revelation in the fourteenth year of the reign of Domitian, about 95. Released after the death of Domitian in 96, John returned to Ephesus where he later wrote the gospel (90-100). Incipient Docetists misinterpreted the gospel, forcing John to write his first letter as a guide for understanding and interpreting the gospel. As tension arose between the Johannine community and the Great Church, John's missionaries were unwelcome in some of the communities of the Johannine church; thus John wrote to these local churches in his second and third letters.

These developments are largely accepted today, even if the author John is rarely identified with the apostle; after all, the gospel does not confirm it, and the community problems referred to in the letters would be unlikely, although not impossible, were the author an apostle. Revelation is written by a person who distinguishes himself from the apostles (18:20; 21:14), and Gaius of Rome (beginning of the third century) and Dionysius of Alexandria (middle of the third century) questioned its apostolic authority. Admittedly, Gaius and Dionysius rejected Revelation's apostolic authority because they were fighting millenarianists who used Revelation for their cause. Still, the style of Revelation is notably different and can only come from the same author as the gospel if one presumes a substantial time lapse, vastly different circumstances, and even considerable age difference for the author. Possibly the author wrote Revelation when he was young and the gospel when he was considerably older.

The majority of contemporary writers consider Revelation's author to be a different person from the Beloved Disciple who is the authority behind the gospel, and from its final redactor who also authored the first letter. Some suggest John the Presbyter authored Revelation, and the Beloved Disciple and his school the rest. I will presume the gospel and the letters came from the same school, but not Revelation.

A regional church. John's gospel centers Jesus' ministry in the south of Palestine in contrast to the Synoptics' Galilean focus, leading to the recurring suggestion that the gospel was written in southern Palestine. While this region may account for some of the early traditions eventually integrated into John, the final form shows other influences and problems which necessitate a diaspora context. Important papyri of John have been found in Egypt, suggesting that the gospel may have been written in Alexandria, home of Philo, the hermetic writings, and the Gnostic Valentinus — all proposed influences on John. An early tradition which has found recent support places John in Antioch. Ephrem at the end of his commentary on Tatian's *Diatesseron* claimed that John wrote his gospel in Antioch. Some modern commentators have rekindled this opinion because of suggested affinities between 1 John and Matthew, or between John and Bishop Ignatius of Antioch. Moreover, Theophilus of Antioch wrote the first orthodox commentary on John.

With only a few exceptions, the early Church tradition considered Irenaeus correct when he insisted that John's gospel was written in Ephesus. Admittedly this opinion leaves some unanswered questions: was Ephesus not a pauline foundation, later entrusted to Timothy? Even if John came later, would he not have shown some pauline influence? Timothy's Ephesian Church was monarchically governed, a structure John seems to reject (3 Jn 9). The Synoptic traditions, brought to Ephesus as recorded in Acts, are not present in John.

In spite of these problems, the majority of commentators, ancient and modern, are convinced that John's writings come from the Ephesian region. In addition to the external evidence of Irenaeus and the chain of writers dependent upon him, the gospel has many parallels with Revelation which explicitly claims to have been written near Ephesus and which addresses seven churches in the region. Although having a different author than the gospel, Revelation's parallels with the gospel suggest a common locality. John's controversies with contemporary Judaism, and his anti-synagogue emphasis fit into Ephesian problems (Rev 2:9; 3:9). John's anti-Baptist motif recalls Acts mentioning the same problem in Ephesus (Acts 19:1-7). This Roman regional capital, a Hellenistic city with a strong Jewish community, was also a center for the early development of Gnosticism and Docetism, significant issues in John.

John's second and third letters suggest that the Johannine community, located in a large city, also had other regional churches dependent upon it. The second letter, addressed to Gaius, attests to the latter's hospitality and also refers to the opposition of another local church leader, Diotrephes.

We have already considered the history of John's community, and the redaction history of the gospel. The complex developments, together with our knowledge of Ephesus from the Acts and the Pastorals, make difficult the dating of the Johannine writings. I am unconvinced by the reasons offered for an early dating.[60] Papyrus was the paper of the common people, and fragments dated around 150 (Rylands) and 180 (Bodmer) show that John was already being read by the common people at this time. Moreover, allusions to, and even familiarity with, John in both orthodox and heretical works of the first half of the second century point to a date no later than the turn of the century. His mature theology and the presumed reactions to incipient Gnosticism do not require a date later than this. John's attitude to "the Jews" places his work not only after 70 and the fall of Jerusalem, but also after 80-90 and the expulsion from the synagogues. Perhaps the gospel presents a community in the 80s to 90s and the letters show development and problems around 100.

Chapter Three
PROCLAMATION FOR A NEW AGE

But the hour is coming, and is now here, when true worshipers will worship the Father in Spirit and truth. (Jn 4:23)

John's gospel begins with the same words as the book of Genesis and, like the latter, goes on to present the creative Word of God proclaiming the birth of a new age. Unlike Matthew and Luke whose infancy narratives, tracing Jesus' ancestry to Abraham or Adam, show he is the expected one, John's prologue shows the unexpected and wonderful origin of the incarnate Lord and how radically new is the age he inaugurates. Abraham, willing to sacrifice his only son, began a new age of faith and covenant, but with Jesus we see "the glory as of the Father's only Son, full of grace and truth" (1:14). In fact, Abraham rejoiced to see the dawning of this age of Jesus Christ (8:56).

God spoke to Moses, establishing a new community, and detailing the reciprocal obligations of God and the people. However, "while the law was given through Moses, grace and truth came through Jesus Christ" (1:17).

The story of this gospel is the story of a new world order, it is a work of transformation from a judged and condemned world to a new age of grace and peace. "The ruler of this world has been condemned" (16:11), and Jesus can claim "take courage, I have conquered the world" (16:33). The new age is judged by different criteria: it is an age of new life, light, truth, manifestation of God in glory, real spiritual food, and genuine direction from the Good Shepherd. "For God so loved the world that he gave his only Son, so that everyone who believes in him might not perish but might have eternal life" (3:16).

This world is passing away, a world full of "blind men who claimed to see (9:34-41), men in bondage who thought they were free (8:31-36), men condemned by their own hope (5:45-47), men who believed yet asked for signs (6:30).[1] Jesus is not another in a long series of great religious leaders, rather he proclaims the final age of God, claiming "I came into the world as light" (12:46), "I do testify on my own behalf" (8:14), and "My teaching is not my own but is from the one who sent me" (7:16). Moreover "whoever comes to me will never hunger, and whoever believes in me will never thirst" (6:35); thus "whoever hears my word and believes in the one who sent me has eternal life" (5:24).

The new age is centered on Jesus is such a way that John interprets all history to focus on Jesus; in fact, in him the final events of salvation history are already realized. John further sees that all the significant questions of life are answered in Jesus and the world must understand Jesus' constant reminder "without me you can do nothing" (15:5). In this new age of Jesus all reality is in light or darkness, can see or is blind, has truth or falsehood, is of heaven or of the world; people let themselves be guided by spirit or by flesh, possess life or death. Constantly contrasting the old order with the new, John, from the first lines of the prologue, presents a vision of a new age come in Jesus Christ.

John's Understanding of History

A new age made known in history. John's gospel although very different from the Synoptics is based upon the same historical person, Jesus. It is no longer possible to claim that the Synoptics' focus is historical, whereas John's is theological, since it is obvious that all four are theological works, as it is equally obvious that authentic theology is rooted in history. John's spiritual emphasis, use of symbolism, stress on the inward experience of Christianity, and focus on eternity, do not lead to a disregard of the actual events of history; on the contrary his work is intended to contribute to his community's understanding of those events. In fact, the truth of events is of critical importance in the Fourth Gospel, and "John's stress on the truth serves as a warning against seeing him as an incurable theological romancer."[2] He builds up a series of witnesses who guarantee the reliability of events of critical theological significance: the Baptist (1:32), Nathaniel (1:48-49), the disciples at Cana (2:11), the blind man (9:24-34), Martha and Mary (11:25-29), the witness of the passion (19:35), Peter and the other disciple at the tomb (20:3-8), Thomas (20:26-28), and the redactor (21:24).

John recounts events in Jesus' life in order to lead to faith (20:30-31). He may alter the order of historical facts to accommodate them to his thought and theological emphases, but his information is authentic and reliable. His first letter rejects exaggerated spiritualism and shows the dangers of a false spirituality which rejects the importance of real material facts and events, since it is John's conviction that the glory of God and a new age for humankind appear in the visible historical Jesus. John interprets these events to persuade and evangelize, telling his audience not only what happened but more particularly what these events mean for them. These interpretations of the theologian-evangelist remain grounded in history.

The Fourth Gospel gives many topographical details of Jesus' ministry not found elsewhere: "Bethany across the Jordan" (1:28), Cana in Galilee (2:1), "Aenon near Salim" (3:23), and "The region near the desert ... a town called Ephraim" (11:54). His precise descriptions of the area around Jerusalem are also remarkable: the pool of Bethesda with its five porticoes (5:2), and the pool of Siloam (9:7). The Johannine Jesus makes several visits to Jerusalem (2:13; 6:4; 13:1), knows well the Kidron valley and the Garden of Gethsemane (18:1).

John's narratives are packed with details, especially numbers (1:35; 2:6; 4:18; 5:5; 6:9; 12:5; 19:23, 39; 21:8, 11), and the characters in the stories come alive: Andrew (1:40-41; 6:8-9; 12:22), Philip (1:43-45; 6:5-7; 14:8-9), Nathaniel (1:45-51), and Thomas (11:16; 14:5; 20:24-29).

John gives accurate historical information concerning John the Baptist, Jesus' baptizing ministry, the longer public ministry, several journeys to Jerusalem, the important Judean ministry of Jesus, the reason for the final journey to Jerusalem, details of the Last Supper, background to the accusations of the trial, details of the Roman trial, a picture of a provocative Jesus who arouses his enemies, Jesus' attitude toward the Sabbath, and a deeper appreciation of the significance of healings.

John's detailed Judean ministry helps us understand how Jesus could have become so influential with the crowds and so threatening to the Jewish leaders, whereas the Synoptics' very brief Jerusalem ministry leaves us confused. John's account of the Roman trial and the High Priest's reasons for encouraging it, give us background to understand the execution of Jesus. Jesus' seemingly inexplicable final journey to Jerusalem is understandable when John points out that Jesus went to cure his friend Lazarus, at Martha's request. The Synoptics' account of Judas' betrayal of Jesus is a stunning surprise, but not for John who knew Judas had been stealing funds for some time. The Synoptics pack all the events of Jesus' ministry in Jerusalem into one week, but John spreads it over about three years and helps us appreciate the dynamics of a growing opposition to Jesus so that the clamor for his death is not unexpected.

John is concerned about the historical reliability of events on which faith is founded. He is, in places, more accurate than the Synoptics and, although the historical events form a departure point for his theology and faith, he is careful to show they are reliable.

John's concept of history. John's gospel is presented to his postresurrection Church to clarify what was really happening on a supra-historical level in the events of Jesus' life. Rooted in history, he considers it inadequate to appreciate the salvific and cosmic significance of these events which can only be recovered by faith. The mere chronological understanding of history yields to a God-given perception of salvific truth made known in and through history. John's doctrine of history integrates the facts of Jesus with a faith-filled penetration of their truth; history is important precisely because it is the history of Jesus.

The story begins with a creation hymn heralding a new and final era of God's grace. The Baptist (1:29-30) and early disciples (1:35-51) recognize Jesus as the Lamb of God, the Spirit-filled teacher, Messiah, King of Israel, and Son of God. Six days of introduction (1:29, 35, 43; 2:1) prepare us for the great day of rest, when God's grace is brought to the world, grace that is experienced in seven wonderful signs. The first sign, at Cana in Galilee (2:1-11), shows us how Jesus transforms the water in the jars of Jewish ritual into the choice and abundant wine of messianic times. The hour of salvation (12:20-32) is anticipated (2:4), heralding a new covenant.

Appreciation that we are in a new period of history is the interpretative key to reading John. It is Jesus who makes sense out of history and gives meaning to all events — past, present, and future. Only a believer can truly understand history, for the life of Jesus is the center of the realization of the plan of salvation.

John presents three perspectives in his Christ-centered doctrine of history: "the preexistent, eternal; the past, historical; and the present, Christian."[3] The preexistence of Jesus, his mission from the Father, and his return to union with his Father are the nonhistorical factors giving meaning to history. "For if you do not believe that I AM, you will die in your sins" (8:24). The past, historical perspective helps us appreciate that he who had glory with the Father before the world began (17:5) in a specific historical framework "came to what was his own, but his own people did not accept him" (1:11). To those who believed he declared, "Whoever has seen me has seen the Father. . . . Do you not believe that I am in the Father and the Father is in me?" (14:9-10) This past, historical framework has two moments: expectancy in Israel, often seen in prophecy; and fulfillment in Jesus, often seen in typology.

The present, Christian era is relevant to John's community. Unlike apocalyptic writers who see the future as giving meaning to the present, John sees the past, historical time of Jesus as clarifying the Christian's present.[4] At times the clarification is for a community, but often it is the history of an individual believer's welcoming of the Lord into life. John's only theme of history is the presence of Christ in eternity, in history, and extended and repeated in the future.[5] This salvific presence is directed by the Father, a direction so emphasized by John that the gospel in places uses deterministic-sounding language.[6]

The eternal, the past, and the Christian present are three

facets of the same picture; often they merge, and frequently a sense of timelessness and eternity permeates all three.

Reinterpretation of tradition. John's account of the life and message of Jesus includes many early traditions that the redactor claims are based on the reliable testimony of the Beloved Disciple; "we know that his testimony is true" (21:24). We have also seen that many episodes in the Fourth Gospel may be more accurate than Synoptic accounts. However, "it is an outdated view of history that 'facts' can be established quite apart from the interpretation of the historian."[7] The very first post-resurrection traditions of the Church are already interpretations of the Jesus event. Add to this awareness the fact that John and the Synoptics belong to different times, cultures, and community needs, and the likelihood of notable differences emerges, giving the Fourth Gospel a new perspective, horizon, and theological synthesis.

John does not write his gospel in opposition to the Church; rather he sees himself within a tradition: "we saw his glory" (1:14), "From his fullness we have all received" (1:16), "we know that his testimony is true" (21:24). Although "we" clearly indicates the community experience, the gospel's final presentation remains very different from other New Testament writings. John's interpretation is much more developed than the Synoptics', with Jesus even speaking in Johannine language.

John articulates the message of Jesus for a mixed Hellenistic audience. He restates the message with the philosophical, cultural, and literary aids of his time and location, so that in places Jesus appears as a Greek philosopher.

However, John's story of Jesus is more than a reinterpretation for a new age in a Hellenistic world; it is "a deliberate attempt to rephrase Jesus' thought in more universalist categories, in terms more relevant for a worldwide situation."[8] He calls his mixed community, living with its own tensions and anxieties, to look to his new answers as a source of vision that can sustain their changing community.

He urges them to "stop judging by appearances" (7:24; 8:15), and to penetrate to the mystery revealed in the simple events of history. Jesus' works manifest who he is (10:38), and he can claim "You search the scriptures, because you think you have eternal life through them; even they testify on my behalf" (5:39). A new perspective on life is needed, a Spirit-life, for "no one can see the kingdom of God without being born from above" (3:3), or "born of the Spirit" (3:8). "Everyone who listens to my Father and learns from him comes to me" (6:45). The community's faith is reinforced as they deepen their conviction that "They shall all be taught by God" (6:45).

John's universalist interpretation sees all the historical events of Jesus' life through the lens of his preexistent divinity. The fact that the Word, who was in God's presence and was God (1:1), came to his own people (1:11) to share the fullness of God's love (1:16), leads the believer to interpret all history, past, present and future, in a new way.

John's reinterpretation of the tradition is a little exceptional. He places less emphasis on the facts than on their interpretation and sees less need for authority than for inward experience in faith. This will provoke a clash with the Great Church, but when the clouds settle the Great Church will have absorbed John's faith-filled vision of Jesus and his supra-historical analysis of the events of Jesus' life.

Eschatology in the Fourth Gospel

Eschatology. John's gospel does not contain a major discourse on the end of the world; moreover, it also lacks the apocalyptic flavor found elsewhere in the New Testament. Nevertheless, a broad understanding of the events of the end of time appears in the Fourth Gospel, even though less frequently than in the other three.

The last day will bring judgment: "Whoever disobeys the Son will not see life, but the wrath of God remains upon him" (3:36). This judgment will be on one's faithful acceptance of Jesus and the power of his words: "Whoever rejects me and does not accept my words has something to judge him: the word that I spoke, it will condemn him on the last day" (12:48). Together with judgment by the Son of Man, the end will bring the general resurrection of the dead: "Do not be amazed at this, because the hour is coming in which all who are in the tombs will hear his voice and come out, those who have done good deeds to the resurrection of life, but those who have done wicked deeds to the resurrection of condemnation" (5:28-29). The last day is a joyful rebirth for the just, since as Jesus claimed, "For this is the will of my Father, that everyone who sees the Son and believes in him may have eternal life, and I shall raise him [on] the last day" (6:40; also 6:39, 44, 54). For such believers the reward will be eternal life in union with Jesus. "Whoever serves me must follow me, and where I am, there also will my servant be. The Father will honor whoever serves me." (12:26). Before his passion and death Jesus confidently assures his disciples that he is going to his Father to prepare places for them, and then "I will come back again and take you to myself" (14:3). Once in these dwelling places of the Father's house, the disciples will witness the glory of Jesus in eternal life (17:24). The end is also the transition into the kingdom of the Son: "My kingdom does not belong to this world. . . . my kingdom is not here" (18:36).

Although John presents indications of his understanding of the end, "his eschatology no longer emphasizes the end and the future, but the beginning and the abiding."[9] Thus, Jesus can say "they are your gift to me ... because you loved me before the foundation of the world" (17:24). This inter-relationship between time and eternity in Jesus already determines the end. Recent major works on Johannine eschatology all argue that John's christology determines his eschatology: "the eschatological teachings of the evangelist are rooted in and constitute little more than extensions of his view of the person and work of Christ."[10]

Thus, although the Fourth Gospel's eschatological emphasis is not as strong as the Synoptics', it is certainly faithful to the common New Testament tradition. The Johannine letters complement the gospel, even adding the unusual teaching on the Antichrist, a unique New Testament concept, repeated five times in the letters. John's special contribution to eschatology is to see it in light of Jesus' preexistence; one's understanding of the last things is conditioned by one's understanding of the first things.

Realized eschatology. Since for John christology determines eschatology, the end time is encountered in Jesus. Faithful to traditional emphasis that the final hour of God's manifestation, of the general resurrection, and of judgment is coming (4:21; 5:28-29; 16:2, 25), John complements this future emphasis with a conviction that future climactic events are already realized in Jesus (4:23; 5:25; 16:32). The "hour," the end, the final judgment, and God's definitive revelation, are manifest in Jesus. That hour which is coming is paradoxically already here (4:23; 5:25).

Jesus, talking to Nicodemus about the Son, says "Whoever believes in him will not be condemned, but whoever does not believe has already been condemned, because he has not believed in the name of the only Son of God" (3:18). Jesus informs the Samaritan woman, "But the hour is coming, and is now here, when true worshipers will worship the Father in Spirit and truth" (4:23).

The evangelist focusing on Jesus can claim: "We saw his glory" (1:14); "Behold, the Lamb of God who takes away the sin of the world!" (1:29); "This is the verdict, that the light came into the world, but people preferred darkness to light, because their works were evil" (3:19); "Look up and see the fields ripe for the harvest" (4:35).

On a particularly solemn occasion, when Jesus challenged his audience to rethink their approach to the Sabbath, he affirmed "so also does the Son give life to whomever he wishes. . . . I say to you, whoever hears my word and believes in the one who sent me has eternal life and will not come to condemnation, but has passed from death to life" (5:21, 24). When he makes a similar claim before raising Lazarus (11:25-26), Martha expresses the belief which turns eschatology into christology: "I have come to believe that you are the Messiah, the Son of God, the one who is coming into the world" (11:27).

For John, eternal life and the future salvation it offers are made available in the present moment of Jesus' revelation and salvific self-gift. The future, second coming of Jesus is realized in the present experience of the gift of the consoling Spirit. Thus, the believer through faith already shares in eternal life and union with the Son.

John is faithful to the common tradition of future fulfillment but adds the creative insight that the blessings of the future are attainable in the present through faith. A futurist eschatology and a realized eschatology are not opposites but rather complement each other, even appearing side by side in the text (5:21-25 and 26-30).

John's own faith convinces him, "Now is the Son of Man glorified, and God is glorified in him" (13:31). As a result he appreciates the blessings of the present moment, portraying Jesus as already glorified and endowed with the power of judgment and salvation. It is faith that sees the end as already attained in Jesus. John's radical reinterpretation of eschatology into a realized eschatology opens the doors to a new focus on our present blessedness, a new optimism, gratitude, and peace, and a challenge to deepen this faith in others.

Judgment. John's original emphasis on realized eschatology brings to the present not only the hopes of the people and the blessings of God, but also personal crisis, judgment, and the battle with "the ruler of the world" (14:30). Even during Jesus' ministry some in the crowd rejected the moment of grace, claiming "This saying is hard; who can accept it?" (6:60) Tension arose among Jewish adherents regarding the extent of their faith in Jesus, some finding belief in him incompatible with their Judaism. Others accepted Jesus secretly, and still others experienced persecution because of their faith.

John portrays life as a continuing struggle, and many suffer because of their faith in Jesus. But a decision must be made for or against Jesus, and Peter, speaking for the disciples, confesses "Master, to whom shall we go? You have the words of eternal life. We have come to believe and are convinced that you are the Holy One of God" (6:68-69). Although others may try to sit in judgment over Jesus (9:13-41; 18:28-40), the fourth evangelist insists that Jesus alone is judge. "And he gave him power to exercise judgment, because he is the Son of Man" (5:27). Thus, Jesus claims: "I came into this world for judgment, so that those who do not see might see, and those who do see might become blind" (9:39). It is not that Jesus wishes to see anyone condemned. "For God did not send his Son into the world to condemn the world, but that the world might be saved through him" (3:17). Once someone acknowledges Jesus as the one who determines the final orientation of life, there results a self-sifting and self-judgment.

"Whoever lives the truth comes to the light, so that his works may be clearly seen as done in God" (3:21). As a result, "whoever hears my word and believes in the one who sent me has eternal life and will not come to condemnation, but has passed from death to life" (5:24).

John's eschatology, filtered through his christology, concludes "Nor does the Father judge anyone, but he has given all judgment to his Son" (5:22), who alone faithfully interprets the Father's will. "Even if I should judge, my judgment is valid, because I am not alone, but it is I and the Father who sent me" (8:16).

The events of the end time are present in Jesus' activity. The final crisis and decision for or against God are made now through one's faithful commitment to Jesus. He is the measure of faithfulness, the giver of eternal life, and the measure of one's own self-condemnation. Sent by the Father, Jesus unites time and eternity, and in him believers realize and experience their own future.

Dualistic Concepts

John proclaims the establishing of a new age in which the values of the future kingdom are anticipated in Jesus' judgment that separates the good from the bad. John describes a set of tensions between opposing forces: light and darkness, sight and blindness, truth and falsehood, heavenly values and worldly values, spirit and flesh, life and death. However, John's deep-seated dualism is not a physical or essential dualism, such as is found in Gnosticism. Rather, "the Johannine dualism is one which comes about historically through man's decision. It is an ethical dualism."[11] His very effective dualism is another presentation of his realized eschatology.

John's dualistic concepts are varied ways of presenting the disciples' acceptance or rejection, an acceptance or rejection which is not dependent exclusively on human decisions but results from the forces of two entirely different worlds: Christ's final salvific kingdom, and the poisoning forces of evil. The eternal values are offered to believers in the new age Christ inaugurates: an age of life, light, love, and truth; whereas the power of evil is perverted, leading to death, darkness, hatred, and lies. "Hence there are two ways of existence open to persons — the way of evil and pretense of independence, and the way of truth and acknowledgement of dependence upon God."[12]

John's dualism is not abstract, but is a very concrete emphasis on the results of faith. His language of life, light, love, and truth permeates the twelve chapters that precede the passion, but echoes also throughout the passion account, even though such terms are less frequently used.

Light or darkness. These concepts are not opposed in the Old Testament as they are in John. The Old Testament, however, would see light as a symbol for the Law (Psalm 27:1; 105:39; 119:105; Isaiah 42:6; Daniel 2:22). John likens the coming of Jesus to the shining of a light in a world of darkness. "The light shines in the darkness, and the darkness has not overcome it" (1:5); "the light came into the world, but people preferred darkness to light, because their works were evil" (3:19); "I am the light of the world. Whoever follows me will not walk in darkness, but will have the light of life" (8:12); "While I am in the world, I am the light of the world" (9:5); "The light will be among you only a little while. Walk while you have the light, so that darkness may not overcome you" (12:35); "I came into the world as light, so that everyone who believes in me might not remain in the darkness" (12:46). Jesus' coming brings light to believers and darkness to the blind and disbelieving. People's attitude toward the light "is expressed by receiving it or not receiving it (1:5), by coming to it or not coming; by hating it or loving it (3:20-21); and even by believing in it (12:36)."[13] In fact, it can be claimed that "Light is a Johannine metaphor of salvation closely related to truth."[14] "Whoever lives the truth comes to the light, so that his works may be clearly seen as done in God" (3:21).

Jesus is the source of light, the light which brought the blind man out of darkness when he was washed in the one sent from the Father (9:5-7). The same illumination offered to the Pharisees is rejected and provokes a deeper blindness that is sinful (9:39-41). The whole story is presented as a trial scene in which judgment depends on the acceptance or rejection of the light, that same light which John immediately describes as the Good Shepherd (Chapter 10). After all,

"Whoever walks in the dark does not know where he is going" (12:35), whereas Jesus' "life was the light of the human race" (1:4), empowering them to become children of God through their faithful acceptance of the light (1:12).

Truth or falsehood. The person who "comes to the light" is the one who "lives the truth" (3:21). Again John sees the dualism: truth or falsehood, knowledge or misunderstanding, as a judgment on one's relationship to Jesus. He is the source of truth (8:40; 14:6; 18:37), bears witness to the truth (18:37), and speaks the truth (8:40-46; 16:7). This liberating truth (8:32) is the enduring word of the Father (17:17), which is communicated through the Spirit (14:17; 15:26; 16:13). Disciples must act in the truth (3:21) and be consecrated in truth (17:19).

"Truth," in Hebrew thought, emphasizes the moral value of faithfulness. In the new age, the truth of Jesus steadfastly remains as the category of judgment. They who accept the truth are made free (8:32), whereas they who reject it are enslaved (8:34), and Jesus condemns them: "You belong to your father the devil and you willingly carry out your father's desires. He was a murderer from the beginning and does not stand in truth, because there is no truth in him" (8:44).

Truth is not simply a value to which the disciple gives intellectual assent, rather it is a progressive penetration of Jesus' revelation. It is a personal knowledge of God in Christ; it is a personal union with Jesus. The new age is divided between those who want to get to know more of Jesus and those who wilfully reject him and his personal revelation. The words "truth" and "true" are used more in John's gospel than in all the rest of the New Testament. The truth of Jesus' revelation is "seen," "known," and "believed."[15]

The rejecting world does not see or know or believe, but misunderstands. "Misunderstanding" is also a recurring theme, but implies a culpable misunderstanding, a willing acceptance of falsehood (8:44-45). In fact, "no one can see the kingdom of God without being born from above" (3:3; also 4:10-15). Thus, Jesus could say to many what he said to the Samaritan woman: "I have food to eat of which you do not know" (4:32). To those who disbelieve he gives the warning "you will die in your sin" (8:21), whereas to the believers he can say: "I say to you, whoever keeps my word will never see death" (8:51).

For disbelievers everything about Jesus is obscure: the nature of his messiahship, his origins (7:27), and his relationship to his Father (8:27-59). The reason for this misunderstanding and disbelief is that some have given themselves to carrying out the wishes of their chosen father, the devil, who "does not stand in truth, because there is no truth in him" (8:44).

At the end of his ministry Jesus can pray to his Father: "The words you gave to me I have given to them, and they accepted them and truly understood that I came from you, and they have believed that you sent me" (17:8). The truth is a special knowledge of the new age; it is a characteristic of new life in the Spirit. "The Fourth Evangelist can speak of ... knowing and seeing God, ... it is the presupposition of his whole view of religion that the Age to Come has come: eternal life is here."[16]

The other world or this world. While teaching in the Temple, Jesus took occasion to warn a group of unbelievers: "You belong to what is below; I belong to what is above. You belong to this world, but I do not belong to this world" (8:23). A radical separation divides two groups of people: those who value this world; and those whose lives are directed to the eternal values of the world to come, and who believe those values are already present in Jesus.

Although Jesus can claim: "My kingdom does not belong to this world" (18:36), he still insists: "I came into the world as light, so that everyone who believes in me might not remain in darkness" (12:46). As he ministers, he proclaims: "Now is the time of judgment on this world; now the ruler of this world will be driven out. And when I am lifted up from the earth, I will draw everyone to myself" (12:31-32). To those who reject him, he says: "Why do you not understand what I am saying? Because you cannot bear to hear my word" (8:43). Rejected by this condemned world, Jesus withdraws from the world (Chapter 12) until its powers resurface at his arrest (18:1-9); and during this withdrawal "Judas, not the Iscariot, said to him, 'Master, what happened that you will reveal yourself to us and not to the world?'" (14:22) However,

Jesus has already appreciated that "The one who is of the earth is earthly, and he speaks of earthly things" (3:31).

John uses "world" in three ways: God's creation (1:9; 3:16; 16:21; 17:24); humanity loved by God; and unbelieving and rejecting people who are self-satisfied and hostile to God's merciful love. The third category, which is characteristic of John, presumes that these people have committed themselves to the "the ruler of the world" who is "coming" (14:30), bringing darkness to his followers (13:30). "The 'world' symbolizes . . . a way of living in which the human tries to be something he or she is not, namely, an independent being having no need of the One responsible for existence."[17] Even the brothers of Jesus fall into this trap and are rebuked by Jesus (7:6-7). John sees Judas as the embodiment of these forces of the evil world. "His role is determined 'from the beginning' (6:64). He is picked by the devil (13:2) and controlled by him (13:27). He is in fact 'a devil' (6:70; cf. 13:18)."[18] This world directs its hatred to believers of the new age of Jesus (15:18-27).

With the coming of Jesus, "Now is the time of judgment on this world; now the ruler of this world will be driven out" (12:31; also 16:11). Jesus does not even pray for this world (17:9) but appeals to the Father to protect his own, telling him "I protected them in your name that you gave me, and I guarded them . . . I gave them your word, and the world hated them, because they do not belong to the world . . . keep them from the evil one" (17:12-15). With Jesus' departure there comes "the Spirit of truth, which the world cannot accept" (14:17). He will continue Jesus' task, and "will convict the world in regard to sin and righteousness and condemnation" (16:8), and will guide the disciples into the truth of the new age.

Spirit or flesh. John is opposed to an essential or physical dualism. He is not against the material world. In fact, of all the gospels, John's is the most physical, highlighting the union of the spirit and flesh in Jesus' incarnation. Moreover, Jesus' passion is provoked by the miracle of giving life to the decaying body of Lazarus (11:1-44). In fact, "just as the Father raises the dead and gives life, so also does the Son give life to whomever he wishes" (5:21).

The distinction between spirit and flesh is a further way of categorizing those whose whole life is oriented to God in a new age of light, truth, and eternal values, and those whose whole life is directed to the values of darkness, falsehood, and earth-bound vision. This spiritual orientation of life implies a sensitivity to a new set of values: "So it is with everyone who is born of the Spirit" (3:8). This direction, that believers and unbelievers give to their lives, is a process of constant growth or constant regression, for "What is born of flesh is flesh and what is born of spirit is spirit" (3:6); "It is the spirit that gives life, while the flesh is of no avail" (6:63). On the feast of Tabernacles, Jesus refers yet again to the new life he wishes his followers to have, and the evangelist points out that "He said this in reference to the Spirit that those who came to believe in him were to receive" (7:39).

In the new age men and women have the opportunity to direct their lives by Christ's values, to dedicate themselves to his vision of life. By doing so they are spirit-filled and heaven-bound. Those who reject Jesus and dedicate themselves to the devil are filled with self-gratification, earth-bound children of a dark world of selfish values. The latter live in sin, are slaves to sin, and will die in their sins (8:21). Jesus tells the former: "I say to you, whoever keeps my word will never see death" (8:51).

Vision of a New Age

The Prologue. John's gospel begins with a prologue that summarizes the major purposes of the entire gospel, presenting this overview in such a way that it recalls the creation story in the Old Testament. This summary of the major convictions of the gospel presents Jesus as the one who "made his dwelling among us" (1:14), like the Old Testament tent of meeting where people could encounter God. Jesus is more than a meeting place; he is the expression of the Father's wisdom and revelation to the world. As Word of the Father, the expression of personalized Wisdom, Jesus does not humble himself in the incarnation, but remains as a manifestation of the Glory of God which the Old Testament and early Christians expected to encounter in the Age to Come. The prologue affirms the gospel's first conclusion "that Jesus is the Messiah, the Son of God, and that through this belief you may have life in his name" (20:31).

The prologue that describes Jesus as "Word," "grace," and "fullness," also points out that he is superior to the lawgiver Moses in his exodus and Sinai experiences (1:17-18); and greater than the prophet John in whom the disciples had mistakenly placed their faith (1:6-8, 15). Unlike the Synoptics which anticipate the post-resurrection glory of Jesus in the transfiguration, John begins by affirming "we saw his glory, the glory as of the Father's only Son, full of grace and truth" (1:14).

Authors debate whether this prologue is Johannine, or preJohannine but Christian, or extra-Johannine and possibly Gnostic. Various writings claim: "The Prologue is saturated with Johannine vocabulary"; it is an early Christian hymn; it is an adaptation of Gnostic material; it is a combination of some of the above; it is a later addition to the gospel since some authors consider its vocabulary uncharacteristic of John.[19] Whatever its origin, it is now the major overture to the good news according to John. He presents the Word as preexistent, as creator, as lifegiver, as the conqueror of darkness, as in possession of the fullness of God's life, which he gives to those who believe. It is a vision of Jesus' cosmic significance: he begins a new age, empowers people to become children of God, fills them with enduring love, and establishes his own with an unexpected fullness of life. "These claims for the cosmic, extra-worldly existence and behavior of the Logos are poetic and imaginative in the most profound sense. They are means of expressing the significance and status of Christ in the personal lives of the Christian community."[20]

The prologue leads into a full week of inaugural activities (1:9 — 2:11) in which a series of individuals bear witness to Jesus as the Lamb of God (1:29), the Messiah (1:41), the one spoken of in the Law and the prophets (1:45), and the King of Israel (1:49). To all these Jesus adds: "I say to you, you will see the sky opened and the angels of God ascending and descending on the Son of Man" (1:51). John tells us that Jesus "was in the beginning with God. All things came to be through him, and without him nothing came to be"

(1:2-3). The new age John proclaims is the age of Jesus, of his values, and of his life.

The Baptist's testimony. Historically, John's community may have accepted previous followers of the Baptist. The Baptist is treated here not as a rival to Jesus but rather as a witness to him, as one who "came for testimony, to testify to the light, so that all might believe through him" (1:7). The Baptist acknowledges the preexistence of Jesus when he proclaims: "This is he of whom I said, 'The one who is coming after me ranks ahead of me because he existed before me'" (1:15, 30). The Fourth Gospel's Baptist quotes Mark's scripture, asserting "I am the voice of one crying out in the desert, 'Make straight the way of the Lord'" (1:23) He goes on to acknowledge his own insignificance before "the one who is coming after me, whose sandal strap I am not worthy to untie" (1:27).

John publicly proclaims that God has singled out Jesus as the one who would "baptize with the holy Spirit" (1:33) and declares: "Behold, the Lamb of God, who takes away the sin of the world!" (1:29) Later, when Jesus begins attracting more followers than John, the latter, who has already referred to himself as the forerunner, now claims he is only the friend of the bridegroom, arranging events for the bridegroom himself (3:29). He "rejoices greatly at the bridegroom's voice. So this joy of mine has been made complete. He must increase; I must decrease" (3:29-30). The Baptist, with typical Johannine insight, perceptively appreciates: "No one can receive anything except what has been given him from heaven" (3:27).

When criticized because of his attitude to the Sabbath, Jesus reminded his audience that John testified as to who he was (5:33), and forcefully adds "But I have testimony greater than John's. The works that the Father gave me to accomplish, these works that I perform testify on my behalf that the Father has sent me" (5:36). Towards the end of Jesus' ministry the crowd expresses the evangelist's conviction: "but everything John said about this man was true" (10:41).

The Fourth Gospel's Baptist is a witness to Jesus. He may be "a burning and shining lamp" (5:35), but he was always a reflection of the true light that comes to disperse the darkness (1:5).

The Baptist acknowledges the coming of a new and final age of baptism "with the holy Spirit" (1:33). In this final age there arises a new leader of the flock, "the Lamb of God, who takes away the sin of the world" (1:29). The Baptist directs his own disciples to Jesus (1:35-37). He also challenges leaders to acknowledge the absolutely exceptional nature of this new leader and redeemer from above who, John knows, ranks ahead of all because he is before all. This exceptional prophet calls attention to the beginning of a new age and then withdraws.

A new order replaces the old. The fourth evangelist addresses the issue of a new order replacing an old one on several occasions, further presenting the conviction that with Jesus we start a new age. At a Jewish wedding in Cana Jesus filled their water jars, used for ritual cleansing, with choice wine of a new age, and in doing so "revealed his glory, and his disciples began to believe in him" (2:11).

As the Jewish Passover was near, Jesus went to Jerusalem and confronted the business practices of the Temple, driving out those who bought and sold there. This cleansing of the Temple was more like a temporary shut down of its activities. When challenged — "What sign can you show us for doing this" (2:18) — Jesus prophesied the complete replacement of the Temple with himself as the place to encounter God. The former place of worship has ended, and Jesus becomes the center of our worship and our channel to God (2:19-22).

Jesus debates Nicodemus and surprises him by insisting that "no one can see the kingdom of God without being born from above" (3:3). Later, Jesus, or maybe the Johannine community, insists "we speak of what we know and we testify to what we have seen" (3:11). This new birth comes through God's only Son who came "that the world might be saved through him" (3:17). The Son brings salvation and opens others to judgment; he brings light, letting others see their darkness; he brings truth, but some prefer a life of falsehood (3:18-21).

When Jesus visited Shechem he met a Samaritan woman near Jacob's well. She was drawing water, and Jesus said to her: "Everyone who drinks this water will be thirsty again; but whoever drinks the water I shall give will never thirst; the water I shall give will become in him a spring of water welling up to eternal life" (4:13-14). In the discussion on authentic worship which follows, Jesus twice says "an hour is coming," then adds, it "is already here." When the woman says: "I know that the Messiah is coming" (4:25), Jesus announces: "I am he, the one who is speaking with you" (4:26). When the disciples return to find Jesus talking to the woman, he says to them: "I tell you, look up and see the fields ripe for the harvest" (4:35). Jesus throughout this episode contrasts the old order with a new one which has already begun with his coming. The water from Jacob's well is not to be compared to his lifegiving water, and neither the Jewish nor the Samaritan temples and their worship are to be compared to the spiritual worship Jesus announces.

The arrival of some Greeks to speak with Jesus towards the end of his ministry provides the occasion for Jesus to announce "The hour has come . . . when I am lifted up from the earth, I will draw everyone to myself" (12:23, 32). Jesus' coming brings a new order, and his passion is the culmination, when "this world's prince" is finally driven out and the new order is established. Jesus warns those who belong to the new order: "While you have the light, believe in the light, so that you may become children of the light" (12:36).

John: evangelist and interpreter. John is an evangelist, proclaiming the good news of Jesus' coming. But he is also a penetrating visionary who offers his church a new way of thinking about religious issues. Moreover, he also claims that this new way of thinking is "the true interpretation of the original material."[21] It is the quality of faith that makes this vision so remarkable; faithful to the common kerygma, he then pursues to their conclusions those many questions which haunt the believer and seem unanswered elsewhere.

John roots his message in history but interprets all history as centered on the new age of Jesus. This age is really the age to come, already anticipated with its blessings by those who believe. This new order is one of light, truth, eternal values, spirit, and endless life — all qualities that disciples must search for, all titles that Jesus uses of himself.

In John, surface meaning is never the main one; rather he calls the reader to look beyond the passing events to see the presence of a new age of God already among us. To this he bears witness at every opportunity, sharing the convictions of his community of a reality they felt privileged to have experienced.

John calls us to reassess our dedication to the full implications of the kerygma, to be aware that we live in the final age, that our lives are always to be judged by the values of Christ's revelation. In accepting the message we welcome the beginning of an eternal life of light, truth, and spirit, and reject the earth-bound values of darkness, falsehood, flesh, and death. The urgent call to dedicate ourselves to live according to the vision of this new age spurs us on daily: "We have to do the works of the one who sent me while it is day. Night is coming when no one can work" (9:4).

Chapter Four
THE PURPOSE OF JOHN

*Now Jesus did many other signs in the presence
of his disciples that are not written in this book. But
these are written that you may come to believe
that Jesus is the Messiah, the Son of God,
and that through this belief you may
have life in his name.*
(Jn 20:30-31)

Writers rarely undertake their laborious projects motivated by a single overriding purpose, and I doubt that John did either. Commentators spend time and effort to discover the one great idea that moved the author, finding supportive references for their endeavor; but it is more likely that John had several purposes in mind when he first put pen to paper, and other aims developed as his task matured. John is clearly a person of profound faith and enthusiasm, and every reader of his work will hopefully catch the spirit of faith and enthusiasm that filled John.

This chapter will consider some of his many aims, focus on his own hope that "you may have life" in Jesus, and reflect on the reasons he stressed a series of signs and discourses in his work, using them in ways quite different from other New Testament writers.

As we discern the general aims of his work, we should try to enter the spirit of the Johannine community, and let ourselves be swept along with his interests and thought. Catching an appreciation for the writer, his world, and values, can help us identify the directions he took in his work and the reasons he centered on some issues more than others. More than any other evangelist, John is enthralled with the vision of his faith, and it is hard to read him without being affected by the same enthusiasm, and being absorbed in the same faith.

Aims of the Fourth Evangelist

Influences on the purpose of John. In previous chapters we have examined a series of possible influences on the Fourth Gospel: Hellenism, Judaism, diaspora Judaism, or even Gnosticism. Various authors have identified each of these groups as the *Sitz im Leben* for John, the concrete pastoral context which gave rise to the Fourth Gospel. We have also seen how the makeup of John's community could have focused the purpose, as the writer may have tried to motivate, persuade, or convert Gentiles, Hellenistic Jews, followers of John the Baptist, or Jews who had suffered excommunication from the Synagogue because of their faith. Further, we have studied the various opinions suggesting John was written to supplement the Synoptic Gospels, or to replace them. We have also seen the suggestion that John was written to give solid foundation and apostolic authority to the Johannine interpretation of Christian tradition as its community made overtures to the Great Church in view of union. Finally we have reflected on the possible aim of refocusing the kerygma so that it stresses the necessary commitment to a new way of life in a new age.

Whenever considering the gospels a prime aim will always be christological. John has certainly done something special with his interpretation of Christ's life, ministry, and salvific death. His high christology, although different than portraits in the Synoptics, is the interpretation which the Great Church eventually accepts, and could well be the motivation for the writing.

All the above are valid motives for the evangelist's work and may well have been contributing aims to the gospel. After all, the gospel has vocabulary characteristic of a Hellenistic environment, suggesting a restatement of the tradition for the Hellenistic world. Its focus on Jerusalem, its presentation of Jewish objections to Christianity, and its anti-Jewish polemic indicate it cannot be considered exclusively as a work for Gentiles. The possibility of combining its Hellenistic influences and Jewish concerns lead to suggestions of a diaspora context. The Gnostic connections of the gospel persuaded some, even Irenaeus, Jerome, and other Fathers, that John wrote to refute this heresy.

The Fourth Gospel's unusual apologetic against the messianic claims of the followers of the Baptist highlights one of the pastoral problems the writer faced, as does that part of the anti-Jewish emphasis expressing anger at the excommunication from the synagogue which seems to have afflicted some of the members of John's community.

The purpose of John's gospel is more difficult to identify than is that of the other gospels. The complex history and development of the Johannine community, together with the commonly-held opinion that the redactional history of the gospel is equally complex, lead to an appreciation that various purposes may be found as motives at each stage in the community's and the gospel's history.

Finally, the letters of John that post-date the gospel indicate attempts to clarify some issues in the gospel, issues that could be considered important enough to be part of the original motive for writing. Thus, the pastoral responses to incipient Docetism, or to Diotrephes' possible abuse of power or structures, come to light.

Recent studies of John's gospel. Since the '60s there have been many excellent studies on John, some surveys of the studies, and many fine articles giving summaries of recent developments.[1] Works have focused on literary criticism, the gospel's relationship to the Synoptics, sociological questions, community history, theology, tradition history, and specific concerns the community may have faced. Commentators have offered a variety of insights and conclusions, but a consensus has not developed on the major questions concerning the gospel. Four areas of recent studies are useful for our consideration because they throw light on the purpose of the work.

Attempts at *source criticism* proved unsuccessful as writers tried to show John's dependence on the Synoptics (Barrett 1955) or on some hypothetical source (Bultmann 1941, Fortna 1970 support a sign source; Lindars 1971 accepts a discourse source; Temple 1975 sees a core made up of a narrative-discourse source). Moreover, as commentators became

convinced of the literary unity of John, there was less interest
in a study of the sources (Dodd 1963, D. Moody Smith 1975).
While form criticism has been a useful tool for analysis, it is
difficult to apply to John with anything more than preliminary
success. "The entire document is pervaded by a distinctiveness
which makes analysis of passages in terms of pre-literary
history most difficult, and some would say, unnecessary."[2]
Nowadays, rather than deal with sources, Johannine scholars
direct their interest to the tradition behind John. They use
redaction criticism to distinguish between his editorial contributions and the traditions he depends on, appreciating that
the traditions he has chosen and the editorial additions
he makes offer good indications of purpose (Martyn 1968).
Some of these redactional studies have focused on the presence or absence of ecclesiology, or sacramentalism in the
tradition, and whether or not these are due to the redactor
(Kysar 1975).

Some Fourth Gospel criticism has focused on *the development of John's community* (Brown 1979), seeking to identify
the origin and nature of the community (Cullman 1976,
Käsemann 1968), and to retrace its history and experience
(Brown 1966). The situation of the community (Martyn 1968)
and the specific traditions of the Johannine church proved
to be interesting areas of study, while the theology of the
gospel has been viewed as a community theology resulting
from the work of a Johannine school (Culpepper 1975).
Under this same thrust some writers have delved into the
special concerns of the community behind this gospel.[3]

This final category leads to a third group of studies which
emphasize *John's theology*. Although known from early
times as "the theologian," John does not offer a systematic
theological presentation. Nevertheless, a series of theological
convictions weave their way through the text. John's christology has received prime attention (Moloney 1976), as have
his eschatology, wisdom motifs, use of signs (Fortna 1970),
and challenge to faith (Schnackenburg 1968). Moreover, the
debate on his ecclesiology and sacramentalism also continues.
In places his work is so clearly structured and so evidently
demands reflection, it has also been proposed that the author
aims at a liturgical use for his work (Borgen 1965).

Study of the text itself has led to a critical analysis of *the text's effects on readers* (Culpepper 1983). Early studies focused on John's readers as Gentiles, or diaspora Jews, or Christians of Asia Minor, listening to instruction or to evangelical exhortation; now the emphasis is on a consideration of the text in its entirety, and its influence on readers as an integral piece of literature. This combination of narrative criticism and reader-response criticism has opened new avenues in our approach to John and our determination of his purpose.

Pastoral concerns and interests. John's gospel is a profound integration of a wide spectrum of Christian traditions, and he unquestionably had several motives for his work. In addition to the specific responses to his environment and the emphases resulting from an examination of recent studies, this section focuses on some of the pastoral concerns and interests that also motivated him.

Different authors are very convinced of the audience for which John wrote. J. B. Lightfoot says John wrote for Jews since the gospel "smells of the soil of Palestine." W. C. van Unnik says John wrote for a synagogue in the dispersion. B. W. Bacon claims John wrote to vindicate Paul's vision of Church. C.K. Barrett feels that the depth of thought in John presumed an audience that had a good grasp of the gospel and basic Christian theology, and so must have been written for informed Christians. Others think he wrote for Gentiles; still others point to the heretics' welcome of John. It is amazing what a wide variety of people can find an echo in this work and this suggests a universalist approach rather than a continuing battle over which one group predominates. John's presentation offers some appeal to a wide range of people: there is something here for everyone, which cannot be said of the other gospels.

John evidences a polemical tone. There are signs of open controversy with the Jews, and particularly strong reactions to the legislation of Jamnia and its anticipation in the local practices of excommunication from the synagogues. There are indications of confrontation with Pharisaic interpretations of the Law, as the author seems to struggle to guarantee that his disciples of Jewish origin do not make the same mistakes

as their Palestinian counterparts. He bluntly presents his
view of Jesus, a view which not only disturbed the Jews but
also Christians of the Great Church. A flavor of trial permeates
the narrative, but the author seems little disturbed by the
constant need to defend his faith. John does not show a nasty
streak in his approach to opposition, but he is certainly
willing to confront opposition, and to go to any lengths to
defend his interpretation of faith. He presents his views
so they will be well received in the Hellenistic world, and
while heresies arise in this environment, he challenges them
as well as the incipient Docetism.

Besides his universalism and constant willingness to confront opposition, John is a leader with considerable pastoral
skill and enthusiasm. He does not explain everything: rather
he bears witness to what Jesus gives us; he invites us to
see, to understand, to experience; he tells us what he has
seen and how convinced he is; and then he leaves us to
draw our own conclusions and mature our own faith.

John has a clear interest in ecclesiology, although he does
not develop it along lines to which we are accustomed. His
teachings on love, unity, and community are very strong but
refer almost exclusively to the members of the community,
with little suggestion of outreach to others. Moreover, his
gospel contains no church structure, no intermediate channels
of authority, and little similarity to known practices in the
Great Church.

Universalism, controversy, and defense of faith, invitation
to enthusiastically share faith, and an unusual approach to
Church: these are some of the interests which, added to the
motives that influenced his work and the suggestions of
recent scholars, give us a clearer idea of his general aims.

Structure of John. There is reasonable agreement on the
division of John's gospel into major units. Most commentators
accept a break at Chapter 13, seeing 1-12 as one section
and 13-20 as another; the former presents Jesus' ministry,
the latter his passion. Thus we have a commonly accepted
general outline.

```
I.  INTRODUCTIONS IN THE PROLOGUE   1:1-18
II. THE BOOK OF SIGNS               1:19 – 12:50
```

III. THE BOOK OF GLORY 13:1 – 20:31
APPENDIX 21:1-25

The Book of Signs offers the progressive self-revelation of Jesus in his early ministry, in his several journeys to Jerusalem, and in the period immediately preceding his passion. Throughout this part of the gospel there are series of signs, discourses, and religious feasts — the author using each for significant furtherance of his purpose. Part III deals with the glorification of Jesus in his passion. The gospel ends with the addition of an appendix. A detailed outline appears below which clearly indicates how John uses his structure to present his major aims.

I. INTRODUCTIONS

1:1-18 Prologue: the presentation of Jesus

II. THE BOOK OF SIGNS

Initial testimonies to the Lord

1:19-34	The Baptist — Lamb of God
1:35-39	Two disciples — Teacher
1:40-42	Andrew — Messiah
1:43-44	Philip — the one in the Law and prophets
1:45-49	Nathaniel — Son of God, King of Israel
1:50-51	Jesus' self-declaration as Son of Man

Early public ministry

2:1-12	Cana: water to wine — Sign 1
2:13-25	Cleansing of the Temple
3:1-21	Discourse with Nicodemus
3:22 – 4:3	Baptizing ministries of Jesus and John — John acknowledges a new age
4:4-42	Discourse with the Samaritan woman

4:43-54	Healing of official's son — Sign 2

Journeys to Jerusalem for the feasts

Sabbath

5:1-15	Cure at pool of Bethesda — Sign 3
5:16-47	Discourse on the Father's work for Jesus

Passover

6:1-15	Feeding of the 5000 — Sign 4
6:16-24	Jesus walks on the water
6:25-71	Discourse on the Bread of Life

Tabernacles

7:1-13	Jesus journeys to the feast
7:14-36	Discourse: Jesus and the Law of Moses
7:37-52	Discourse on living water
[7:53 — 8:11	The adulteress — a non-Johannine interpolation]
8:12-30	Discourse on the light of the world
8:31-59	Discourse: Jesus and Abraham
9:1-41	Healing of blind man — Sign 5
10:1-21	Discourse on the Good Shepherd

Dedication

10:22-24	Feast of the Dedication
10:25-39	Discourse on Jesus and the Father
10:40-42	Jesus withdraws to Jordan

Prelude to the passion

11:1-44	Raising of Lazarus — Sign 6
11:45-54	Meeting of Sanhedrin and plot
11:55-57	Last Passover
12:1-11	Anointing of Jesus at Bethany
12:12-19	Triumphant entry into Jerusalem
12:20-36	Greeks ask to meet Jesus — Discourse on life through death
12:37-43	Evaluation of Jesus' ministry

PURPOSE OF JOHN

12:44-50 — Final challenge to unbelievers

III. THE BOOK OF GLORY

The meal
- 13:1-20 — Washing of disciples' feet
- 13:21-30 — Prophecy of Judas' betrayal
- 13:31-35 — New commandment
- 13:36-38 — Prophecy of Peter's denial

Final discourses
- 14:1-31 — First farewell discourse
- 15:1 – 16:33 — Second farewell discourse
- 17:1-26 — Jesus' apostolic prayer

The Passion
- 18:1-12 — Arrest in Gethsemane
- 18:13-27 — Appearance before Annas and Caiaphas — Peter's denials
- 18:28 – 19:16 — Trial before Pilate
- 19:17-30 — The Crucifixion
- 19:31-37 — A final testimony
- 19:38-42 — Burial

The Resurrection
- 20:1-10 — Peter and another disciple discover empty tomb
- 20:11-18 — Appearance to Mary Magdalene
- 20:19-23 — Appearance to the disciples
- 20:24-29 — Appearance to the disciples and Thomas

CONCLUSION

20:30-31

APPENDIX

21:1-14 — Jesus appears to disciples

21:15-19   Peter the shepherd and martyr
21:24-25   Second conclusion

The Gift of Life

John's rich proclamation fulfills several goals, but clearly the fostering of faith in Jesus was a major focus of his entire enterprise. Before the addition of a brief appendix in Chapter 21, the original conclusion of John's proclamation was 20:31 in which he claims to have recorded the message to help his community "believe that Jesus is the Messiah." However, John's is not only an intellectual project that gives information, persuades readers of the greatness of Jesus, or challenges them to an orthodox formulation of faith. The last line of the conclusion rings out the consequence of faith: "that through this belief you may have life in his name." Faith leads to salvation, life, fullness of life, and it is to these Johannine insights that we now turn.

Life in Christ. We have seen that John's understanding of Christianity was that it is primarily a new way of existence in a new age of God. It is above all a qualitatively different life. In fact, while the notion of life is exclusively future in the Synoptics, it is both future and present experience in John. He never uses the word "life" (zoe) for natural existence, but only for the true, real, eternal life, that is already experienced because of Jesus. While Matthew uses the word "life" seven times, Mark four, and Luke five, John uses it thirty-five times in the gospel, as well as thirteen times in the first letter. Of the thirty-five gospel uses, there are thirty-two in the first twelve chapters and only three in the book of the passion (Chapters 13-20) and the appendix. This significant change of terminology is also seen in terms such as "to live," "to give life," "light," and "to light."[4]

Jesus is the source of life:[5] "For just as the Father has life in himself, so also he gave to his Son the possession of life in himself" (5:26). Like a Good Shepherd (10:14-15), Jesus offers life-giving food (6:35) in revealing God's saving love (1:17-18). This revelation brings salvation, brings life. In fact, Christ, salvation, and life are identical terms for believers. "John's most characteristic word for salvation, then, is life, and ultimately it is not a quality, a state, to which Jesus brings men, but Jesus himself. 'I am the resurrection and the life' (11:25; cf. 14:6)."[6] Thus, Jesus claims "the one who feeds on me will have life because of me" (6:57); and elsewhere he succinctly states the great message of John's work: "you will see me, because I live and you will live" (14:19).

Jesus, "the way and the truth and the life" (14:6), like a grain of wheat, dies in order to produce life (12:24); he gives his flesh for the life of the world (6:51). In fact, he claims: "This is why the Father loves me, because I lay down my life in order to take it up again" (10:17). Although Jesus' life-giving mission is referred to most frequently in the first twelve chapters, it is particularly at the raising of Lazarus that he spectacularly demonstrates his Father's gift: "whoever believes in me, even if he dies, will live, and everyone who lives and believes in me will never die" (11:25-26).

Life was a central concept for John. He saw Jesus as the Word of God, in whom "What came to be through him was life" (1:4). Jesus is greater than the Baptist, and "Whoever believes in the Son has eternal life" (3:36). He is nourishment for the thirsty Samaritan woman, and claims "the water I shall give will become in him a spring of water welling up to eternal life" (4:14). He is the revelation of the Father, who reveals that "whoever hears my word and believes in the one who sent me has eternal life" (5:24). Jesus is the new way God providentially feeds his pilgrim people; "I am the bread of life" (6:35). When Jerusalem celebrates the Lord's gift of water, Jesus announces he is the "living water" they seek (7:37). Before his encounter with the blind man in chapter nine, Jesus had already said: "I am the light of the world" and assured his followers that they would "have the light of life" (8:12). He is the Good Shepherd who says "I came so that they might have life and have it more abundantly" (10:10). While some of his opponents celebrated the dedication of the Temple as the place of spiritual nourishment and encounter with God, Jesus insists: "I give ... eternal life" (10:28). Thus John related each of these descriptions of Jesus to his lifegiving activity, indicating that much of this gospel can be grouped around this central concept of life.

A disciple of Jesus "has passed from death to life" (5:24); he or she has entered a new way of living with God. It is as if the Synoptics' notion of kingdom is replaced by entering into life. This new existence is not just something for oneself, but is life-giving for others, too: "Let anyone who thirsts come to me and drink. Whoever believes in me, as scripture says: 'Rivers of living water will flow from within him' " (7:37-38). While Jesus is the primary source, believers also become sources of that life for others.

Conditions for receiving life. No one earns the life that Jesus brings; it is a gift which disciples receive with open hands. The prologue, which sets the stage for the entire gospel, is structured in inverted parallelism, or chiasm, and centers on 1:12b "he gave power to become children of God."[7] The whole prologue pivots on this fundamental awareness that Jesus empowers; the helpless disciple receives. Thus the task of the believer is to be open to God, for Jesus reminds all: "No one can come to me unless the Father who sent me draw him" (6:44). The disciple is drawn to a preliminary appreciation of Jesus by the reading of the scriptures: "search the scriptures . . . they testify on my behalf" (5:39). Elsewhere we read that Moses announced Jesus in the Bible: "he wrote about me" (5:46). Open to the channels of God's word, the believer must be sensitive to the challenges of the Holy Spirit since "It is the spirit that gives life" (6:63), who will "remind you of all that [I] told you" (14:26), and "will guide you to all truth" (16:13).

This openness to God must be complemented by belief in Jesus and acceptance of his words. This challenge, most notably stressed in the gospel's solemn conclusion (20:31), is also well expressed by Peter: "Master, to whom shall we go? You have the words of eternal life" (6:68). The disciple must be willing to come close to Jesus in order to receive his gift of life (5:40). Those of whom Jesus says "my word has no room among you" (8:37) have chosen another kind of existence than what Jesus offers; they "will not see life, but the wrath of God" (3:36). However, those who are receptive to Jesus' message find that "the one whom God sent speaks of the words of God. He does not ration his gift of the Spirit"

(3:34), and those who believe in him will find the life they seek (3:36).

The disciple needs openness to God, belief and acceptance of Jesus' word, and also the experience of a new birth before entering the new life of a child of God. Jesus' passion was "to gather into one the dispersed children of God" (11:52; also 3:14-15). Reception of life, for John, means becoming a child of God through a rebirth: this is how one passes from death to life, from darkness to light, from bondage to freedom.[8] In his discourse with Nicodemus Jesus points out that the Holy Spirit is the agent of this new birth into the life of faith. A new birth implies the surrender of a previous way of life, and union with the death of Jesus (3:14-15). Through this the disciple is born into a community of God.

Once born again, the believer must abide in Jesus, as one who "remains in me and I in him" (6:56). The parable of the branch, which gets life from the vine, admirably portrays the need for a constant commitment: "Remain in me, as I remain in you. . . . because without me you can do nothing" (15:4-5). When the disciple abides in faithful obedience and love, Jesus gives assurance, "Whoever loves me will keep my word, and my Father will love him, and we will come to him and make our dwelling with him" (14:23).

Thus, among the conditions for receiving life from Jesus are openness to the Lord, belief and acceptance of Jesus' words, a new birth, and a willingness to abide in God.

Fullness of life. When these conditions are met, "Whoever believes in the Son has eternal life" (3:36). "For this is the will of my Father, that everyone who sees the Son and believes in him may have eternal life" (6:40). Eternal life, which consists in knowing the Father, and the one whom he sent (17:3), is not something one receives in the future; rather it is a present possession. Such a one already "has eternal life" (5:24), for "I say to you, whoever believes has eternal life" (6:47). This realized gift is also a pledge of final resurrection (6:54); Jesus complements the eternal, yet present, characteristic of life with the assurance of final resurrection (5:28-29) and with the consoling promise that he will prepare places for true believers (14:2-3). Their reward will include the reality that "they shall never perish" (10:28) even though they die they will come to life (11:26).

The fullness of life given by Jesus as a result of faith is knowledge, vision, and present experience of God. It means already seeing the reign of God and entering his kingdom (3:3, 5). Since final resurrection and eternal life are already present in Jesus, "For the believer there is not 'then' without a 'now,' and because of what happens 'now' the importance of what will happen 'then' — for it is not denied — is greatly reduced."[9] John's is the good news that eternal life is a present option: "I came that they might have life and have it more abundantly" (10:10).

John constantly refers to eternal life: he uses the phrase eighteen times and "life" seventeen times. It implies the abandonment of false security in self and this world's prince, and appreciating that one is secure in the saving love of the Father. "Whoever loves me will be loved by my Father, and I will love him and reveal myself to him" (14:21). Reborn to a new life, we are empowered to live as a family and can do so confidently. "For the Father himself loves you, because you have loved me and have come to believe that I came from God" (16:27).

A part of this security is the resulting gift of Jesus' peace. He can say to those who have life in his name: "Do not let your hearts be troubled" (14:1); "Peace I leave with you; my peace I give to you" (14:27; 16:33). And with this peace goes joy, even amidst present hardships (15:11; 16:20, 24; 17:13). The life of God means freedom, especially from the slavery of sin (8:34-36). A committed follower is willing to lose life in order to truly save it (12:25).

The fullness of eternal life offered by Jesus is understandable only as love. "From his fullness we have all received, grace in place of grace" (1:16). To be born as a child of God means being born into a loving community, for which Jesus prays "Holy Father, keep them in your name that you have given me, so that they may be one just as we are" (17:11). This "new power of saving love, glorious in its faithfulness and tenderness,"[10] comes from the Father and Jesus (15:14-17). This new relationship with Jesus produces new relationships with others (15:12-13), a deeper sense of unity (17:11, 21), and an awareness that we are all part of the Lord's flock for which he gave his life (10:11).

John calls all to find a new life, fullness of life in faith in Jesus. While he stresses believing throughout, and especially in the conclusion (20:31), "believing for John is only the means and not the end that the writer has in view. The goal he has in mind is 'life.' Therefore, to call the Gospel of John 'The Gospel of Believing,' . . . is inadequate."[11] The real revelation is that faith leads to fullness of life, anticipated now and prolonging itself in eternity. This life is eternal, a pledge of final resurrection, and leads to the abandoning of all false securities and the finding of one's peace and love in God. This fullness of life means love of God and love of the community, which produces a deep unity among all.

The Signs

Nature of Johannine signs. In the Old Testament the signs and wonders performed during the Exodus were the creative and salvific actions of God, revealing his nature and his loving care for the people. This Old Testament usage is very similar to John's and may well provide a significant background to his use of signs.

The Synoptics focus on the miraculous power of Jesus and recount many more of Jesus' miraculous deeds than John does: healings, exorcisms, nature miracles, and raisings from the dead. Each Synoptic gospel contains at least three times more miraculous acts than John does. Particularly noticeable is John's complete omission of exorcisms, especially since the conquest of demonic power is important in each of the Synoptics, and even dominates the wondrous acts of Jesus in Mark. Perhaps John's omission is not so surprising, since in the Synoptics Jesus acknowledges that others besides himself cast out demons, whereas John has selected the most extraordinary stories as clarifications of Jesus' glorious life. John's gospel has no parables. Rather he presents a small selection of Jesus' mighty works as acted parables that achieve much of what the Synoptic parables do.

"John's Gospel is notable not for the many deeds of Jesus it records but for the profound exposition of the few it selects."[12] John says little about the miracles' accompanying circumstances that highlight Jesus as a wonder-worker. Instead, he calls the miracles "signs," revelations of who Jesus is; they are outward signs of the inner reality of Christ, manifestations of his divinity. John takes these signs, heightens the remarkable presence of Jesus, and uses each as "a window into the reality of that which Jesus always was and always is and always did and always does."[13]

John, then, refers to Jesus' miracles as signs: "Jesus did this as the beginning of signs in Cana in Galilee" (2:11). Following, the healing of the official's son we read, "[Now] this was the second sign Jesus did" (4:54). In his conclusion (20:30) John says, "Jesus did many other signs in the presence of [his] disciples that are not written in this book." Jesus twice uses "signs" to describe his activity, complaining "Unless you people see signs and wonders, you will not believe" (4:48), and elsewhere, "I say to you, you are looking for me not because you saw signs but because you ate the loaves and were filled" (6:26). Even the crowd uses the word, asking, "What sign can you do, that we may see and believe in you?" (6:30). On all other occasions Jesus refers to his miracles as "works." In fact, he sums up the whole of his ministry as the work the Father had given him. Elsewhere he includes his preaching as part of his great works. "The words that I speak to you I do not speak on my own. The Father who dwells in me is doing his works" (14:10). This broad concept of "work" Jesus uses especially of his miraculous deeds. "The works that the Father gave me to accomplish ... testify on my behalf" (5:36). "I told you, and you do not believe. The works I do in my Father's name testify to me" (10:25, 37). More solemnly he can say, "Believe me that I am in the Father and the Father is in me, or else, believe because of the works themselves" (14:11). During the Last Supper Jesus laments, "If I had not done works among them that no one else ever did, they would not have sin; but as it is, they have seen and hated both me and my Father" (15:24).

Jesus' comments indicate that the works are the Father's mandate to him (5:36); they witness to who Jesus is (10:37-38); there is blame in rejecting them (15:24); and they show the close relationship between Jesus and the Father (10:38; 14:11).

Each sign is closely associated with a discourse which explains and interprets the meaning of the sign. In fact, sometimes the presentation of the sign is brief but the discussion of its meaning prolonged, for example, the healings of the sick man and the blind man. "It would hardly be overstating the case to say that miracle story plus discourse constitute sign-narrative for John."[14] Together they witness to and reveal facets of John's christology. "Moreover, they are presented in their deepest sense ... as works of the Father performed by Jesus. The unity of Christ and God in action is the motif of the signs, and they invite men to ascertain that unity, if they will."[15] They demonstrate Jesus' divine power, prove his authority, and show he is the one who can give life and give it to the full (10:10).[16]

Structure and number of the signs. John's presentation of Jesus' signs is a major part of the work. In fact, the main section of his gospel is often called the Book of Signs. Some authors, such as Bultmann and Fortna, suggest that John had a source made up of sign material. Many miraculous deeds are referred to by John, and called signs, not all in the Book of Signs (2:23; 12:37; 20:30). Moreover, other non-miraculous acts of Jesus seem to fulfill the same purposes as the signs: the cleansing of the Temple (2:13-22) and the washing of the disciples' feet (13:1-20) are certainly acted parables with revelationary value.

Apart from general summary statements on Jesus' wondrous activity (2:23; 12:37; 20:30), John presents a small list of extraordinary miraculous actions of Jesus: the miracle of wine at Cana in Galilee (2:1-12); the healing of the royal official's son (4:43-54); the cure of the sick man at the pool of Bethesda in Jerusalem (5:1-15); the feeding of the 5000 (6:1-15); the walking on the water (6:16-24); the healing of a man born blind (9:1-41); the raising of Lazarus from the dead (11:1-44); and the extraordinary catch of fish (21:1-14).

The miracle at Cana, the cure of the man at Bethesda, the healing of the man born blind, and the raising of Lazarus have no Synoptic parallels; however, some commentators suggest John's story of Lazarus is a personal construction based on his theology and the parable on Lazarus in Luke (Lk 16:19-31). The healing of the official's son is probably

a different version of the stories of Matthew (Mt 8:5-13) and
Luke (Lk 7:1-10). The feeding of the 5000 and the walking on
the water are closest in context and order to the Synoptics
(Mk 6:32-51; Mt 14:13-33; Lk 9:10-17). The Johannine post-
resurrection miraculous catch of fish has some similarities
with Luke's expanded version of the call of Peter (Lk 5:1-11).
Brown, having examined similarities between the stories,
states: "The similarities listed above make it reasonable to
conclude that independently Luke and John have preserved
variant forms of the same miracle story."[17]

Does John use all these stories as signs of Jesus' self-
revelation? There are two which require further consideration.
I doubt that John intended the story of Jesus walking on
the water to be considered as an independent sign. Chapter
6 presents the feeding of the 5000, clearly based on God's
providential care of his people during the Exodus, feeding
them with manna, whereas Jesus now gives his own flesh
to eat. John probably includes the walking on the water
because he found it joined to the feeding in his sources;
he could see how this episode of crossing the water is a
suitable ending to a narrative based on the Exodus and
spoken by Jesus at the Passover. No independent discourse
follows this miracle, and unlike the other sign stories it
produces no faith-response in participants. In fact, it is
followed by the discourse on the bread of life, affirming yet
again its relationship to that previous episode. This story is
to be read as part of the feeding; it is probably not viewed
by John as a miracle at all, and certainly not as a sign.[18]

The other miraculous event requiring further reflection
is the catch of fish, which has no accompanying explanatory
discourse. It is a post-resurrection appearance of the glorified
Lord, rather than a pre-resurrection sign revealing that Jesus
is the glorified one. It is not a call to faith and an invitation
to encounter Jesus in the sign; it is a proof, a post-resurrection
confirmation of the signs. If it has any other purpose, it is
to proclaim the extraordinary apostolic mission of the Church.

Some commentators accept all the above eight miracles
as Johannine signs. Others restrict their use to the so-called
Book of Signs; thus they exclude the catch of fish and retain
the other seven, aware of John's clear use of a pattern of

sevens.[19] Smalley has an interesting summary. He accepts the basic six signs but excludes the walking on the water. These six are preceded by the prologue which describes the incarnation and is an anticipation of what the signs will reveal. The six signs are concluded in the resurrection which is the fulfillment to which the signs point. He sees the catch of fish as a seventh sign, a postresurrection revelation.[20]

The six acceptable signs in the Book of Signs precede the passion of Jesus, which is a further revelation of his glory, a sign of his power and union with his Father. The six anticipatory signs have the same revelatory purpose. Along with others, I would see that "the first six signs are incomplete and look forward to the seventh at Jesus's great hour of death and glorification, when he will be lifted up and draw everyone to himself."[21]

The seven signs are arranged chiastically: 1. *Transformation* of wine at Cana (A), 2. Official's *dying* son (B), 3. *Cure* at Bethesda (C), 4. Feeding of the 5000 (D), 5. *Cure* of a blind man (C'), 6. Raising of *dead* Lazarus (B'), 7. *Transformation* sacrifice of Jesus (A'). Thus the signs parallel each other in inverted order: 1 and 7, 2 and 6, 3 and 5, with the new salvific exodus of 4 being the hinge that unites them.

Teaching of the signs. Reactions to the signs varied considerably: after Cana the disciples began to believe; later in Cana the official and all his household believed; the sick man at the pool did not know who cured him, and when he found out he betrayed Jesus; after the feeding many disciples abandoned Jesus; the blind man believed but the Pharisees turned against Jesus; Martha and Mary believed in Jesus at Lazarus' rising; a small church community supported Jesus at his death but no expression of faith was made. "In order for signs to contribute in a positive way to the birth and growth of religious faith, they must be perceived in a certain way."[22] People need to question what is happening, but to do so with an openness that presupposes a minimal faith. For some in Jesus' audience the signs meant nothing and aroused no positive religious response (12:37), rather at times they even harden people in their hatred of God (15:24). The raising of Lazarus led some to betray Jesus (11:46). The Book of Signs ends with a summary evaluation of Jesus' ministry as a failure: "Although he had performed so many signs in their presence they did not believe in him" (12:37). The general response to Jesus was not unlike the Egyptian's response to Moses' signs (Exodus 10:1; Numbers 14:11, 22; Deuteronomy 7:19).

Are signs meant to lead to faith, or is it faith that precedes the signs? At one time John suggests the former (2:11; 4:53), on another occasion the latter (4:48; 14:11). One author suggests that John has combined two traditions, "one which understands signs as having a legitimating function, and another which has Jesus refusing to grant signs as a means of initiating faith."[23] The legitimating of Jesus' messiahship is clearly a function of the signs, but possibly only in so far as it reinforces faith for those who already believe.

Weddings and banquets are Old Testament symbols which Jesus often used in the Synoptics to describe messianic fulfillment. The dramatic action in Cana — the replacement of water by wine, the best wine kept until Jesus intervenes, the filling of the ritual jars with Jesus' gift, the abundance of wine and joy — all represent the inexhaustible gifts of the new age that Jesus inaugurates, and his superiority over all that preceded him. The event takes place "on the third day" (2:1) and points to Jesus' final establishment of new life in his resurrection.[24]

The second sign, the healing of the royal official's son (4:46-54), although brief and not followed by a discourse, focuses on two issues critical for the rest of the gospel. The first is faith, which is rewarded in the official, but which is also contrasted with too much reliance on signs. The second issue is life, as Jesus restores life to a dying boy, giving a clear direction to the rest of the narrative.

The third sign takes place in Jerusalem at the Bethesda pool. It is not just the healing which is important; the real sign is that it is a Sabbath healing. Thus this sign is followed by the discourse on Jesus' Sabbath work and his relationship to his Father. The sad outcome of this sign is that it fails to evoke faith. However, it is a critical point in Jesus' ministry, leading to the early decision to put him to death, because he "called God his own father, making himself equal to

God" (5:18). John thereby draws out for us the meaning of this sign.

The feeding of the five thousand, together with the great discourse on the bread of life, is a central event in John's gospel. It takes place near Passover, portrays the crowd murmuring (6:41, 60) as they did with Moses, and ends with a passage over water. This exodus, in which Jesus is seen as a leader and deliverer who providentially feeds his people, summarizes the major thrusts of the whole gospel. Jesus manifests himself to the people, and offers them eternal life; some choose, and others walk away.

The Sabbath cure of the man born blind is a masterpiece of Johannine literary and theological skills. The blind man is challenged to immerse himself in a pool called "sent," to reveal to all their need to be immersed in the one sent by the Father. The man sees, and he believes, and thus anticipates the Beloved Disciple's postresurrection faith (20:8). The dialogue and interrogation which follows portray the man's courageous confession of Jesus under pressure and make him a model for the Johannine community. The event is another portrayal of the new age since Jesus is the light of the world (9:5), and what happens has never been seen since the world began (9:32).

The Lazarus story is a dramatic conclusion to the ministry of Jesus, showing Jesus as the source of life. It not only heralds a final resurrection but insists on the redemption from death and the gift of new life that faith in Jesus already brings (11:25-26) because of his constant union with his Father (11:41-42). This sign leads to Jesus' death, and to Caiaphas' prophecy that his death happened so that all could live (11:50-52).

All of these signs lead to the seventh sign of Jesus' self-gift in death. These signs "express as well as symbolize their basic meaning: that eternal life is given by God to the believer through Jesus the Messiah."[25] Although the stories are different there is a remarkable common emphasis on the gift of new life in Jesus.

The Discourses

John's use of the discourses. A series of major dialogues punctuates the gospel of John. Some authors have been convinced that a long discourse or dialogue follows every sign as an interpretation of it. Thus, for these authors, the seven signs/discourses become the main structure of the entire gospel. For some there is a progression in John's thought through the seven signs/discourses, whereas for others each sign/discourse "is so constructed that each several episode contains in itself the whole theme of the Gospel."[26] Clearly some discourses are directly related to a sign. Thus the Bread of Life discourse interprets the feeding of the five thousand. Other significant discourses or dialogues are not related directly to a sign: Jesus' discourse with Nicodemus, even though Nicodemus does refer to the astounding signs of Jesus (3:2); Jesus' dialogue with the Samaritan woman. There are also significant discourses outside the Book of Signs.

A large portion of this gospel is in discourse or dialogue form. The discourses are solemn, difficult to understand, profound theological reflections, often used as explanations of the signs. Some authors consider that John had a discourse source available to him, but this seems less likely than in the case of the signs-source. A consensus seems to have emerged that "The dialogue and discourse material in the fourth gospel has in most cases arisen from redaction."[27] It is hardly likely that Jesus himself would have spoken like the mystical theologian of the discourses.

These original literary creations of John are unlike the Synoptics; their language, concepts, and style are different, though, as Dodd points out, Synoptic-like sayings are embedded in the discourses, and at times John uses imagery already in the Synoptics. Even an entire dialogue, such as that with Nicodemus, could be a Johannine reinterpretation of Jesus' discussion with the rich young man.[28]

John uses the discourses for theological purposes, each being basically a theological reflection. They are artificial constructions, similar in style and purpose to the great patriarchal discourses in the Old Testament. In the New Testament the Pastoral letters taken together form one literary, yet artificial, presentation of the final will and testament of Paul, and 2 Peter serves a similar function. John likewise felt free, along the lines of ancient historians, to put major speeches in the mouth of his master. Jesus speaks, but in Johannine terms, since the speech writer is John, even though some of the material may have been already combined in the community's evolving oral tradition.[29] These speeches are long, involved, difficult to follow, and so unlike the speeches of Jesus we know from the rest of the New Testament, they cannot be considered historical. It seems most unlikely that John ever expected people to think they were, since he presents most discourses as spoken by the postresurrection glorified Lord. Moreover, some speeches recorded in detail claim to have been given at very private meetings — that with Nicodemus, for example, or the chance encounter with the Samaritan woman.

These very important Johannine constructions exemplify typical stylistic characteristics of the redactional parts of the gospel — parallelism, contrast, irony, and use of key words — a further indication of John's authorship of them. Sometimes a discourse imperceptibly merges into a monologue, as in the encounter with Nicodemus; sometimes a dialogue merges into a discourse, as in the case of the Good Shepherd. One of the farewell discourses becomes a long prayer of Jesus.

Although clearly artificial, these speeches contain authentic approaches of Jesus, and John offers them as a reliable synthesis of the truths he has discerned in the message and life of Jesus. He composes these discourses to address major issues in his community as can more easily be seen in those discourses where it is clear "that it is the risen Lord who is speaking and that the hearers are Christians living in John's own day."[30]

These revelatory discourses, profound christological statements, deal with the gift of life that Jesus brings. They start with the birth of this life in the Nicodemus discourse and present various facets of this fullness of life.

The teachings of the discourses. The first major discourse summarizes Jesus' encounter with Nicodemus. It follows the sign at Cana and the prophetical action of the cleansing of the Temple and states, as they do, that a new age begins with Jesus and that disciples must break with the past and be reborn in God (3:5-6). The discourse, with its focus on new birth, Spirit-life, and the lifting up of Jesus, is programmatic of the whole gospel. While speaking of new life this first discourse describes that life as water (3:5), belief (3:12), light (3:19), and truth (3:21), thereby immediately making links with key concepts of later discourses. This discourse is also a marvellous summary of John's christology. Jesus is the one sent, the Son of Man, the one lifted up, the only Son, and the light.

Jesus' dialogue with the Samaritan woman contrasts the outcast's faith with the tentativeness of Nicodemus, Israel's teacher, and presents an early example of Jesus' opposition to religious and cultural rationalizations of injustice. It may also be an indication of a Samaritan group in John's community, desirous of showing Jesus' success in that region through the shared ministry of the woman. Living water (4:10-15), authentic worship in Jesus (4:16-26), and true food (4:27-38) are the themes that focus this dialogue and link it with other discourses. It should be mentioned that the importance of lasting relationships and commitment plays a significant role, as it must for all disciples (4:16-18).

Following Jesus' Sabbatical cure of the man at the Bethesda pool in Jerusalem, we have the third main discourse on the authority of Jesus and his relationship to his Father. Although dealing with Sabbath work, this discourse focuses on the Son's authority to grant life and some of the conditions for its acceptance. The new age is here and the separation of the two ways of life is already underway. Consequently Jesus' power to give life is also a power of judgment (5:26-30).

The multiplication of loaves is a critical turning point in Jesus' ministry. The crowd was ready to support him as a political messiah (6:15), and he had to give a clear focus to his own messiahship. Continuing the previous discourses' emphasis on a new age, and following from birth, nourishing water, and the authority of Jesus, this discourse presents Jesus as the leader of a new exodus in which he providentially cares for and feeds the people. The truth of the new age is complemented by a life sustained by feeding on Jesus on whom "the Father, God, has set his seal" (6:27). The Israelites died, although they had eaten the manna; Jesus promises eternal life (6:58). It is an original focus on the centrality of Jesus. He is "the bread of life" (6:35), as he is "the light of life" (8:12), and the "Word of life" (1 Jn 1:1). The fact that Jesus uses three "I am" formulas (6:35, 48, 51) is a very important claim to divinity which we will look at elsewhere.

The feast of Tabernacles lasted a week, celebrating God's gift of water in the desert, and the gift of light in the pillar of fire that guided the wandering Israelites. This discourse has three parts, interrupted by the non-Johannine narrative of the adulteress (7:53 — 8:11). In the first part (7:14-36), Jesus claims to be greater than Moses who led the wandering nation; in the second part (7:37-52), he claims to be living and lifegiving water; in the third part (8:12-59), he claims he is the light of the world and goes on to show he is greater than Abraham who had given life to the whole nation. Also in the third part, there are five "I am" statements, which add to the great solemnity of this Johannine christology.

The sign and subsequent trial of the man born blind is followed by the discourse of the Good Shepherd. Jesus has just claimed to be "the light of the world" (9:5), pointing out yet again that this means separation into the two ways of life, and judgment (9:39-41). Only his way is acceptable and leads to light and life, for he is the only gate (10:7). Those who choose Jesus' way "will be saved"; "will come in and go out, and find pasture" (10:9); will "have life and have it more abundantly" (10:10). This discourse adds two new ideas. First, Jesus says: "I have other sheep that do not belong to this fold" (10:16), a statement with ecclesial, evangelizing, and missionary significance. Secondly, we read a clear affirmation of Jesus' sacrificial death for others: "I lay down my life ... I lay it down on my own. I have power to lay it down, and have power to take it up again" (10:17-18). New life is given by Jesus through his own death.

The feast of the Dedication of the Temple gives John the opportunity to speak about Jesus' relationship to his Father, which after all is the reason he is the source of new life, the living water, the bread of life, the light of the world, and the Good Shepherd. Those who believe understand this truth, disbelievers do not (10:25-26). Jesus confirms the eternal life given to his disciples and assures them: "No one can take them out of my hand" (10:28). New life is guaranteed because of belief. The brief discourse ends by pointing yet again to the importance of belief in Jesus' signs (10:37-38).

The death and resurrection of Lazarus prophetically anticipates Jesus' own death and resurrection; and a hope-filled encounter with Greeks gives Jesus occasion to think of his coming hour and to discourse on his conviction that the new life he has so frequently proclaimed is attained through his death (12:24), as it will be for his disciples (12:25-26). This life-giving death is the culminating judgment on the world (12:31-32), and Jesus makes a final appeal: choose the life of light and faith of the new age so that "darkness may not overcome you" (12:35).

The ministry ends with a brief evaluation and a final summary of the basic points proclaimed in the previous discourses.[31]

John's gospel is a profoundly rich proclamation of Christ and his message. Many aims weave their way through the text, and reflection on the gospel's influences, scholars' commentaries, and the writer's general interests, bring several of these aims to the surface.

We focus on the author's interest that belief in Jesus leads to fullness of life. This Johannine purpose is mentioned frequently. In fact, his is a revelation of life, confirmed by the constant emphasis of the signs and the discourses.

Chapter Five
PORTRAITS OF GOD

*And I will ask the Father,
and he will give you another Advocate
to be with you always." (Jn 14:16)*

John's portrait of God is multidimensional. He gives insights into God which have inspired the Church for two thousand years. His is a mystical-religious document that begins where others leave off; and it may well be that the exposition of these portraits of God was among the major pastoral and evangelizing motives of this gospel. John's presentation focuses on Jesus, who now manifests the glory of God that previously descended on the Temple (1:14; 2:11). John's christology is eminently trinitarian. It is not merely historical, but speaks of the Jesus of the Church's present and future.

John's presentation of God is not abstract but vitally relevant to our individual and communal lives, and its universalism and experiential aspects assure its enthusiastic welcome. His innovative synthesis combines human values with mystical insight into the awesome glory of God: "And the Word became flesh . . . and we saw his glory" (1:14). In this chapter we journey to the deeper understanding of God that is John's gift to the Church. Mindful of Jesus' words, "Whoever loves me will keep my word, and my Father will love him, and we will come to him and make our dwelling with him" (14:23), we approach this task with openness, a commitment to deepen our faith, and a thirst for the living waters that enrich and satisfy.

The Father

"The Father possesses life in himself." The Father speaks but once in this gospel, on the occasion of Jesus' reflection on the arrival of his hour. Encouraged by the approach of a group of Greeks, Jesus concludes the episode: "Father, glorify your name!" to which the heavenly voice of the Father replied: "I have glorified it and will glorify it again" (12:28). Jesus' prayer for the coming of the new age is answered with the reassuring words of the Father. Apart from this statement, we only know the Father through Jesus' teaching concerning him: "Whoever has seen me has seen the Father" (14:9).

Jesus states explicitly, "I honor my Father" (8:49); and he refers to the Father as the light (3:21), the truthful one (3:33), and says that "God is Spirit" (4:24), the one God (5:44), "the only true God" (17:3). Elsewhere Jesus calls God "Holy Father" (17:11) and "Righteous Father" (17:25).

Although there is little evidence that Judaism used the title "Father" for God, preferring to focus on God's power, Jesus speaks of God very personally and reveals God as Father; this title John uses one hundred and twenty times in the gospel in contrast to the sixty-four times it is used in the Synoptics. Although no one has seen God except "The one who comes from heaven" (3:31), the revelation that God is Father becomes "the central and creative dogma of [John's] Christianity."[1]

"The Father loves the Son" (3:35; 5:20), has shown him everything he does, and has given everything to him. The Father's love is especially seen in his appreciation of the Son's willingness to accept death (10:17). The love of the Father becomes the model of Jesus' love for his own disciples (15:9). This loving Father seeks authentic worshipers who will adore in Spirit and truth. "The Father seeks such people to worship him" (4:23). The Father works still (5:17), raises the dead (5:21), bears witness to Jesus (5:37; 8:18), and gives bread for the life of the world (6:32).

The Father works through Jesus, giving him followers (6:37) and loving those who love Jesus (14:21; 16:27); responding to requests they make in Jesus' name (15:16; 16:23); being glorified by the success of their ministry (15:8); guiding them after Jesus' departure by sending the Holy Spirit (14:26); and establishing heavenly dwelling places for the faithful (14:2).

The Jewish Temple was the Father's house (2:16), and

Jesus zealously condemned anyone who misused it, for he knows that whoever lives in disobedience, "the wrath of God remains upon him" (3:36). This judgment is a personal choice, and personal self-judgment, since "Nor does the Father judge anyone" (5:22).

"The Father has life in himself" (5:26; 6:57), and the power of judgment (5:27), glory (8:54), and honor (12:26), and he is the Son's source of all these, as he sets his seal on the Son's ministry (6:27).

The awesome Father is not directly accessible; rather the faithful approach him through Jesus' mediation (14:6). Jesus claims "the Father is greater than I" (14:28), and "I love the Father and that I do just as the Father has commanded me" (14:31; 15:10).

When Jesus leaves the world he is "going back to the Father" (16:28), and he does so with profound confidence in the Father, knowing that the Father will guard the disciples, consecrate them, unite them, dwell in them, and love them (17:9-26).

John's beginning conviction is "No one has ever seen God. The only Son, God, who is ever at the Father's side, has revealed him" (1:18; 6:46).

God's love for the world. God in his love uttered his revealing Word and "to those who did accept him he gave power to become children of God" (1:12). The Word comes from the Father, "Full of grace and truth" (1:14), and willing to manifest this love by taking "away the sin of the world!" (1:29) The ministry of Jesus, which is the completion of the Father's plan, is a manifestation of the Father's love. "For God so loved the world that he gave his only Son, so that everyone who believes in him might not perish but might have eternal life" (3:16). The new age of the Father's love is an age of individual decision; some love the darkness, others' "works may be clearly seen as done in God" (3:21). The Father's love respects decisions and grants freedom even to those who reject him: "For God did not send his Son into the world to condemn the world, but that the world might be saved through him" (3:17).

As Abraham was willing to sacrifice his only son for the fruitfulness of the chosen people, so the Father "gave his only Son," whom he loved, for the salvation of the world. In fact, the Father takes the initiative in the salvation of humankind, sending Jesus (10:36), and giving him all that is his (3:35), so that the Son imitates the Father's love for the world (13:1).

As signs of his love, the Father gives the world living water (4:10), life (5:21), the healing signs of Jesus (5:36), heavenly life-giving bread (6:33), sight (9:3), and eternal life (17:3). The loving Father is the model for Jesus' role of Good Shepherd (10:15), and when Jesus heals or gives life he acknowledges the Father's power at work in him (11:41-42). As the hour of death looms, Jesus' request that it pass is momentary; immediately he reaffirms, "But it was for this purpose that I came to this hour. Father, glorify your name!" (12:27-28) Even when arrested, his love moves Jesus to protect his disciples and assure their safety (18:8-9). However, that same love urges Jesus on: "Shall I not drink the cup the Father gave me?" (18:11) The Father's love for the world is well expressed by Caiaphas: "nor do you consider that it is better for you that one man should die instead of the people, so that the whole nation may not perish" (11:50). John adds: "and not only for the nation, but also to gather into one all the dispersed children of God" (11:52). This love for the world is eventually symbolized in the universal inscription placed on Jesus' cross (19:19-20).

The Father's love for the world, a love which motivates Jesus, is the parting gift and command to disciples (15:9-17). This love must be preserved even in the experience of being hated (15:18-27). However, disciples will be supported by the Father's love for them individually (16:27) and as a community (17:21).

Although the Father is absolute power and life, John reveals his interest, love, and personal involvement in our world. Through his own loving Son, the Father shows the world the depth of his salvific love. It is an extraordinary religious revelation, so powerful it becomes a motive for disciples' reflection and conversion. The Father has unlimited love for humanity, and this gospel, focused on Jesus, tells of the depth of the Father's love.

The Father and Jesus. The Johannine Jesus states that the

Father taught him (8:28), knows him (10:15), glorifies him (8:54), consecrates him (10:36), and sends him into the world (1:14). Jesus insists: "My teaching is not my own but it is from him who sent me" (7:16; also 8:28; 12:50; 14:24), and he asserts that "the works of God might be made visible through him" (9:3), as if there is complete conformity between his mission and the Father's will (5:36; 10:32, 37-38; 14:10). Jesus prays to the Father (12:27), expressing thanks for his gifts (6:11), and confidence that his prayers will be heard (11:41). The first impression is of Jesus as an obedient Son, "My food is to do the will of the one who sent me and to finish his work" (4:34; 6:38). This is further confirmed by Jesus' awareness that the Father gives success to his ministry: "Everything that the Father gives me will come to me" (6:37); "No one can come to me unless the Father who sent me draw him" (6:44); "No one can come to me unless it is granted him by my Father" (6:65). This part of the portrait is well summed up by Jesus when he says: "The Father is greater than I" (14:28).[2]

There is another dimension of the portrait, for Jesus alone claims direct experience of God (8:38), to have a mission from the Father, to speak his words, and to come with his power. "The Father loves the Son and has given everything over to him" (3:35). This means power over all humankind (17:2), including judgment (5:22, 27), the gift of the right words to say (12:49; 17:8), knowledge of the divine name (17:11-12), personal glory (17:22), and the power to have life in himself (5:26). The relationship is not only one of shared power; Jesus also reveals God as Father and is clearly aware of his own special relationship with "the Father who sent me" (12:49).[3] Jesus is "The only Son, God, who is at the Father's side, has revealed him" (1:18).

The mutual knowledge of Father and Son is so profound it leads Jesus to proclaim "The Father and I are one" (10:30). This deep union is a mutual knowledge (10:15), a sharing in the nature of the Godhead (14:10; 1:18). To refuse honor to one means refusing it to the other (5:23); faith in one is faith in the other (14:1); and the works of one are the works of the other (14:10).

The Father has spoken through Jesus, "the Son of God"

(1:34), and grants eternal life to those who believe in Jesus (6:29, 40). John's theology centers on christology: "Whoever has seen me has seen the Father" (14:9). The implications for discipleship are evident. However, John wishes readers to penetrate this relationship even more, to realize the obedient Son and his access to special experience, mutual knowledge, intimate union. The Johannine Jesus explicitly states "I am the Son of God" (10:36; 11:4).

The awesomeness of God, whom no one has seen, is enriched by awareness that he has a profound love for the world, and this love is brought through Jesus. In the next section we will reflect further on some of these ideas, and expand our vision of John's portrait of Jesus.

Jesus

John's portrait of Jesus is substantially different from the presentations of other New Testament writings. He makes explicit what is only implicit elsewhere, and takes to logical and theological conclusions ideas simply suggested by other writers. John's work is essentially a christology; all other characters in his narrative are there to serve this purpose and draw out the fuller picture of John's high christology. The constant question on every page is "who is Jesus?" Chapters 2 and 3 of the gospel tell us to look beyond appearances to "My Lord and my God" (20:28). Jesus does not change or grow in awareness of his mission, as some commentators think he does in Mark. There is no difference between the pre-resurrection and post-resurrection Jesus such as disciples may find in Luke.[4] John neither explains nor develops his portrait of Christ; he simply expresses his intuitions and faith and leaves the reader to draw conclusions. Some may ask: Is John's a credible Christ? Marsh thinks John is trying "to enable his readers to see, perhaps for the first time, what sort of portrait the synoptists had drawn."[5] At the feast of Dedication a group of Jews say to Jesus: "How long are you going to keep us in suspense? If you are the Messiah, tell us plainly" (10:24). In John's gospel we all get our answer, as "Jesus talks at length about himself and his mission. He talks about Christology."[6] By the end of the gospel no doubts remain regarding John's claims. Even in his earthly life Jesus is the glorious Christ, "that eschatological revealer and mediator of salvation through whom alone true information and knowledge of God and his world, genuine communion with God and share in the divine life, are to be obtained."[7]

This section considers John's christological synthesis under the title "we saw his glory," viewing Jesus as preexistent, Word, Son, and Savior. Then, since Jesus' ministry in John does not lead up to glory but presupposes it, we will leave the ministry to a second consideration "the Word became flesh," reflecting on Jesus' ministry, Last Supper, passion, and resurrection.

"We saw his glory."

The preexistent Lord. The gospels of Matthew and Luke begin with the infancy narratives, and Mark's at the start of Jesus' public ministry, but John's begins in heaven and stresses the preexistence of Jesus. The Johannine Christ's ministry is one of self-revelation. In all his statements about the Father, it is still the Son who is being revealed. We know the Father in the Son, who dwells among us as the Shekinah, or presence of God; and John's community confesses: "We saw his glory" (1:14). Christ's preexistence is stated in the first line of the gospel (1:1); it is acknowledged in the Baptist's first public statements (1:15, 30); it is claimed by Jesus himself (6:62), who also repeated it in his final prayer (17:5). It is implied when Jesus speaks of himself as bread from heaven (6:33, 50, 58); when he speaks out on the feast of Tabernacles (7:28-29; 8:14, 23, 26, 42); when he responds to questions on the feast of Dedication (10:36); and finally it is referred to in one of the farewell discourses (16:28). Frequent references to Jesus' glory (1:14; 2:11; 11:40; 17:5) and to his omniscience (4:16-17; 5:6; 6:6, 61-64; 11:14) are indirect confirmations that he comes from God. John's description of Jesus as Word is closely associated with the Old Testament concept of wisdom, itself seen as preexistent (Proverbs 8:22-31; Wisdom 8:4-6).

The Johannine Jesus proclaims his own dignity, preexistence, and equality with God with the use of the divine name, which was announced to Moses in the episode of the burning bush (Exodus 3:14). The expression used then, "I AM," was subsequently used as the name of God, and it is spoken by Jesus on several occasions. When used without a predicate, as it is on four occasions (8:24, 28, 58; 13:19), the concept, while having some connections with the Hellenistic world, is more clearly intended for Jewish readers.[8] Jesus says: "For if you do not believe that I AM, you will die in your sins" (8:24); "When you lift up the Son of Man, then you will realize that I AM, and that I do nothing on my own" (8:28); "I say to you, before Abraham came to be, I AM" (8:58). Having prophesied his own betrayal, Jesus adds "From now on I am telling you before it happens, so that when it happens you may believe that I AM" (13:19). The above four uses of "I AM" are explicit uses of the divine name. There are other "I AM" statements that have an implied predicate and could mean "It is I." However, both uses (6:20; 18:5) are in the context of theophanies and could be a surrogate form of the divine name. A third group of "I AM" statements do have an expressed predicate. However, they are still revelationary formulas closely associated with the other "I AM" statements, and they do express "a revelation of the divine commitment involved in the Father's sending of the Son. Jesus is these things to men because he and the Father are one."[9] Thus, Jesus' self-proclamation includes: "I am the bread of life" (6:35, 51), "I am the light of the world" (8:12; 9:5), "I am the gate for the sheep" (10:7, 9), "I am the good shepherd" (10:11, 14), "I am the way and the truth and the life" (14:6), "I am the true vine" (15:1, 5). Some commentators would add other self-declarations of Jesus (4:26; 8:18, 23). These "I AM" sayings are often seen as post-resurrection utterances made for Jesus by prophetical witnesses in the community.

The preexistence of Jesus is further presented in John's use of the term "God" for Jesus at key places in the gospel. In eternity "the Word was with God, and the Word was God" (1:1). In Jesus' ministry of revealing God's love to the world, John insists: "No one has ever seen God. The only Son, God, who is at the Father's side, has revealed him" (1:18). The gospel's concluding confession comes from Thomas, who acknowledges Jesus as "My Lord and my God!" (20:28)

John presents Jesus as the pre-existent Word, who identifies himself with God in the "I AM" statements, and whom John confesses as God. This focus on preexistence is further confirmed by some of the titles John uses — Son of Man, Word, the one sent — which we will look at later.

The Word. John's gospel begins with a creation story in which Jesus is referred to as the creative and revealing Word of God. This expression is confined to the prologue, never occurring again in the gospel. The background for this significant designation of Jesus is found in the Old Testament creation story. It is also found in the concept of the Word of God, which is seen as light and life (Psalm 119:105, 107, 130; Deuteronomy 30:14); as revealer of God; and eventually as personal (Isaiah 55:10-11; Wisdom 18:15-16).[10] The background is also seen in the presentation of Wisdom as revealer of divine glory, incarnate, instructor and motivator of the people, and eventually as God's gift that is rejected.[11] Thus, Jesus is the Word, that is, the creative and revealing expression of the wisdom of God. Anticipated in the Word of the prophets (Jeremiah 1:4), the Johannine Word is the full proclamation of God.

Jesus is the revealer, the light of the world (1:4), rejected by the wicked (3:20), but the pledge of eternal life to those who listen and receive (8:12; 12:46). Sent by the Father, Jesus reveals the Father's teaching (12:49; 14:24), testifies to the truth (8:32; 18:37), and glorifies the Father (17:4). He especially reveals the divine mystery of God's love (1:18; 5:36) and is our access to the Father (3:11).

"Word" also refers to the whole sequence of the Father's saving and revealing actions to the world. Thus, Jesus can say "I gave them your word" (17:14), which is the same as "I revealed your name" (17:6), or "the words you gave to me I have given to them" (17:8). Jesus' word calls to faith (4:41; 5:24), believers put their trust in it (4:50), but nonbelievers reject it (5:38; 8:37; 12:48). Jesus' proclamation draws people to God: "The words I have spoken to you are spirit and life" (6:63), as Peter also recognized; "Master, to whom shall we go? You have the words of eternal life" (6:68). Jesus claims "Whoever belongs to God hears the words of God" (8:47). This word purifies (15:3) and consecrates in truth (17:17). This message, however, is not distinct from

Jesus himself. It is Jesus who has been made known, and entrusted to the faithful. The commandments, word and truth, that Jesus teaches are further self-disclosures.

As Word, Jesus is the Father's expression of salvation and brings the assurance that believers will become children of God. In Jesus as Word "the Father himself becomes word in Jesus' words. One hears the Father in the words of Jesus when one hears him correctly."[12] Thus, Word is a title of power, privileged access to the Father, reliable teaching; it states that Jesus has the authority of God.

Although the Word is used only in the prologue, many commentators see the prologue as a table of contents for the entire work: thus, the Word is preexistent, light, creator, and revealer in the verses of the prologue and throughout the entire narrative.[13]

The Son. Jesus is the preexistent Word who reveals the Father because "the one who is from God; he has seen the Father" (6:46) and can thus reveal him. Jesus can lead us to the Father precisely because he is the Son, the one sent from the Father, who lives in constant union with the Father. Jesus has preexisted with the Father (3:11; 7:16; 14:9) and is the authentic messenger of God (3:11, 31-34; 5:30; 7:16; 8:28, 38, 40; 12:49-50; 14:10, 24). Besides Jesus, "No one has ever seen God" (1:18), "No one has gone up to heaven" (3:13). But Jesus is "the one who has come down from heaven" (3:13; 6:33, 38, 42, 51); he comes from the Father (8:42; 13:3; 16:27, 28, 30; 17:8); he as "light came into the world" (3:19; 9:39; 11:27; 12:46; 16:28; 18:37).[14] Jesus comes from the Father, accomplishes his mission, and then returns "to the one who sent me" (16:5), saying, "Now I am leaving the world and going back to the Father" (16:28). In fact, Jesus' death is described as a return to the Father (7:33; 8:14; 13:1, 3; 14:28; 16:5, 28).

John refers over thirty times to Jesus as the one sent by the Father. As a true emissary, he does not act on his own but does the work of the one who sent him (5:30; 7:17, 28; 8:28, 42; 12:49; 14:10). Jesus is irresistibly committed to completing the Father's will and revealing his message through his words, testimony, and signs, in complete obedience (10:18; 12:49; 14:31).

Jesus, "the one who comes from above" (3:31; 8:23, 42), is contrasted with "the one who is of the earth" (3:31; 8:23, 44). These two approaches to life are the two kingdoms. Believers enter God's kingdom by self-immersion in the one sent from God, just as the blind man is told to wash in a pool called "sent" (9:7).

This portrait of Jesus as the one sent from God has no parallel in the Synoptics. He can claim, "the one whom God sent speaks the words of God. He does not ration his gift of the Spirit" (3:34). He does God's will, claiming: "My food is to do the will of the one who sent me and to finish his work" (4:34). But Jesus is sent so that others may be sent and the work of revelation may continue: "As the Father has sent me, so I send you" (20:21).

Jesus claims not only to have been sent with authority, but also a deep union with the Father (11:22; 17:5). He alone is "Son," while all believers are children of God. Jesus refers to God as "My Father" (5:17) and asserts a close union "because I always do what is pleasing to him" (8:29). So he knows the Father's mind (15:15), judges in his name (5:22, 27), gives life in his name (3:3-15; 6:53; 17:1-2), and works closely with him (5:17-18). But Jesus claims even more: "Whoever has seen me has seen the Father" (14:9); "The Father and I are one" (10:30); "The Father is in me and I am in the Father" (10:38). This profound unity is "because you loved me before the foundation of the world" (17:24), at a time when the Son was "at the Father's side" (1:18).

The lasting relationship of love between Father and Son, this mutual communion and love, is an enduring relationship (8:29; 16:32) so that concerning the Father, Jesus can say, I "remain in his love" (15:10), and "I have life because of the Father" (6:57)

The unity between Father and Son is "a unity of action and purpose. The Son loves, wills, acts, as the Father loves, wills, and acts."[15] It is not a metaphysical unity. The writer is struggling to express his faith in the intimate unity of Jesus and the Father and the origin of Jesus in God. He suggests a mutual indwelling of Father and Son (especially in Chapter 17). Eventually this union will become the model for the relationship between Christ and his followers.

Savior of the world. Jesus is acclaimed as Savior only once (4:42), but several titles in the Fourth Gospel refer to Jesus' saving mission, and we will group them together here. The Book of Signs begins with a series of testimonies concerning Jesus. John the Baptist, who plays such a key role for both the gospel and the Johannine community, speaks in Johannine theological terms and acknowledges Jesus' preexistence (1:15, 30). Once John's witness opens the narrative, we are introduced to a series of first disciples who proclaim Jesus as rabbi, teacher, Messiah, the one Moses announced, Son of God, King of Israel, and Son of Man. Raymond Brown sees this easy accumulation of christological titles as "the indication that Jesus regards these titles as inadequate and promises a greater insight — they will eventually see that it is in him that heaven and earth meet (1:50-51)."[16] All these titles are inadequate expressions of christology for John. They are conclusions for the Synoptics but a point of departure for John, who then moves to give us a clearer vision of his community's portrait of Christ as preexistent Word, and Son of God. The many titles used for Christ in this gospel must all be filtered through the awareness that "we have seen his glory: the glory of an only Son coming from the Father, filled with enduring love" (1:14). Jesus is "Word," "Light," "only Son," "Lamb of God," "God's chosen One," "Teacher," "Messiah," "King of Israel," "Son of God," "Son of Man," "Savior," "the Way and the Truth, and the Life," "Bread of Life," "Good Shepherd," and "Vine."

The first time the Baptist saw Jesus coming toward him, he said "Behold, the Lamb of God, who takes away the sin of the world" (1:29, 36). This episode could be a Johannine rewriting of the Synoptics' account of Jesus' baptism; but here not only is Jesus not baptised by John, but the latter acknowledges his preexistence. "Lamb of God" is a term with several meanings. It could refer to the Suffering Servant who is described as a lamb (Isaiah 53:7; also 42:1-4; 49:1-6; 50:4-9; 52:13 — 53:12). It may also imply the paschal lamb, a concept which is part of the Johannine theology of Jesus' death (19:14, 29, 36). Reference has already been made to Abraham's willingness to sacrifice Isaac, and links to Jesus' sacrifice are also possible. We also find some references to the lamb as triumphant leader, such as in the book of Revelation (5:6-14). It may be that John understood this title as an equivalent for Messiah; at least that is the conclusion Andrew draws after hearing the Baptist (1:41). Since all these meanings develop in the early Church, they could be implied by John. Jesus is leader, servant, loving Son, offered in sacrifice for the sins of the world.

After the multiplication of loaves the crowd declared of Jesus, "This is truly the Prophet, the one who is to come into the world" (6:14); and on the feast of Tabernacles, some in the crowd who heard Jesus asserted, "This is truly the Prophet" (7:40). This title, which the Baptist explicitly rejected for himself (1:21), refers to the eschatological prophet, foretold by Moses (Deuteronomy 18:15-18). It looks as if John uses the Prophet as equivalent to the Messiah (6:14-15).

During the feast of Dedication a group of frustrated Jews asked Jesus: "How long are you going to keep us in suspense? If you are the Messiah, tell us plainly" (10:24). The Baptist had refused the title (1:20, 25; 3:28). Andrew used it of Jesus (1:41), and when the Samaritan woman mentioned the Messiah, Jesus replied "I am he, the one who is speaking with you" (4:26); she then proclaimed Jesus as Messiah to the townspeople (4:29). On the feast of Tabernacles some of the people asked, "Could the authorities have realized that he is the Messiah?" (7:26); and later, "When the Messiah comes, will he perform more signs than this man has done?" (7:31) However, one problem remained for the crowd, which John uses to press the reader to think more deeply: "When the Messiah comes, no one will know where he is from" (7:27 also 7:41-42). Later, a further clarification is asked when Jesus hints at his departure. The crowd says, "We have heard from the law that the Messiah remains forever" (12:34). Jesus' origin is known to the readers, and it is the very reason he can remain with his people in unthought-of ways. The title Messiah was important to the community. In fact, acknowledging Jesus as Messiah became the reason for the excommunication of some members from the synagogues (9:22).

According to the prophet Ezekiel, the Messiah is a shepherd (Ezekiel 34:23-24); and following the messianic feeding of the five thousand, Jesus gives a discourse referring to himself as the Good Shepherd (10:1-18). He declares the sheep recognize his voice, he leads them, they follow him, he knows his sheep, and he will lay down his life for them. Even in the appendix to the gospel, Jesus speaks again of his sheep, as he entrusts them to Peter (21:15-17).

A further term used of Jesus is "King." In fact, John uses it fifteen times, almost twice as many times as any other gospel. The Synoptics speak of vineyard and kingdom, but the terms become personal in John — vine and king. Moreover, in Matthew and Mark the title "king" is only given to Jesus in mockery, whereas in John it is also a confession, as in the case of Nathaniel (1:49). After the multiplication of bread the crowd tries to make Jesus a king (6:15); and when he enters Jerusalem it is in triumph as a king (12:13). When Jesus is brought to trial before Pilate, he is asked "Are you the King of the Jews?" (18:33) and Jesus explains the nature of his kingship (18:36-37). This is an excellent theology of Christ as King, written in inverted parallelism, the crowning with thorns at the center (19:5). Jesus reigns by his death, and the nature of his kingship is a life of truth. We return again to the new age and a personal choice between the two kingdoms: "Everyone who belongs to the truth listens to my voice" (18:37); "Shall I crucify your king? . . . 'We have no king but Caesar' " (19:15). John's Christ dies as the King of the Jews (19:19, 21-22).

Several commentators consider the expression "Son of Man" as the title John prefers to express "his central christological theme," "the heart of johannine christology," viewing it as "the most important christological title in John's gospel."[17] Used thirteen times, twelve of which are in the Book of Signs, this title is not a confessional formula but is a self-designation by Jesus. Jesus corrects the inadequate confessions of the first disciples by stating "you will see the sky opened and the angels of God ascending and descending on the Son of Man" (1:51). Jesus instructs Nicodemus that only the Son of Man has come down from heaven (3:13), and that the same Son of Man must be lifted up in death to give life to believers (3:14). The Father has given to the Son of Man the power of judgment (5:27). The Bread of Life is given by the Son of Man (6:27) which is his flesh (6:53). This Son of Man will ascend to heaven (6:62), but first he will be raised up in death (8:28). The blind man is asked if he believes in the Son of Man (9:35), and the discussion with the Greeks signals the hour of glorification for the Son of Man (12:23) who is to be raised up (12:34). The description is still not clear as we read the last statement in the Book of Signs; the crowd asks "Who is this Son of Man?" (12:34). The only reference in the Book of Glory is after Judas' departure from the supper room when Jesus says "Now is the Son of Man glorified" (13:31).

The title combines the typical Johannine emphasis of preexistent glory, incarnation, vicarious death, and return to the Father. "The Johannine Son of Man is the human Jesus, the incarnate Logos; he has come to reveal God with a unique and ultimate authority and in its acceptance or refusal of this revelation the world judges itself."[18]

Jesus' saving mission is expressed in the titles Lamb of God, Messiah, Shepherd, King, and Son of Man. This last one, in particular, combines the glory and the incarnation, and thus most clearly expresses John's convictions regarding Jesus' saving presence to the world.

"The Word became flesh."

The ministry. John emphasized the glorious union of Jesus with his Father, and the resulting portrait, while not as human as the Synoptics', still adequately presented the humanity of Jesus. He comes from Nazareth (1:45), the presumed son of Joseph and Mary (6:42), gets "tired from his journey" through Samaria (4:6), depends on the Father (5:19; 7:16; 10:29; 14:28), is deeply moved by Mary's weeping at Lazarus' death (11:33), is himself troubled in spirit (11:38), and weeps at the loss of his friend (11:35). He is anxious as he approaches his hour (12:27), and is clearly upset at the anticipated betrayal by a follower (13:21). John does not show us Jesus ignorant of events, or surrounded by friendly children, but his portrait is not that of a shadowy spiritual being such as the Docetists and Gnostics may have wanted. In fact, in response to heretical interpretations, the Johannine Jesus is very physical: "Give me a drink" (4:7); "eat the flesh of the Son of Man and drink his blood" (6:53); "he spat on the ground and made clay with the saliva, and smeared the clay on his eyes" (9:6). He lets the woman anoint his feet (12:1-8), washes his disciples' feet (13:1-11), drinks the wine raised to his lips on the cross (19:29), and tells Thomas to touch his hands and side (20:27). This gospel also shows the violence of Jesus overturning the money changers' tables (2:13-22), and angrily debating with his opponents (9:40-41). John gives no information on Jesus' early life, except for two comments that might imply knowledge of the virgin birth (8:19, 41).

The chronology of Jesus' ministry in John differs notably from that in the Synoptics. He is based in Jerusalem and travels to Galilee where he is welcomed (2:1-12; 4:43 — 5:1; 6:1 — 7:14). Jesus spends three Passovers in Jerusalem, implying a longer ministry than the Synoptics, and after Chapter 10 he is in Jerusalem for the best part of a year. Several Synoptic episodes are omitted for theological reasons; the temptations, baptismal theophany, and transfiguration are out of place for John for whom the glory of Jesus is visible from the beginning. The narrative begins with the Baptist's Johannine confession, has the first disciples saying things they do not conclude until late in the Synoptics, shows Jesus inaugurating the new age and cleansing the Temple. These conclusions are all early in John, setting a different tone for the whole narrative. After reading only two chapters the end of the ministry is clear: Jesus ends the efficacy of Judaism, dialogues with Jews and Samaritans open to his word, and begins a commitment based on faith in him and attained through his death. The public ministry focuses on the progress to Jesus' hour and its salvific significance (2:4; 7:6, 8; 8:20; 12:23; 13:1; 17:1). He experiences hostility from the first days (2:18-22), and throughout his ministry (6:66-67; 7:19, 23, 25, 30, 32, 44; 8:59; 10:39). Jesus' opposition to Jewish interpretations of the Sabbath is a particularly thorny problem but again it focuses more on who Jesus is. Eventually he is accused of blasphemy (10:33). As opposition increases in Chapters 5 to 8 we see the separation into two kingdoms, and after Chapter 12 Jesus spends his time alone with his disciples and there are no more disputes and plots but only the friendship with his own (12:44-50).

John's Jesus is always in control of events, "did not need

anyone to testify about human nature. He himself understood it well" (2:25), and deals with controversy as a Hellenistic philosopher or wise rabbi (7:14 – 8:59). His debates are not about the Law, as they are in the Synoptics, but rather about Jesus' own identity.[19] In fact, Jesus' responses do not leave room for reconciliation; they give the impression of formulations of post-Easter positions that already irrevocably separate the Johannine community from Judaism (3:18, 36; 5:42-43; 9:28, 41; 10:24-25).

The Last Supper. In the Synoptics, Jesus' last meal with his disciples was on the evening of the feast of the Passover. He was tried and executed in the morning and afternoon of the Passover, a day being calculated from sundown to sundown, not midnight to midnight. In the year that Jesus died, the Passover feast lasted from sundown on Thursday to sundown on Friday. John's gospel presents these events twenty-four hours earlier, so that Jesus dies on Thursday afternoon, the end of the full day before the Passover. This was the Preparation Day when the paschal lambs were slaughtered for the next day's feast. Thus, Jesus' Last Supper is not the Passover, and John's chronology is probably correct.[20] Nevertheless, the meal is a Passover-type meal, and John, like the Synoptics, takes advantage from the imagery. John's supper also excludes the institution of the Eucharist, substituting the washing of the disciples' feet.

The washing of the disciples' feet is an act of humility by the servant Jesus, symbolic of his humbling in death for the redemption of others. It is not so much the gesture itself which is important – actually the Johannine high Christ is not a servant of others. The gesture of footwashing, which probably took place when the guests arrived, is transferred into the heart of the celebration by John. The gesture becomes an acted prophecy of Jesus' future redemptive death for others. This dedication to love is followed by the betrayal by Judas and the anticipation of the denial by Peter.

Chapters 14 to 17 contain the farewell discourses of Jesus. Like the typical Old Testament patriarchal final speech, these chapters summarize the basic teachings of Jesus. It is the risen Lord who is speaking to the Johannine community, but he does not refer to the Synoptic apocalyptic or parousia expectations since the Johannine Jesus is already glorified. There are three discourses: 13:31 – 14:31; 15:1 – 16:4; 16:4b-33. The first deals with Jesus' departure, the second with the community's conflict with the synagogue, and the third with the community's intense experience of Jesus' absence. Each successive discourse builds on the previous one and focuses on particular crises in the Johannine community.[21]

The first discourse addresses Jesus' impending departure; the disciples' sadness and Jesus' reassurance; the effectiveness of prayer to the Father in Jesus' name; the coming of the Paraclete; faithfulness to Jesus; and the gift of peace. The second discourse could be the combination of two originally distinct sections (15:1-17 and 15:18 – 16:4a).[22] While repeating some of the themes of farewell, this discourse challenges deviation from the Lord and his teachings, and probably has in mind the apostasy resulting from the threat of excommunication from the synogogue. The third discourse returns to the theme of the absence of the Lord, the work of the Paraclete, and the Father's lasting love.

The supper discourses end with a final prayer of Jesus, which summarizes the basic ideas of John's christology. This part of the disciples' instruction is given in the form of a prayer to indicate "that the disciples' fate does not rest in their own hands."[23] Addressed by the risen Jesus to John's community, it is a prayer for unity, either for the disciples with Jesus or for the Johannine community with the Great Church. The prayer is in three parts: Jesus prays to his Father and this becomes a summary of Johannine christology (17:1-5); he prays for the perseverance of his immediate disciples (17:6-19); and he prays for future believers and their unity (17:20-26).

The entire supper narrative is characterized by Johannine concepts and terminology. It has no counterpart in the Synoptics and constitutes about a fifth of the Fourth Gospel. We will return to it in Chapter 7.

The Passion. All of the gospels present an account of Jesus' passion, but John's is told in light of his glorified Christ. The hour of passion is the hour of glorification (7:30; 8:20; 12:23;

13:1; 17:1). Anything that goes against that image of majesty is left out. There is no agony, no formal trial by the Jews, no silent Jesus, no supportive women following, no need for Simon of Cyrene, no mocking of Jesus as he hangs on the cross. Rather, John now gives a detailed presentation of the kingship of Jesus. The general scheme is similar to the Synoptics but John's is an independent tradition.[24]

The Romans crucified Jesus under the governorship of Pontius Pilate (26-36), when Caiaphas was High Priest (18-37), probably around 27-34. The narrative begins with the arrest of Jesus in a garden on the far side of the Kidron valley. John presents no agony scene even though he may have known the tradition (12:27). Opposition to Jesus, which had begun early in the ministry (5:16), climaxed with the raising of Lazarus (12:10-11). Judas arrives with Roman cohort and Temple guards. "The forces of darkness, fully equipped with lanterns and torches, approach him who is the light of the world and do not recognize him in their light, which is only darkness."[25] Judas does not identify Jesus; rather Jesus freely steps forward, proclaiming "I AM" (18:5-6), a reference to the divine name that provokes worship. Jesus, again in control, obtains the release of his disciples, while he is taken to Annas.

There is no formal trial by the Sanhedrin, and Annas' interrogation of Jesus is bracketed with the denials of Peter. This questioning was not official, but Annas was the power behind the office, since he was formerly High Priest himself (6BCE-15) and five of his sons and his son-in-law, Caiaphas, held the office. The role of the Jewish leadership is minimal in John: no formal trials, no interrogation by Caiaphas, no mockery by Temple guards. Jesus is slapped by a guard and sent, bound, to Caiaphas. Jesus responds to the questioning with authority and challenge. In general, John takes care not to implicate the Jewish nation in Jesus' death.

The trial before Pilate, the Roman authority, is the only trial scene in John, and the accusations against Jesus are political. This is unique to John and seems to reverse the common Christian practice of defending the Roman Empire and placing the blame on the Jews. The trial is a confrontation between two kingdoms in their extreme form: the kingdom of truth for which Jesus dies to save others, and the irreligious world of Pilate who kills in order to save himself. Pilate tries to manipulate events, using an innocent man to degrade and humiliate the Jews: making them acknowledge they have no power in law (18:31); leading them to choose a criminal (18:39-40); taking Jesus out scourged and crowned as a mock-king of Jews (19:5); taunting them to crucify Jesus when he and they know they have no power to do so (19:6); and ending with the Jews blasphemously acknowledging "We have no king but Caesar" (19:15). Once Pilate has cruelly played with the conquered Jews, he disdainfully hands Jesus over to be crucified (19:16).[26] The Jews use the secular power they hate to help them put to death an innocent person; they talk of friendship for Caesar, and helplessly appeal to the irreligious Pilate to crucify their king. Johannine irony permeates the narrative. Jesus is presented with dignity and authority as he freely goes to his death to save others. The trial explains the crucifixion: it is the result of the evil machinations of the world of darkness driving out the unwelcome Light.[27]

Like Abraham's beloved son Isaac (Genesis 22:6), Jesus carries his own cross; he does not fall, no women follow him, no help is given by Simon of Cyrene. In fact, there is no description of the journey to Calvary in John. Jesus is in charge: "I lay down my life ... No one takes it from me, but I lay it down on my own" (10:17-18). Jesus is not mocked by the crowds or priests. He is the high Christ in constant control, and from his throne of the cross forms the first Christian Johannine community (19:25-27), committing it to unity (19:23-24), and granting it his Spirit (19:30).[28] Once this final gesture of love is accomplished, Jesus allows his death to proceed (19:28). He dies at the time of the slaughter of the paschal Lamb; thus John adds the signs of Passover to his death — hyssop, wine, and unbroken bones.[29] Jesus' death is the great sign of his faithfulness to his Father, his love for the world, and the fullest revelation of the nature of God. Jesus' body is embalmed and buried by secret Jewish disciples in a garden tomb near Calvary.

The death is Christ's glorification, for the Son, who had come from the Father's side, was now returning to him, having shown the world how much it is loved. John's presentation of the death draws together several theological emphases, which he sees rooted in the death: union with the Father, control over death, redemptive love, the gift of the Spirit, and the formation of Christian community.

The Resurrection. On three ocasions in the gospel we read that the Son of Man will be raised (3:14; 8:28; 12:34), meaning raised on the cross and raised up in glory. The empty tomb stories in the gospels differ considerably; John's tells us how Mary Magdalene, finding the tomb empty, tells Peter and the Beloved Disciple who run to the tomb and find things as Mary Magdalene had said. The episode of running toward resurrection faith is possibly a reference to the Johannine community and the Great Church. The Beloved Disciple of the community gets to the empty tomb first but respectfully waits for Peter to enter. As soon as the Beloved Disciple entered, "he saw and believed" (20:8), arriving at resurrection faith without the appearance of Jesus.[30]

The appearance to Mary Magdalene, which follows, is unusual in that it emphasizes a very human and affectionate encounter, unusual for John's high christology. John also preserves reference to the ascension (20:17), even though in his view "the ascension has in effect taken place in the crucifixion-resurrection."[31]

The next pair of appearances are to the disciples without Thomas and then to Thomas. The risen Lord appears, greeting the disciples with the salvational gift of peace (20:19, 21; see Isaiah 53:5; Psalm 85:8). Jesus still bears the wounds, as the Graeco-Roman world thought that people did after a violent death. Jesus commissions his disciples: "As the Father has sent me, so I send you" (20:21); and then conveys the promised gift of the Spirit, which he had said would be given when he was glorified (7:37-39). The power to forgive, often restricted to the sacrament of penance, is to be understood, broadly here, as the commission to the disciples to proclaim forgiveness in their evangelizing ministry.

The appearance to Thomas, a Johannine episode and construction, seems directed to Christians who want physical evidence as a source of faith, an attitude Jesus had condemned (4:48). Raymond Brown states: "Thomas is to be reprimanded on two counts: for refusing to accept the word of the other disciples, and for being taken up with establishing the marvelous or miraculous aspect of Jesus' appearance."[32] Fortunately, when Jesus offers Thomas the chance to examine the evidence, he stops, and without the proof formulates his great confession: "My Lord and my God!" So we are taken back to the beginning of the gospel: "the Word was with God, and the Word was God" (1:1).

The gospel's first conclusion (20:30-31) is followed by an appendix, which describes a further appearance to the disciples by the Sea of Galilee. Written after the formal conclusion, yet always a part of early manuscripts, this addition brings together three episodes, though the links between them are rough, possibly indicating separate sources. Vocabulary and context have much in common with the gospel, but there are a few distinctive features that suggest to some commentators a distinct author-redactor for this part. The miraculous catch of fish, an episode with many common elements to Luke's call scene (Lk 5:1-11), is presented as the third appearance; it is actually the fourth in John but reads like a first.

The commissioning of Peter follows, serving as a Johannine presentation of the importance of Peter in the Great Church. It is also a rehabilitation of Peter after his threefold denial of the Lord. The prophecy of his death speaks about the quality of his discipleship, and shows Peter as a model shepherd who will lay down his life (10:14-18).

A brief episode follows on the fate of the Beloved Disciple, artificially connected by means of verse 20. It explains that Jesus never claimed the Beloved Disciple would not die and suggests that he has now died after a long ministry in the community; thus, a misinterpretation of Jesus' saying is now cleared up. Some commentators also suggest that the redactor may intend a comparison between Peter's martyrdom and the non-martyrdom of the Beloved Disciple, clarifying that the manner of death is not what is important but that each remembers, "You follow me" (21:22).

The gospel's second conclusion affirms the Johannine community's belief that the Beloved Disciple is the authoritative source for their tradition of the Lord Jesus, of whom they believed "We saw his glory," the glory of the Word made flesh.

The Holy Spirit

"God ... does not ration his gift of the Spirit." John's theology is basically a christology. Jesus' revelation of the Father is a self-disclosure; and here with the Spirit the focus remains on Jesus and John's high christology. There is no mention of a conception by the Spirit; or of Spirit-filled witnesses that welcome Jesus' coming; or of being driven into the desert by the Spirit; or returning to minister in the power of the Spirit; or indication of any commissioning or impetus to ministry due to a pouring out of the Spirit — all Synoptic episodes. In John "the Spirit is presented less as the divine power that has directed Jesus' ministry than as the divine power that continues and completes it."[33]

The Baptist told the crowd that God had promised to identify God's chosen one through the presence of the Holy Spirit: "I saw the Spirit come down like a dove from the sky and remain upon him" (1:32). Although the Spirit is a sign for the Baptist, John also states that he saw the Spirit "come down and remain upon him" (1:32-33). The verb John uses suggests a permanent abiding of the Spirit with Jesus. The Spirit remains with him throughout his ministry, as Jesus becomes the bearer of the Spirit. This messianic anointing is indicative of the traditional view of Jesus fulfilling the prophecies that the Messiah would be filled with the Spirit of God (Isaiah 42:1-4; 61:1-3). The Baptist also teaches that Jesus will baptize with the Holy Spirit, thus bringing the new age to believers.

In the episode with Nicodemus, Jesus teaches "no one can enter the kingdom of God without being born of water and Spirit" (3:5). This passage complements the expectation of an individual outpouring of the Spirit on the person of the Messiah, with the communal outpouring on the community (Joel 2:28-29). The new birth is through the life of the Spirit, which John will later state takes place at Jesus' glorification in resurrection (7:37-39). After the digression on the final witness of the Baptist, the writer returns to

Jesus' discourse in which he states: "God ... does not ration his gift of the Spirit" (3:34), thereby affirming the boundless life of the new age.

Jesus' discussion with the Samaritan woman eventually deals with authentic worship, stressing that in the new age only those who possess the gift of the Spirit will be able to authentically worship the Father (4:23). All others belong to the kingdom that does not understand (4:22). God wants authentic worshipers because "God is Spirit, and those who worship him must worship in Spirit and truth" (4:24). This description of God, very like describing God as light or truth, implies that this is a characteristic of believers too. They receive the Spirit, live in the Spirit, and return Spirit-filled worship to God.

A similar reflection is made when some disciples leave Jesus after the discourse on the Bread of Life. Jesus says: "It is the spirit that gives life, the flesh is of no avail" (6:63). In other words, the new age leads to the way of life through the Spirit, and those who do not accept are left in darkness and death, in the ways of the flesh.

The feast of Tabernacles celebrates the gift of water. Water was used in the Old Testament as a symbol of wisdom and Spirit, and here Jesus claims: "Let anyone who thirsts come to me and drink. Whoever believes in me, as scripture says: 'Rivers of living water will flow from within him'" (7:37). There is excellent balance in the phrases: "Anyone who thirsts" balances with "come to me and drink;" and the other two parts also balance. From this reading it is clear that the source of the Holy Spirit is Jesus who, as John clarifies, gives the Spirit when glorified. This is the preferred interpretation, although another worth mentioning is based on a different reading and punctuation. "If anyone thirsts, let him come to me; let him drink, Who believes in me, Scripture has it: 'From within him rivers of living water shall flow.'" In this latter case the believer becomes a source of the Spirit for others.

The Paraclete. During the farewell discourses John five times uses the term "paraclete" (14:15-17, 26; 15:26-27; 16:7-11, 12-14) and identifies him with the Holy Spirit (14:17, 26; 15:26; 16:13). The word "paraclete" is unusual and has been variously translated as attorney, advocate, intercessor, consoler, and comforter — words that never give the full meaning of his role, for he is all these and more. Brown considers that the concept is based upon a tandem relationship: a leader passing on his spirit to a follower, like Elijah did for Elisha (2 Kings 2:9-10, 15); and the protecting presence of a guardian angel, an idea from late Jewish angelology. To these he adds the ideas of the Spirit of God as a prophetic gift to disciples, and the understanding of personified Wisdom. He believes the Paraclete in John is the integration of all these roles.[34] Culpepper considers that the Paraclete is modelled on the Johannine community's understanding of the role of the Beloved Disciple. What the latter had been to the community, the Paraclete will be.[35]

The *Sitz im Leben* of the Paraclete passages is the changing circumstances in the Johannine community which, having previously "lost" Christ in his return to his Father, and now having lost the Beloved Disciple in death, seeks assurance of the continued presence of the Lord in their community. The passages on the Holy Spirit, which we have seen in Jesus' ministry, all refer to the future and show the Spirit as a gift to the post-Easter Church. The Johannine community has formulated a daring theology. Their authority for this is shown to be the Holy Spirit, who can assure them in the present and strengthen them for the future, since he is their teacher of faith, source of love, and guide to hope.

Those who in this new age dedicate themselves to Jesus in faith and love are told, "I will ask the Father, and he will give you another Advocate to be with you always; the Spirit of truth, which the world cannot accept" (14:16-17). This second Paraclete — Jesus being the first — remains with those who have chosen love, faith, truth, as an assuring presence in the life they have chosen. Those who have not chosen life in the new age will not even be able to recognize him (14:17).

This permanent, truthful presence of the Holy Spirit guarantees and authenticates instruction in the Johannine community and their spiritual ability to recall the essence of Jesus' teaching (14:26).

Similar ideas are presented in the second farewell discourse.

The Spirit will testify to Jesus, thus maintaining the continuity in the Church's teaching (15:26). Yet again, we hear echoing the theme of the Spirit, coming from the Father and from Jesus, as a Spirit of truth.

The third discourse also focuses on the Paraclete. Jesus says the Paraclete will not come unless he goes to send him. The Paraclete's task is here specified as an ongoing discernment of life for the new age. He is constantly identifying and confronting the false values of an age filled with the sin and injustice of the prince of this world (16:7-11). The same Spirit of truth will guide those who choose truth: reminding them of Jesus' message; highlighting the future; and thus building the age of Christ and giving him glory (16:12-14).

In the absence of Jesus, the Paraclete is the principle of new life for believers, their sanctifier, and their guide. He dwells in the hearts of believers as a new presence of Jesus, and through disciples completes Jesus' work. In the Johannine community's loss and crisis, this assurance of Jesus' new presence is a consoling gift from the Father.

John's portraits of God touch the heart of his thought and faith. Centered on christology, his understandings of Father and Spirit become further clarifications of his high christology. John's community believes that to have seen Jesus as they have is to have seen the Father (14:9); and they also believe that the Holy Spirit reminds them of Jesus (14:26). With John, the New Testament reaches its climax in its portrayal of God. Even the modern reader cannot help but think that the writer speaks from profound religious experience and calls to the same.

Chapter Six
DISCIPLESHIP IN JOHN

*As the Father loves me,
so I also love you. Remain in my love.
If you keep my commandments, you will remain
in my love, just as I have kept my Father's
commandments and remain
in his love. (Jn 15:9-10)*

John uses the word "disciples" seventy-eight times. He seems uninterested in the concepts "apostles," which he never uses, and "the Twelve," which appears only four times. His concept of discipleship is broad and is equivalent to faith. Unlike the Synoptics for whom discipleship implies detailed requirements, John's is more contemplative and indicates a more mystical-passive approach. The Synoptics emphasize, though not exclusively, what we should do as disciples, whereas John tells us what to be. John has no discipleship discourse, such as Matthew's Sermon on the Mount; or Luke's handbook on discipleship given during the journey; or Mark's central journey to Jerusalem with its illumination of the disciples' lifestyle.[1] John has the instructions of the final discourses, but, inspiring though they are, their focus is more restricted regarding requirements for discipleship than are the Synoptics'.

John is often referred to as a mystical writing, and this is justified. The characteristics of mysticism are passivity, simplicity, ineffability, and experience. John's writing is based on experience, and calls for it. It speaks of our wonderful relationship to God in ineffable, indescribable ways. There is a simplicity in its constant focus on a few important, profound issues. It presents discipleship as the result of union with God in Christ rather than as an asceticism of daily struggle,

though it does include an ascetical component. One of the
great advantages of a mystical approach is timelessness — it
can speak to us in new ways as the years pass. It focuses
on essentials, leaving concrete applications to people in their
own circumstances. Thus we find no antitheses and their
applications, as we do in Matthew, no discourse on discipline
within the community, no series of ethical requirements.
Rather, John focuses on the quality of life that ought to
be ours in this new age of God, presuming that, if one's life-
orientation is right, the details will take care of themselves.

This chapter will consider the nature of discipleship in
John; look at some models of discipleship that he presents;
review his challenge to reject the sinful world; focus on the
central commitment in faith; and see the implications of our
life in God. These reflections on discipleship will need to
be complemented with the communal aspects of the disciple's
life in the following chapter on the Church.

Nature of Discipleship in John

Disciples are Jesus' own. The first words of Jesus in the
Fourth Gospel are "Come, and you will see" (1:39). This
invitation to learn about him is really a call to be with him.
The result is the growth of a group of followers that Jesus
can genuinely call "his own" (13:1). In fact, John generally
uses the expression "his disciples" (2:11), rather than disciples
— a usage that both emphasizes intimacy, and is probably
very early.

In the Synoptics, disciples struggle to appreciate who
Jesus is, some rejecting aspects of Jesus' messiahship as does
Peter (Mk 8:32), and others disbelieving right up to the end
(Mt 28:17). In John, disciples recognize who Jesus is from
their first encounter, and thus the writer can emphasize the
depth of their relationship. Jesus came to his own (1:11),
and loved them (13:1), for they were the Father's gift to
him (17:6, 24).

Jesus does not call his own to repent; in fact, the word
does not appear in John. Jesus purifies them with his word
(15:3), and they become his friends who receive his confidence and hear the wisdom of his revelation (15:15; 17:26).
Privileged with his instruction, they must recall that "no

slave is greater than his master nor any messenger greater than the one who sent him" (13:16). Their humble awareness of dependence on Jesus will maintain the blessings of their lives (13:17; 15:4).

Jesus' invitation to his own friends includes the grace of response (6:44, 65); however, the invitation must be accepted by the believer (1:12; 5:43). Believing, used with the Greek preposition "eis" and the accusative case, is used thirty-six times by John and "means not merely accepting Jesus' doctrine but giving oneself to him, to his allegiance (12:11), setting the whole of one's life in movement towards him, 11:25f."[2] The disciples want to be his own. They are drawn to Jesus, stay with him, and find their own identity in him, so that even in difficulties Peter can say "Lord, to whom shall we go?" (6:68)

Jesus comments on his leadership of his disciples in the allegory of the Good Shepherd. He says he knows each one by name and leads them personally (10:3). He knows they recognize him and will follow no strangers (10:4-5). There is a mutual knowledge and life experience between disciples and Jesus (10:14), and the relationship is so profound that Jesus willingly dies for his own (10:11, 15, 17).

Mark speaks of disciples as Jesus' own, but in John the idea is deepened; disciples are Jesus' own friends to whom he entrusts all that he is, and his self-gift actually makes them who they are.

Discipleship — a transforming gift. Jesus comes to empower his disciples to become children of God (1:12). Disciples are begotten by God (1:13), like the blind man who from natural birth had lived one life but, after faith in Jesus and baptism in the pool called "sent," begins a new life.

The ministry begins with a very clear orientation: Jesus' revelation is a new creation, and all former rituals are superceded, the Temple is finished, the Sabbath yields to another life; for one who is greater than all these, greater even than Moses and Abraham, is now here. This new life is a gift from on high (3:27), making disciples children of God even in this life.

This aspect of discipleship as a new creation and a new birth is so important that John deals with it in Jesus' first major discourse, with Nicodemus. "I say to you, no one can see the kingdom of God without being born from above" (3:3). This is the new birth that gives disciples entry into the life of the new age. John actually describes this new life as God's kingdom (3:3, 5), the only use of this very common Synoptic concept.

This new birth, which is God's transforming gift to disciples, is a birth "from above," "of water and Spirit," a spiritual birth. The second part of the speech, preceded by a confessional statement of the Johannine community (3:11), goes on to theologize about the transforming birth, claiming it is based on faith in Jesus: "Everyone who believes in him might not perish but might have eternal life" (3:16). The new birth is to eternal life. The faith in Jesus that produces a new birth through the Spirit is elsewhere indicated to be obedience to the commandments (14:21), acceptance of the words of Jesus (12:48), and acting in truth (3:21).

The discourse with Nicodemus, stating that disciples are "born of water and Spirit," is thought by some to have a baptismal implication. Although Nicodemus could not have understood any baptismal interpretation, the Johannine community would certainly read this as a reference to the disciples' new birth through baptism. This reference to water is in all the texts. Very few commentators think Jesus said it; those who consider the speech as Johannine, and not from Jesus, think it was a later addition, possibly from a redactor. The gospel is never without it, and the phrase clearly indicates the community's belief that the transforming birth, a gift from above, comes through the Spirit and is externalized in baptism.

Active responses. Jesus' gift of new life requires acceptance and a response that calls for sacrifice. "Whoever loves his life loses it, and whoever hates his life in this world will preserve it for eternal life" (12:25). Jesus goes on in the same section to speak of "whoever serves me," and "my servant" (12:26). Disciples are his own, but they must be willing to live as he does. Their response includes believing in Jesus (14:11), doing the works he does (11:12), obeying the commandments (14:15, 21), loving Jesus (14:21), being true to his word (14:23), going out and bearing fruit (15:16), loving one another (15:17), witnessing (15:27), and asking in Jesus' name for needed blessings (14:13).

The response is that of one totally dedicated to Jesus in absolute loyalty. The attitudes of authentic discipleship are referred to as pursuing the light, truth, and life. John speaks of the disciple as "whoever hears my word" (5:24); "Everyone who listens to my Father and learns from him" (6:45); "Whoever belongs to God hears the words of God" (8:47); "The sheep hear his voice" (10:3, 27). This attentive listening to God becomes the source of the disciple's life-direction.

The disciple's active response to God's transforming gift of making the follower one of Jesus' very own is particularly seen in the critical decisions that disciples must make for the new age and against the prince of this world. Facing life with discernment and judgment, they choose light instead of darkness, truth instead of falsehood, heaven instead of earth, spirit instead of flesh, and life instead of death. These choices are made when one chooses God and the new age, but they are lived out each day. "Whoever lives the truth comes to the light, so that his works may be clearly seen as done in God" (3:21).

This active response will be complemented by considerations of an active rejection of this world, mature believing, love, building unity, and service — ideas we will see developed later in the chapter.

Abide in me. The union between the Father and Jesus is the model for the disciples' union with Jesus. In his final discourse Jesus proclaims, "If you remain in me and my words remain in you, ask for whatever you want and it will be done for you" (15:7). The life of the disciple is an ongoing deepening of the union between believer and Jesus: "Remain in me, as I remain in you" (15:4), and elsewhere, "Remain in my love" (15:9).

Abiding in Jesus is the ongoing life of the disciple, the source of constant strength and fidelity. "Whoever loves me will keep my word" (14:23); "whoever believes in me will do the works I do, and will do greater ones than these" (14:12). This mutual presence enables the disciple to recognize the Holy Spirit (14:27), and leads disciples to bear fruit (15:4-5).

When disciples live in the presence of Jesus, he directs

them to "ask for whatever you want and it will be done for you" (15:7), especially they are directed to ask for fruits that endure (15:16). Disciples who abide in Jesus receive the promise that the Father will protect them (17:11), guard them from the evil one (17:15), consecrate them by means of truth (17:17), and bless even future disciples brought to the Lord through their work (17:20). Finally, Jesus prays for those who abide in his love: "Father, they are your gift to me. I wish that where I am they also may be with me, that they may see my glory that you gave me" (17:24). In the meantime he says he will continue to reveal the Father to them and endow them with the Father's love.

Jesus gives his life for those who are truly his. In fact, he nourishes their abiding union with his own flesh (6:51). Those who are the Father's gift to Jesus (6:37) are blessed with the present experience of eternal life with Jesus through his gift of living bread. This is his way of preserving union (6:53-55). "Whoever eats my flesh and drinks my blood remains in me and I in him" (6:56).

All these disciples who are Jesus' own have received a transforming gift of new life, and actively respond to the gift. Jesus' hope for them is always the same: that "the love with which you loved me may be in them and I in them" (17:26).

Disciples in John

Jesus works great signs and delivers challenging discourses. The crowds are impressed, seek him out (6:22-24), and speak well of him (7:31). Often potential disciples accept the signs but reject his words (6:60, 66; 12:37). Jesus could say to all: "I will not reject anyone who comes to me" (6:37). Jesus becomes, for all, the focal point of their choice for light or darkness, truth or falsehood, life or death.

The first disciples. The ministry opens with a series of confessions from disciples who acknowledge Jesus with significant titles and express an enthusiastic commitment. The calling of these first disciples is not in Galilee as in the Synoptics. The first disciples are former followers of the Baptist and become models for those in John's community who had made a similar transformation. After the Baptist's witness, they follow Jesus asking "Where are you staying?" (1:38) On a more profound level this question has already been answered; Jesus is "at the Father's side" (1:18). On the level of discipleship it still has to be answered, when Jesus tells them he will live on in them and make his dwelling in their hearts (14:23; 15:4-10). Jesus' reply, "Come, and you will see," also has the deeper meaning of coming to Jesus and seeing the Christ of the Johannine community.

The writer now sets in motion a series of reactions which become his initial understanding of discipleship: human testimony, hearing, following, seeking, finding, coming, seeing, remaining with Jesus, and telling others of the experience. Thus as each one encounters Jesus and learns to acknowledge him as teacher, Messiah, the one spoken of by Moses, Son of God, and King of Israel, each new disciple ends by evangelizing someone else. Thus Andrew calls Simon, Philip seeks out Nathaniel, and later the Samaritan woman proclaims Jesus to the townspeople.

John does not give us the names of the Twelve, nor does he call them apostles. He stresses the call of these first five disciples, some of whom surface again in the ministry. Simon, whom we will consider in the next chapter, is already Peter in the first meeting with Jesus. Philip is the only one whose call is explicitly described; barely mentioned in the Synoptics, he plays a role, in John, in the feeding of the five thousand (6:4-7), is the mediator between the Greeks and Jesus at the end of the ministry (12:21), and is the one who asks Jesus to "show us the Father and that will be enough for us" (14:8-9). Philip seeks out Nathaniel, who in John appears as a disciple and beomes a model for true Jewish believers who join the Johannine community. "Here is a true Israelite. There is no duplicity in him" (1:47). Jesus implies to Nathaniel that these first disciples' confessions of him are inadequate, and greater insights and revelations lie ahead. Nathaniel is again referred to after the resurrection (21:2).

The call of these first disciples is a paradigm of discipleship. The episode starts with four powerful and symbolic words: follow, seek, stay, and see.[3] It then moves to confessions which, although inadequate for John, are the conclusions of Synoptic faith and important formulations in John's community. This core of disciples stays with Jesus and receives the revelation he promised.

Other models of discipleship. "Now there was a Pharisee named Nicodemus, a ruler of the Jews. He came to Jesus at night" (3:1-2). John's community has members who are practicing Jews, but secretly Christian, and Nicodemus becomes a model for such people. He starts like them, coming to question Jesus in secrecy. He acknowledges "we know that you are a teacher who has come from God, for no one can do these signs that you are doing unless God is with him" (3:2). For John this is an inadequate faith based on signs. As usual, Jesus is in control and directs the whole discussion and its subsequent discourse to the topic of new birth. It becomes a strong challenge to conversion away from Judaism to the high christology of the Johannine community. Nicodemus no doubt came to discuss important questions with Jesus, but Jesus turns the encounter into a personal challenge, and the Johannine Church sees its communal implications. Nicodemus returns during a Sanhedrin meeting, where he speaks for Jesus with justice and fairness: "Does our law condemn a person before it first hears him and finds out what he is doing?" (7:51). He represents balance and open-mindedness amidst the growing prejudice and opposition of the rest of the governing body of the Jews. Nicodemus was also one of the two who buried Jesus, a gesture that required visibility in going to Pilate and in taking care of the burial (19:39). Possibly Nicodemus illustrates a process of faith for secret Christians. Whether the burial is an act of devotion from a faithful Jew or a sign of conversion to Jesus is left unclear.

The man born blind is an excellent model for a faith that illumines and leads to authentic confession of Jesus as Son of Man, a title that combines well John's high christology and belief in the incarnation. The fact that the blind man washes in Siloam, a word that means "sent" (9:7) would have baptismal significance for John's community.

The first time Thomas appears is when Jesus announces that Lazarus is dead. Thomas says to the other disciples "Let us also go to die with him" (11:16). This burst of loyalty contains a touch of Johannine irony since following Jesus will imply dying with him (12:25). During the Last Supper Thomas bluntly expresses his lack of understanding regarding Jesus' teaching (14:5): he is one of the four disciples — Peter, Thomas, Philip, and Judas (not Iscariot) — to ask for clarifications during Jesus' last discourses. The final episode concerning Thomas shows us the doubter (20:24-25), which climaxes, as we have seen, in his rejection of the need for physical evidence and his great formulation of faith: "My Lord and my God!" (20:28)

Women disciples in John. There are seven instances in the Fourth Gospel where Jesus meets women (2:1-11; 4:7-30; 8:3-11; 11:1-44; 12:1-8; 19:25-27; 20:1-2, 11-18). They describe Mary at Cana, the meeting with the Samaritan woman at the well, the inserted story on the adulteress, Martha and Mary at Lazarus' burial and raising, Mary's anointing of Jesus for burial, the women at the foot of the cross, and the appearance to Mary Magdalene. The role of Mary, the mother of Jesus, we will leave until the next chapter, since hers is a special case and not a Johannine comment on femaleness, or feminism. We will also omit the inserted story on the adulteress, since this is not part of the original Johannine gospel.

Some events in the scene with the Samaritan woman pick up discipleship themes: seeking living water, conversion to a new age, new forms of worship in spirit and truth, and apostolic zeal in proclaiming Jesus to others. The episode would be an encouraging indication of Jesus' Samaritan ministry for any Samaritans in John's community.

The relationship between Jesus and Martha and Mary is interesting because, while they are disciples, the episode focuses on friendship and love (11:3, 5, 11, 36). Martha and Mary inform Jesus "Master, the one you love is ill." Addressing him with a title of faith, they leave to Jesus the response. Martha expresses belief and confidence in Jesus, culminating in the Johannine credal statement "Yes, Lord. I have come to believe that you are the Messiah, the Son of God, the one who is coming into the world" (11:27). Thus is a creed expressed before the sign takes place. Then, following a common practice of disciples in John, she goes off to tell someone else, namely Mary, who then expresses the same

initial faith as Martha (11:32). While the crowd questions
and doubts, the sisters' faith remains strong, and they witness
a resurrection and the beginning of a new life, which is
what discipleship is all about.

Jesus returned to Bethany six days before the Passover
and his friends gave a banquet for him at which Mary anointed
his feet with precious oils and wiped them with her hair
(12:1-8). Judas Iscariot criticizes her gesture of loving service,
but Jesus defends her, indicating her action is a preparation
for burial. Sandra Schneiders points out that the meal took
place on a Sunday, the day of Christian Eucharist; it was a
last supper for Jesus and those he loves. Martha served at
table, a ministerial office in the early Church, Mary's gesture
is like the footwashing of the Last Supper, and Jesus approved
Mary's religious initiative in spite of Judas' opposition.[4]
Given the above similarities both Martha and Mary emerge
as models of key ministers in the Church.

Mary Magdalene had stood at the foot of the cross of Jesus
(19:25), and she was the first to discover the empty tomb
and to inform Simon Peter about it (20:1-2). She herself
returned to the garden and became the first witness to
the Risen Lord: "I have seen the Lord" (20:18). This is the
only individual appearance of Jesus in John, which assigns
to Magdalene what other gospels assign to Peter: namely
the mission of being the first authoritative witness in the
Church and passing on the Johannine version of the post-
Easter kerygma.

The women in John are outstanding models of discipleship.
Jesus calls the Samaritan woman, even though the disciples
seem to disapprove (4:27), and she proclaims Jesus in the
region. Martha appears "as the representative of the believing
community responding to the word of Jesus with a full
confession of Christian faith. It is analogous to Peter's as
representative of apostolic faith in Matthew's gospel."[5] Mary
carries out a central function in the anticipated celebration
of the Last Supper. Mary Magdalene has "apostolic primacy
as witness to the paschal mystery."[6]

Rejection of the Sinful World

"Do you also want to leave?" Although the Johannine Jesus is presented as being in control and does not reject anyone who wishes to come close to him, Jesus still experiences a number of failures regarding the response of disciples. After the Bread of Life discourse many of his disciples remarked: "This saying is hard; who can accept it?" (6:60), and they "returned to their former way of life and no longer accompanied him" (6:66). When the inner group of disciples reaffirm their commitment, Jesus takes occasion to say, "Did I not choose you twelve? Yet is not one of you a devil?" (6:70) The man cured at Bethesda did not become a disciple (5:15); and concerning Jesus' family we read "his brothers did not believe in him" (7:5). His ministry concludes with the sad acknowledgement that "Although he had performed so many signs in their presence they did not believe in him" (12:37).

John prepares us for the bitter rejection in the prologue: "He came to what was his own, but his own people did not accept him" (1:11). Throughout the gospel Jesus not only knows the Father and reveals him but he also knows humanity. "He did not need anyone to testify about human nature. He himself understood it well" (2:25). He knows that some are "of God" (8:47), belong "to the truth" (18:37), and "do not belong to the world" (15:19; 17:14), while others "belong to this world" (8:23) and speak of "earthly things" (3:31). The former are "his own," and the latter belong to the devil (8:44).

Those who receive Jesus (1:12), who are the Father's gift to him (17:6), accept the light, are his own, and become children of God, and they must reject darkness, the world, the devil, and unbelief. Moreover, without the Synoptics' strong motivation of the approaching end, disciples in John are motivated by faith, love, and union in the present. Their rejection of a sinful world is an interior and spiritual experience that leads to a critical judgment against darkness and for the light. "I gave them your word, and the world hated them, because they do not belong to the world" (17:14).

However, even those to whom the message is revealed may slip away, as many did. Although his own who have received a transforming gift, and for some time remain with Jesus, they too can go out to the empty and condemning darkness (13:30). Some "do not believe, because you are not among my sheep" (10:26), "Because my word has no room among you" (8:37), "But you do not want to come to me to have life" (5:40), rather you willingly carry out the wishes of the evil one (8:44).

The true disciple rejects the evil world of darkness: "Master, to whom shall we go? You have the words of eternal life. We have come to believe and are convinced that you are the Holy One of God" (6:68-69). This new life calls the disciple to "Stop judging by appearances, but judge justly" (7:24; 8:15-16). This discernment leads to the rejection of the world hostile to Jesus. It demands disciples who are humble (13:14-15), can accept mortification (15:2), and live through persecution (15:18-21; 16:1-4, 20).

The threat of the evil world is clearly powerful. Disciples who for a while followed Jesus ultimately rejected him, and two of those who pledged allegiance betrayed or denied him (13:26-30; 18:15-18, 25-27), returning to the darkness of night (13:30) and to a coldness of heart that cannot be warmed (18:25).

Jesus knew his mission would end in this division: "I came into this world for judgment, so that those who do not see might see, and those who do see might become blind" (9:39). The task of discipleship is the daily experience of life in the new age. "I have told you this so that you might have peace in me. In the world you will have trouble, but take courage, I have conquered the world" (16:33).

Prove the world wrong about sin. The Baptist proclaimed Jesus as "the Lamb of God, who takes away the sin of the world" (1:29). Unfortunately "the light came into the world, but the people preferred darkness to light because their works were evil" (3:19). Although Jesus came to remove the sin, people who practice evil hate his very coming (3:20). The sinister dimensions of sin cannot be ignored and the results of one's choice for light or darkness are permanent. "Those who have done good deeds [come forth] to the resurrection of life, but those who have done wicked deeds to the resurrection of condemnation" (5:29). Jesus himself does not judge, but people judge themselves by their own values. To those Jews who rejected him Jesus said "the one to accuse you is Moses, in whom you have placed your hopes" (5:45).

Those who put store by this world are told "its works are evil" (7:7).

The inserted story on the adulteress deals with sin, but when Jesus says, "Let the one among you who is without sin be the first to throw a stone at her" (8:7), the crowd disappears, leaving Jesus and the woman. Even then Jesus refuses to condemn her but adds, "from now on do not sin anymore" (8:11).

The gospel of John contains twenty references to sin, twelve of which are in Chapters 8 and 9. This concentration of references may lead us to John's theology of sin in these chapters. After the discourse on the light of the world, Jesus warns unbelievers: "I am going away and you will look for me, but you will die in your sin" (8:21). By rejecting the light they have irrevocably chosen the reign of darkness and that choice is sin. "You belong to what is below ... You belong to this world ... That is why I told you that you will die in your sins" (8:23-24). Jesus did not accuse Nicodemus of sin, nor even the Samaritan woman with her several lovers, but they who choose to reject the light, truth, and life of the new age are vigorously condemned. They have failed to accept the gift of God, and to recognize Jesus as the preexistent Son who has come to show the world how much the Father loves it. "For if you do not not believe that I AM, you will die in your sins" (8:24).

Jesus discussed with some Jews their commitment to Abraham and their unwillingness to accept "the truth will set you free" (8:32). Jesus' conclusion was that they are slaves to a former way of life and not free to accept his gift of new life, and that is sin. "I say to you, everyone who commits sin is a slave of sin" (8:34). In John's theology there is no grey area: accepting Jesus is life; not accepting him is sin and death, the result of the devil no matter how religiously devout people think they are. So he tells the Jews: "You belong to your father the devil and you willingly carry out your father's desires" (8:44). Jesus further insists "Can any one of you charge me with sin? If I am telling the truth, why do you not believe me?" (8:46)

In the episode of the man born blind Jesus rejected the Jewish connection between sin and sickness. When the disciples asked: "Rabbi, who sinned, this man or his parents, that he was born blind?" (9:2), Jesus replied that neither had sinned (9:3). As the debate between the Pharisees and the cured man unfolds, it becomes clear that the Pharisees' notion of sin is violation of law. Moreover, they were so attached to their petty religious legalism that they denied the obviously wonderful and merciful cure because it was done on a Sabbath (9:16). Even the uneducated, cured man saw the foolishness of their blindness and of their notion of sin (9:31), leading the self-righteous legalists to disdainfully return to the more primitive notion of a link between sin and sickness (9:34).

Jesus' final statement on sin is a summary of John's theology, and simply, but profoundly, explains its nature. "If I had not come and spoken to them, they would have no sin; ... but as it is, they have seen, and hated both me and my Father" (15:22-24). The choice is truth or falsehood, light or darkness, life or sin. The judgment Jesus exercised is then passed on to the Holy Spirit, the Paraclete. "And when he comes he will convict the world in regard to sin, ... sin, because they do not believe in me" (16:8-9). Disciples are called to life and to resist the world of sin. Their choice, for Jesus, is a rejection of sin.

Commitment to Believe

Journeys to faith. John's gospel describes three moments in the community's journey of faith. At the beginning of the gospel the writer makes the possibility of faith clear with a series of episodes (2:1 — 4:54). Then, at the end of the gospel, he shows Peter and the Beloved Disciple, Magdalene, and Thomas expressing mature faith in the risen Lord (20:1-18, 24-28). Thirdly, the evangelist challenges his community to believe, even though they have not seen (20:29). In fact, the writing of the gospel is an undertaking motivated by the desire to help others grow in faith (20:30-31).[7]

Throughout the gospel we meet a wide variety of reactions to Jesus. Nicodemus was impressed by Jesus' teachings and signs but did not believe (3:2); after the multiplication of loaves people expressed faith because of the sign (6:14); when Jesus told those who witnessed the multiplication of bread "This is the work of God, that you believe in the one he sent" (6:29), they asked for another sign; hearing Jesus on the feast of Tabernacles, some placed faith in him because of his signs (7:31), and others because of his words (7:40). The Sanhedrin showed no faith in Jesus (7:48), even criticizing Nicodemus' balanced appeal for justice (7:52), and later claiming to be disciples of Moses (9:28). Admittedly some Sanhedrin members believed in Jesus but were afraid to admit it lest they be excommunicated from the synagogues (12:42).

John uses an early section of his gospel to give guidance on correct and incorrect faith. Once the early disciples have formulated belief with a series of titles from Synoptic conclusions,[8] the actual ministry moves to Cana. Jesus changes water into wine there; he also returned to Cana for his second sign. John's section from Cana to Cana gave him opportunity to theologize on correct and incorrect faith.[9] The first episode at Cana presents Mary, a model of mature faith, who asks for a miracle because of her faith, and whose confidence is unshaken even by Jesus' initial reactions (2:1-11). The second episode at Cana presents the royal official who believes in Jesus' words (4:46-54). Between these two episodes of mature faith we are presented with examples that move from no faith to partial faith to complete faith.

In Jerusalem a crowd, enthralled by the power of religion, admires Jesus' signs but there is no real faith, and "Jesus would not trust himself to them because he knew them all" (2:24). We are then introduced to Nicodemus who "appears to be a man ready to believe but incapable of doing so. Jesus does not fit his categories."[10] But Nicodemus is open and does seek out Jesus, even if under the cover of night. He is a secret disciple, open and accepting of Jesus, but with no real commitment (3:1-21, 31-36). The episode of the Samaritan woman shows a woman who initially has no particular interest in religion. She talks about it to a stranger, however, and ends expressing wonder at Jesus' prophetical insight and formulating an early declaration of faith (4:25-29). The Baptist and the Samaritan villagers are examples of complete faith. The former who had previously expressed the Johannine belief in the preexistent Lord, now adds that he "stands and listens for him, rejoices greatly at the bridegroom's voice" (3:29); and the latter believe Jesus' words and not his signs (4:42). Thus this early section becomes a journey, not only from Cana to Cana, but also from disbelief through inadequate, partial belief to a more mature belief. This is John's initial outline of the issue that will hold his attention throughout the gospel. This simple summary is also a journey from Nicodemus, the orthodox Jew, to the Samaritan schismatics, to the royal official who may well have been a Gentile.

Besides this early summary of John's views on faith, and the climactic belief of Magdalene, Peter, the Beloved Disciple, and Thomas, the gospel keeps the issue of growth in faith as a permanently recurring theme.

The gospel as a whole presents these seven attitudes toward faith.[11]

1. Some disciples' faith is based on signs. This is inadequate. In fact, "some see the signs and do not believe at all (3:19-20; 9:41; 11:47)."[12] By themselves, signs are ineffective in leading to faith (4:48); rather they need faith to be appreciated. "Wondrous works are no sure-fire way of producing faith. There is no certain, experiential foundation for faith in Christ, the evangelist is telling us."[13]

2. The second faith response is that of secret disciples like Nicodemus. Unfortunately their openness to Jesus never leads to real commitment.

3. The third stage in faith-growth is also inadequate. It is the acceptance of Jesus as a wonderworker (2:23-25; 4:45; 6:30, 66; 7:2-5). The man healed at the pool of Bethesda sees Jesus in this way (5:11-12, 15). However, Jesus puts no value on this kind of comfort religion (2:23-25).

4. While faith based on signs is inadequate, some people find that the signs help them to prepare for faith. This was the case with the blind man (9:35-38), as it was for Nicodemus (3:2) and the Samaritan townspeople (4:42). The sign gives them an openness to faith; they penetrate it to see the revelation it contains. It is immature but not bad. For example, following his healing the blind man progressively speaks of Jesus as "The man" (9:11), "a prophet" (9:17), "from God" (9:33), and "Son of Man" (9:35). Faith should not need to

rely on miracles (4:48; 20:29), but for these people faith was started with signs and then went beyond them.

5. The fifth is a mature form of faith based on the words of Jesus. Thus it was for the royal official (4:50), for the Samaritan townspeople (4:42), and for some at the feast of Tabernacles (8:30).

6. A good faith response can include misunderstanding as one's faith seeks greater clarification. This is generally the case with the disciples who misunderstand and ask questions during the Last Supper. It is also true of Martha and Mary who have love and faith but still need to be open to the Lord's revealing instruction.

7. The final response is "paradigmatic discipleship. It blends with the top end of the previous response in that there is no further criticism of those who surmount misunderstandings."[14] These believers see miracles, like Mary did, as signs of Jesus' glory that reinforce and deepen their faith (11:40, 45). However, disciples do not need signs (20:29).

Nature of belief in John. John does not use the word "faith" but rather the verb "to believe," which appears ninety-eight times in his gospel, seventy-four of them in Chapters 1-12. In using the verb, John stresses that belief means active commitment. John has four expressions of believing: first he uses "to believe in" 36 times. He "seems to have coined the expression to denote the dynamic interpersonal relationship set up between Jesus and the person to whom he reveals himself."[15] Second he uses "believe" with a direct object. Thus disciples are called to believe the words of Jesus (2:22). Third, disciples are called "to believe that," followed by a theological statement about Jesus (for example: "that you are the Holy One of God" (6:69)). Finally, John uses "to believe" without an object twenty-five times as a summary of the whole attitude of commitment to Jesus and those objects that reveal who he is.[16]

In John, believing is shown by many formulas, each giving us a moment's insight into John's rich understanding. John describes faith as receiving Jesus (1:12), knowing Jesus and the Father (10:38), and acknowledging Jesus as the one sent (3:16-18). Faith means to come to Christ (5:40; 6:35-45; 7:37-38), to accept and receive him (1:12; 5:43; 13:20), to remain in his word (8:31; 15:7), and to be true to his word (8:51). To see, to hear, to come, to know, to testify, and to remember — all are part of John's dynamism of faith. However, out of his many phrases that refer to faith, there are four concepts of special significance: hearing, seeing, knowing, and believing. "Hearing" is not passive but an attentive listening so that one is always being taught by God (6:45). This constant, discerning hearing is so that one is always true to Jesus' word (8:31, 51). It is the disciples' reception of God's revelation. "Seeing" is a second expression for believing, a natural choice when we remember that light and darkness are descriptions of the two kingdoms. "John seems to have a deep appreciation for the way sensual experiences lead one to faith. The physical, the sensory, the material is the medium by which faith is born."[17] To some in his audience Jesus can say, "although you have seen [me], you do not believe" (6:36; 7:3-5; 11:45-46). Thus, physical sight is not the "seeing" that relates to faith. The latter is a spiritual insight and vision that goes with faith (1:14) and sometimes results from it (11:40). In fact, it is a word that describes the whole faith experience (14:9). Although the intellectual content of faith is important for John, "knowing" means a personal understanding, experience, dynamic interaction, the daily learning of faith. Sometimes knowing and believing seem the same (6:69; 14:9; 17:3, 8).

When John uses "believing in," the object is Jesus. This clearly does not mean knowledge about Jesus but an intimate acceptance of who he is for us. "Do not let your hearts be troubled. You have faith in God; have faith also in me" (14:1; 17:3). This belief in Jesus guarantees eternal life (3:16, 36), and is seen especially in a conviction, inner knowledge, and acceptance "that I AM" (8:24, 28, 58; 13:19). Thus, believing in Christ is a summary of revelation. The disciple also believes the various doctrines and teachings that form part of Jesus' revelation, especially concerning his relationship to his Father, for his words, works, and witness are all identical to self-revelation.

To summarize John's spirituality of faith, he first affirms that believing is a gift from the Father (6:37-40) who draws individuals to Jesus (6:44, 65) and helps them persevere in their commitment (10:29).

Believing is also a personal choice, the human response to the loving and welcoming gestures of the Father (9:35-37). As revelation in Jesus makes God known, the disciple responds with a believing obedience (3:36) and a loving interpersonal relationship with the Son (14:15, 21, 23). Believing is a way of life.

Believing is a dialogue between the disciple and God in Christ, the former empty, the latter "full of grace and truth" (1:14). This constant dialogue daily renews the disciples' new birth. Without this dialogue we lose our way and end in darkness (12:35).

Believing is the ongoing grace of the Father facilitating response and recommitment. "This is the work of God, that you believe in the one he sent" (6:29). This important work of God aids the disciple to abide in Jesus' teaching (8:31).

Believing is a form of vision. Eternal life is the vision of God anticipated in Jesus (14:9). The disciples' vision of faith is not focused on a desire to be faithful to many words of teaching and instruction, but rather a centering on the one and only Word spoken by God.[18]

Believing is witnessing to the Word with whom we abide (15:27; 20:21). John often shows how the work of others prepares for faith. Thus, several believers become evangelizers: Andrew, Philip, the Samaritan woman, and Magdalene.

Believing is a guarantee of happiness for the disciple (13:17; 20:29) who becomes a child of God (1:12). Although suffering will be a part of life (15:18-21; 16:1-4; 17:13-19), and the hour of darkness will be painful (13:19; 14:29; 16:4), the disciple knows this in advance, and is urged not to be anxious (14:1). Moreover, part of the happiness of believing is the love of Father and Son, and the union experienced in Christian community.

Believing is knowing that the Father will protect and guard disciples from evil (17:11, 15). John not only presents a profound picture of belief but an equally profound one of unbelief.[19] "Wilful incredulity is shown in all its malice as satanic opposition to the Father (8:40f, 44), spiritual self-sufficiency and inexcusable rejection of the Light, bringing divine wrath, 5:44; 9:41; 12:43, 47f."[20] For disciples haunted with the fear of disbelief, Jesus prayed the Father would consecrate them and he added "And I consecrate myself for them, so that they also may be consecrated in truth" (17:19).

John's gospel contains only one beatitude: "Blessed are those who have not seen and have believed" (20:29). His gospel is, throughout, an exhortation to faith. The early chapters give some preliminary models of correct and incorrect faith. The Book of Signs centers on believing, leading in the Book of Glory to a refocusing of faith in love. Believing is critical to John's purpose in writing the gospel. "But this purpose is not uniquely the writer's: it is the purpose of the Father (3:16), the Son (10:10b, 28), and the Holy Spirit (16:12-15); it is the purpose of the Disciples (15:27: 20:21) and of the church."[21]

Life in God

Love of God. Disciples who commit themselves to believe can say from experience, "From his fullness we have all received, grace in place of grace" (1:16). John adds, "because while the law was given through Moses, grace and truth came through Jesus Christ" (1:17). We have seen that Jesus' love makes disciples his own and leads them to abide in him (17:26). We have also seen how Christ's coming and revelation show the world how much God loves it (3:16-17). Belief is human response to God's love. The briefest synthesis of teaching on belief could be "As the Father loves me, so I also love you. Remain in my love!" (15:9) As God's revelation of loving compassion is seen in the death of the Son out of love for humankind, so the quality of believers' faith is seen when they have the love of God in their hearts (5:42) and respond to Jesus' appeal: "Remain in my love" (15:9).

The Fourth Gospel is the only one in which Jesus speaks of love for himself. The first such reference clearly links love of Christ as a consequence of the disciples' faith. "If God were your Father, you would love me" (8:42). Love of Christ is shown in obedience to his revelation: "Whoever has my commandments and observes them is the one who loves me" (14:21). This faithful and obedient love produces immediate results for disciples, as they are given the Father's love, Jesus' love, and further revelations of the Lord (14:21). Although Jesus mentions commandments, he gives few in this gospel, and so he can also say "Whoever loves me will keep my word" (14:23). Those who have come to know Jesus and believe in him know that he comes from God. "If you loved me, you would rejoice that I am going to the Father" (14:28). Before his departure Jesus makes his great promise of the gift of the Holy Spirit as a consequence of love. "If you love me, you will keep my commandments. And I will ask the Father, and he will give you another Advocate to be with you always" (14:15-16).

In the appendix Jesus asks Peter three times "Simon, son of John, do you love me?" (21:15-17) What love means is no longer specified but is to be understood as a mature believing.

This call to disciples to love Jesus is an extraordinary revelation in world religions. Moreover, loving Jesus leads to the Father's love for disciples (16:27; 17:23). Loving Jesus leads to a union between believers and the Father (17:21). In fact, the unity of Jesus and the Father is the model for the disciples' unity with God in Christ through their loving commitment to the Lord (17:23).

The love for Christ becomes the thrust of the disciples' lives. One author suggests it leads to a practical orientation in our lives to remove false loves and give growth to true love. Among the false loves he lists love of darkness (3:19-21), love for the glory of others (12:43), love of one's own life (12:25), and love of the world (8:23). Among those loves that can be integrated into our love for Christ, he includes love for the glory of God (12:43), love for the light (3:19), love for Christ (8:42-47), and love of God (5:40-44).[22]

A manifestation of disciples' love for Christ is prayer. "Whatever you ask in my name, I will do" (14:13-14). Elsewhere the link between belief and prayer is more specific. "If you remain in me and my words remain in you, ask for whatever you want and it will be done for you" (15:7).

Jesus is the model of prayer in John: praying in thanksgiving at Lazarus' tomb (11:41-42); for glory at the end of his ministry (12:27-28); in intercession for his disciples and future Church during the Last Supper (17:1-26). He always prays as Son in union with his Father. Jesus teaches disciples to pray in Spirit and truth (4:23-24), to pray in his name

(14:13-14), to pray for perseverance and fruitfulness (15:16), and to pray "that your joy may be complete" (16:24). The Johannine commandment to love Christ challenges disciples to make their faith concrete in loving obedience to Jesus and his words, and in prayerful dependency on his support.

Love of others. The Fourth Gospel has no major collection of ethical teachings such as we find in the Sermon on the Mount, nor, for that matter, do we find ethical commands scattered throughout the narrative as we do in the Synoptics. As we have seen, John's basic orientation is Christ's union with his Father in love, a love that reaches to the world through the incarnation and becomes the model for disciples in their union with Jesus. By believing in Jesus, disciples become children of God (1:12); that is, something of God's very nature is generated in us, and we are told it is that we share in his love (1:16). It is this theology and spirituality that lead to ethics. For John the commands of life focus on love for each other (13:34-35; 15:12-13). Christ calls this "a new commandment" and challenges disciples, "As I have loved you, so you also should love one another" (13:34).[23] As a new covenant is established in the Lord's passion, a new command is given that disciples love each other with the quality of love Jesus has shown to them. Jesus views this commandment as a summary of all his wishes (15:12). In practice this broad challenge includes a willingness to serve others, to wash their feet as Jesus did (13:1-17), and to lay down one's life for others (15:13; 10:18).

Disciples' love is rooted in Christ, which is what makes it so new, but it is visibly shown through service to others. This witnessing to love has extensive consequences: "This is how all will know that you are my disciples, if you have love for one another" (13:35). Jesus not only calls his disciples to love but also to a love that leads to a deep unity among themselves in community (17:11). He goes on to pray that "they also may be one in us, that the world may believe that you sent me" (17:21). This unity is portrayed in the allegory of the vine, but it is "apparent that the key to abiding in the vine is obedience to the love commandment (cf. 15:6-17)."[24] The revelation of God's love leads to faith, faith manifests itself in a love itself rooted in the unity of

Father and Son. Love builds unity among Christians; unity leads others to believe in the revelation. This new commandment is the visible characteristic of disciples' faith in this time of the Church (13:35). It is the way we have of maintaining the revelation in the Lord's absence and thus pursuing and living his will: "remain in my love" (15:9). We find yet again that John's theology is basically christology. "Love one another" is the ethic that is rooted in christology, "because I have loved you."

John is frequently accused of having a narrow view of love, restricted only to the inner community of disciples. This follows Jesus' own attitude since he loved those who chose life but condemned those who did not. The criticism is unjustified. John's community had several internal crises to face, and focusing on unity was a wise pastoral decision. Moreover, there are indications of outreach (10:16), and the point of departure is always "For God so loved the world that he gave his only Son, so that everyone who believes in him might not perish but might have eternal life" (3:16).

John's teaching on discipleship is a further manifestation of his christology. He describes disciples as believers who are truly Jesus' own, who have received the transforming gift of becoming children of God. They live this out in active response and by abiding in Jesus' love. He gives a series of models on discipleship as excellent exemplars of his teachings. Discipleship implies a rejection of the kingdom of this world and its sin. Above all, discipleship is a commitment to faith that manifests itself in love and thus leads to fullness of life in a new age.

Chapter Seven
CHURCH IN JOHN

*I have other sheep that do not
belong to this fold. These I also must lead,
and they will hear my voice, and there will be
one flock, one shepherd. (Jn 10:16)*

Luke gives us a detailed presentation of both the nature of the Church, and how we ought to live as an ecclesial people during this time of waiting for the Lord's return. Matthew has discourses on the Kingdom, on church discipline, and on church ministry. Mark seems well aware of church structures and criticizes some of them.[1] All three deal with structures of authority, the central importance of the Twelve, the early development of church laws, and forms of community ritual. In contrast, John seems little interested in the Church. Rather his focus is christological: Jesus is the word, or encounter, between God and disciples. "It is written in the prophets: 'They shall all be taught by God' " (6:45). Where the other gospels remind us of the mediation of the Twelve, John says "the Holy Spirit . . . will teach you in everything, and remind you of all that [I] told you" (14:26). When Jesus addresses the disciples' concern at his departure, he tells them, "Have faith in God; have faith also in me" (14:1); "Remain in my love" (15:9). When he prays for future followers who will come to believe, he prays that "the love with which you loved me may be in them and I in them" (17:26).

Jesus calls disciples to pursue light, truth, and life, and when he speaks of obedience, it is to his word (14:15, 21); when he speaks of commandments, he is referring to love (15:12, 17); when he speaks of authority, he means the Father.

John emphasizes a personal, individual approach to religion, facilitated directly by God and not by mediating structures.

Moreover, John is writing at a time when other parts of the
Church, such as those influenced by Matthew and Luke,
have already formulated ecclesiological syntheses. John
is so different.

Nature of the Church in John

Church in the Fourth Gospel. Although at first sight John
seems to have no interest in Church, this initial reaction
should not be exaggerated. "John does not unfold the kind
of ecclesiology which the historian would expect to find in
a representative of the Christian Church at the end of the
first century."[2] Nevertheless, ecclesiological concerns are
not totally absent from John's thought, and the following
references scattered throughout the text imply Church life.
After the encounter with the Samaritan woman, Jesus says
to his disciples: "Do you not say, 'In four months the harvest
will be here'? I tell you, look up and see the fields ripe for
the harvest" (4:35). This is similar to a mission charge in
Matthew 9:37-38, or could be compared to "a parable of
the Kingdom of God, like the seed parables in Mark 4."[3]

The episode with the Samaritan woman ends with a
communal commitment to belief based on the words of
Jesus (4:39-42). We have already seen the possibility that
this story was inserted to show the foundation of faith in
Samaria and to encourage the present members of John's
community who were previously Samaritans.

The prophecy of Caiaphas ironically speaks of the future
mission of the Church when he claims that Jesus would die
"to gather into one the dispersed children of God" (11:52).
A first sign of this universal appeal of Christ comes with
the request of the Greeks to see Jesus (12:20-22). The Lord's
reply speaks of producing much fruit through his sacrificial
death (12:23-26). The encouraging intervention of the Father
leads Jesus to say "And when I am lifted up from the earth,
I will draw everyone to myself" (12:32).

In his final prayer to his Father, Jesus speaks of the disciples
as a group, claiming to have instructed them, acknowledging
they are the Father's gift to him, receiving glory in their
faithful choice, protecting them, and praying that the Father
will now guard them, unite them, and consecrate them

(17:1-19). He then continues "I pray not only for them, but also for those who will believe in me through their word, so that they may all be one" (17:20-21).

In the post-resurrection appearance to the disciples on the first day of the week — the Church's day of worship — Jesus commissioned his disciples: "As the Father has sent me, so I send you" (20:21). He follows this with the gift of the Holy Spirit and the power of forgiveness (20:22-23).

The final words of Jesus before the appendix are a response to Thomas' faith, but go on to refer to Jesus' joy in the faith of future disciples too: "Have you come to believe because you have seen me? Blessed are those who have not seen and have believed" (20:29).

These scattered references will be complemented later with John's images and models of Church. Already these are adequate to show that John's approach is not an exclusively individual spiritual commitment. Each of these references implies a communal vision and mission. Moreover, John's dualism implies a separation between two groups, and suggests a strong bonding between those who walk in the light. We saw in the last chapter that the commandment to love is verified in unity, and if John is criticized, it is because this unity seems to be for members only.

To these references we must add a further reflection on the Paraclete. All five passages suggest his role is to the whole community; to support it in Jesus' absence, to instruct and remind it of Jesus' teachings, to witness to Jesus through believers, to understand the full message of Jesus (14:15-17, 26; 15:26-27; 16:7-11, 12-14). "The disciples are called to follow Jesus individually; yet they believe in him together, and after the resurrection experience corporately the indwelling and activity of the Spirit-Paraclete."[4]

John's approach to Church as an institution is reserved. He focuses on christology and faith, even though it must be stressed that faith is not individual but implies a communal knowing and confessing: "we saw his glory" (1:14); "we speak of what we know and we testify to what we have seen" (3:11); this testimony "we know ... is true" (21:24). John's christology leads to faith in the saving action of Jesus, and this soteriology leads to an extension of this vision to others —

it leads to ecclesiology. John's is "a logos ecclesiology and even a logos zoology."[5] Disciples' dedication to Church, and to spiritual life, flows from their understanding of, and commitment to, Christ.

John's principal focus is on individuals, but it is impossible to read the whole gospel in this way. He has been very discreet in presenting his ecclesiology, although Brown has warned against any argument from silence.[6] If John does not mention something, it hardly means he opposes it! If one wanted to conclude he has little interest in Church one could do so, since there really is not all that much to support an ecclesiology. But, "If one would like to find symbolic traces of the Church throughout the gospel, there are also possibilities for this opinion."[7] In fact, there are signs of a special love for future followers whom John calls "the dispersed children of God" (11:52); and Jesus says to them "I will not leave you orphans; I will come back to you" (14:18).

Models of Church in John. John shows no sense of need to develop a theology of Church. This is indeed strange when one thinks of writings before John: Paul and Mark; contemporary with the main formulations of the Fourth Gospel: Matthew, Luke, and possibly the Pastorals or Clement of Rome; and coming shortly after John: Ignatius of Antioch and Polycarp of Smyrna. Nevertheless, the imagery John uses gives us insights into the nature of the Church which enrich the universal Christian body.

The symbol of the vine was often used in the Old Testament for the chosen people, and in 67 CE when Jewish rebels struck their own coins in opposition to Rome, the coins carried the image of a vine with its branches. Jews in Jesus' time, or John's, "would know what the 'genuine vine' meant on the lips of Christ."[8]

Jesus' discourse begins "I am the true vine" (15:1). Thus there is no suggestion of grafting the new group onto Israel; rather, in John, believers form a new community outside of Israel. Jesus is the vine; the Father, the vinegrower; the disciples, the branches who must bear fruit. Fruitful believers are purified by the words of Jesus, and draw their life from the vine through continual union. If disciples maintain an intimate union with Jesus, receiving life from him, they will produce abundant fruit, and the Father is thus glorified (15:1-8). Jesus goes on to comment on the meaning of the image of the vine (15:9-17). "As the Father loves me, so I also love you. Remain in my love" (15:9). Theology leads to christology, which is the basis for ecclesiology. The union Jesus urges implies faithful obedience to the commandments, selfless service to others, friendship with Jesus, and bearing lasting fruit. Jesus also stresses that disciples were chosen by his initiative, and part of their calling is loving union and fruitful service.

This second farewell discourse (15:1 — 16:4) was possibly made from two independent units (15:1-17 and 15:18 — 16:4). One commentator suggests that 15:1-17 constitutes an originally independent discourse, directed to believers who have deviated from the community's emphasis on mutual union as a sign of faith and who are "ceasing to abide as 'friends' in the hierarchy of love."[9] Thus, this image of the vine presents an understanding of Church, and John possibly uses it specifically to address a problem within his church.

A second symbolic discourse that gives a glimpse of John's ecclesiology is that of the Good Shepherd (10:1-18). There are two images, both used twice: Jesus is the Good Shepherd (10:11, 14), and he is the gate to the fold (10:7, 9). The image of Shepherd is used in the Old Testament to describe Joshua (Numbers 27:16-17), David (2 Samuel 7:7-9), and God (Isaiah 40:11; Jeremiah 31:10). Ezekiel speaks of Israel's leaders as bad shepherds and prophesies a new shepherd will come (Ezekiel 34:11-16). The same imagery is also used in the New Testament (Mt 18:12-14; Lk 12:32; 15:3-7; Acts 20:28-30; 1 P 2:25).

In this story the keeper of the sheepfold is God, the shepherd is Jesus, and the sheep, the community. Those who recognize the voice of the shepherd follow him; they know him. The Good Shepherd lays down his life for the flock. The allegory also refers to sheep not yet of the flock who also must be brought into the fold. "There will be one flock, one shepherd" (10:16). John may have in mind Israel as the flock, and the Gentiles as "other sheep."[10] In the same discourse, Jesus is seen as gate through which the flock enters the sheepfold. He is the only gate and "Whoever enters through me will be saved" (10:9).

Jesus as Good Shepherd and as the gate to salvation are both images that imply the Church is a sheepfold. While focused on the Shepherd and gate, this is a delightful picture of essential Johannine christology that leads to ecclesiology.

Jesus establishes a new age for his own, giving them a new commandment of love, sealed with his self-gift in humble service (13:1-17). Returning to table after washing the disciples' feet, Jesus tells the disciples they must now do this for others (13:14-15). Although John does not use the word "covenant," the new relationship between Jesus and his own is a covenant relationship, and the fullness of life disciples receive is the fruit of their commitment. Caiaphas suggests that Jesus will die for the people, and John adds "and not only for the nation; but also to gather into one the dispersed children of God" (11:52). This forming of a new people by the death of Jesus can be seen as at least a suggestion by John that the Church is the People of God, the people of the covenant.[11]

The passion narratives in John are a solemn synthesis of many of his key themes. They are also very carefully structured. "Johannine christological and ecclesiological concerns can be detected as dictating in very large measure the composition of the Johannine passion narrative in these opening scenes."[12] One scene in particular merits attention because of its connections with ecclesiology: it is the execution of Jesus on the cross, the time when the Good Shepherd lays down his life (19:16-42).

Brown, with others, sees this scene as a chiasm.[13] The story can be structured as follows: 1. Introduction (19:16b-18), the elevation of Jesus on the cross; 2. Episode I (19:19-22), Inscription of Jesus as king; 3. Episode II (19:23-24), the seamless tunic; 4. Episode III (19:25-27), Jesus' mother and the Beloved Disciple; 5. Episode IV (19:28-30), Jesus hands over his spirit; 6. Episode V (19:31-37), Jesus is pierced; 7. Conclusion (19:38-42), the burial. In a chiasm the center unit is frequently the interpretive key, and this account focuses on the new Church community formed of the Beloved Disciple and Mary. The narrative speaks of Christ, and his death as king, whose seamless tunic symbolizes Church unity, and whose last accomplishment is to form the Church community. This he does by giving his Spirit and then, as he dies, the first Christian community, assembled at the foot of the cross, looks on him who has been pierced. In chiasm 1 parallels 7, 2 parallels 6, 3 parallels 5, and 4 is the centerpoint. Thus in John's picture of community the unity (3) is established by the Spirit (5); Jesus is king (2) by offering himself to be pierced (6). This is an image of the birth of the Church at the death of Jesus.

One further image deserves mention. The Baptist refers to Jesus as the bridegroom (3:29), implying the bride is the messianic community. While this image has little support in the Old Testament, it was used by early Christians, and John's commmunity could well have understood it in this way.

Although John never uses "church," or "body of Christ," "family," or "temple of God," or other New Testament descriptions of Church, he does not ignore the importance of the new community of Jesus; and while these indications are not developed in detail in his writings, he has certainly opened his community to a deeper appreciation of their common calling.

Living as Church

A sharing Church. John sees the Church as a community of love, based on the Word, and guided by the Spirit. His is not an abstract ecclesiology, but a community of concrete sharing. Although he insists on the exclusive mediation of Christ, there are some indications that the community's love is shown in practical community, ritual, and sacramental gestures.

John gives no detailed list of forms of community sharing such as we find in the early chapters of the Acts of the Apostles. The Johannine Jesus establishes deep friendships (11:3, 5, 11, 36; 13:1, 23), and values the peace (14:27), love (15:9), and joy (15:11) that build a good community. He cultivates among his own a deep union, and they must surely have learned from his example. The gospel offers a few external gestures which may have been rituals of sharing in the early Church, but interpreters vary in the weight they give to these suggested rituals. While Jesus is portrayed as the great sacrament of God's love for humanity, some commentators stress he is the only one, and they believe the Johannine community rejects all ritual sacraments. Others believe John has sacramental emphasis providing simple human rituals by means of which believers externally manifest their desire for the inner transformation Jesus brings.

Commentators who consider John non-sacramental emphasize that Jesus closed down the Temple (2:13-22) and insisted on worship in Spirit and truth (4:21-24). John has no institution of the Eucharist during the Last Supper and no commission to baptize in Jesus' name such as we find in the Synoptics. Do the Synoptics portray a lapse back into a ritualism that Jesus rejected, or is John the one who has lost a significant form of community sharing, or not yet accepted it?

Other writers are positively impressed by the sacramental interests of John. They believe the several visible signs of the gift of life in water, bread, and anointing show life is communicated through these external signs and demonstrate John's is a sacramental gospel. Moreover, early Christian art soon chose episodes from John to visualize the sacraments. Some commentators believe John wrote "to oppose Christian teachers who, as the history of early Christianity progressed, gave too little place to the sacraments in the life of the church," or to reflect "a growing need to give the right emphasis to sacramental teaching."[14] Another writer thinks that some dropouts from John's community proved unfaithful to the word of Jesus, and John played down the sacraments because, in the case of the dropouts, the sacraments had not authenticated true discipleship.[15]

John nowhere explicitly says he is anti-sacramental, but neither does he explicitly support a sacramental system. In the next sections we will examine elements of John's teachings that refer to rituals, and see if those references also show the community's conviction that through these rituals Jesus is present again.[16]

Baptism. John omits the baptism of Jesus as he also omits any final commissioning to baptize in Jesus' name. Some episodes have secondary reference to baptism. The first episode to consider is the scene in which Jesus tells Nicodemus: "No one can enter into the kingdom of God without being born of water and Spirit" (3:5). Although "of water" appears in all texts, commentators still discuss the possibility that it is a late addition by a redactor. While the history of this part of the text would be interesting to pursue, John's community would give this section of Jesus' discourse a baptismal interpretation, and this is our main concern here. Admittedly the reference is secondary since Jesus makes no further mention of water; but "of water" is in all manuscripts, and it has no other interpretation but the act of Christian baptism through which the life of the Spirit is conveyed. In fact, as Brown points out, the whole discourse to Nicodemus deals with new birth and would have a "baptismal significance for the early Church even without the mention of water."[17]

Chapter 9 on the healing of the blind man evidences several indirect references to baptism. The man is born blind and so we are dealing with a new birth. He is told to wash in a pool called "sent," and after the washing, he sees. In addition to the healing power of water, the man is "anointed" with the mud and saliva. The man ends confessing faith in Jesus as Son of Man. The story presents conversion through water and anointing and the result is illumination. Although secondary this is an outline of the nature and effect of baptism. Lindars concludes: "John is not, of course, giving teaching on baptism as such; but his picture of the conversion experience may be influenced by his knowledge of Christian initiation."[18]

Two other references mention water as a source of life, but the context gives no support to a baptismal interpretation. In 7:37-38 Jesus concludes by quoting scripture: "Rivers of living water will flow from within him." The evangelist himself sees this as a reference to the Holy Spirit (7:39). The final reference is the fulfillment of this last mentioned prophecy when "One soldier thrust his lance into his side, and immediately blood and water flowed out" (19:34). While the redemptive significance of baptism is associated with the death of Jesus, there is no reason to think John has it in mind here. Cullman has suggested a baptismal interpretation to the washing of the feet, but that, like the two references above, is not persuasive. Nevertheless the episodes with Nicodemus and the blind man do have secondary baptismal references which would hardly be missed by John's readers.

Eucharist. The institution of the Eucharist is not mentioned during the Last Supper. In fact, although the farewell discourse "breathes a sacramental air,"[19] it contains no Eucharistic language. John seems to have disassociated the Eucharist from the Last Supper. Whether or not this is to resist conflict over the celebration such as we find in 1 Corinthians 11:17-22 is not clear. The only ritual during the Last Supper is the washing of feet. Insofar as this is an acted prophecy it interprets the essence of Jesus' coming sacrifice, but there are not even secondary Eucharistic references during the meal. One writer suggests the reason is "The Sacrament is no longer a rite commemorating Christ's death, but the channel through which is bestowed the gift of eternal life."[20] More generally commentators turn to the feeding of the five thousand and the Bread of Life discourse for any Eucharistic emphasis by John. The feeding is close to Passover (6:4), Jesus does not break the bread but he distributes it himself, not the apostles, and he "gave thanks" (6:11). All of these are elements with some eucharistic links.[21]

After the feeding of the five thousand and the episode on the lake, this new exodus event is extensively commented on by Jesus in the discourse on the Bread of Life. The discourse is commonly divided into two parts (6:35-50 and 6:51-58); the latter is sometimes seen as a doublet of the previous part. The main part of the discourse (6:35-50) presents Jesus as Wisdom (Proverbs 9:4-6; Sirach 24:21), and teaches that believing in Jesus will remove the hunger of life (6:35). "For this is the will of my Father, that everyone who sees the Son and believes in him may have eternal life" (6:40). Some writers, while emphasizing the primacy of a sapiential interpretation to 6:35-50, consider there is a secondary Eucharistic overlay which early Christians would see. However, the Israelites, wandering in the desert, were providentially fed by God, but the Exodus and wandering are not essentially a feeding experience but a revelation. Likewise here, Jesus ascends a mountain (6:3) — the Christian Sinai — and the crowds receive a revelation from the Bread of Life, the light of the life (8:12), and the word of life. The discourse's focus is christological, a further teaching and self-revelation of Jesus (6:35, 40, 45, 47).

There follows the second half of the discourse (6:51-58), and the focus moves from believing to eating: "Whoever eats on my flesh and drinks my blood has eternal life" (6:54). This section, which could have originally been a Eucharistic homily, sees the community's celebration as a messianic banquet (Proverbs 9:5). It is viewed by many as a later addition to John, but it is explicitly Eucharistic. The crowd could hardly have understood it in this way, even if Jesus had actually spoken it, but the Johannine community surely saw it as Eucharistic (6:53). This section, probably added at a late stage in the redaction, clearly speaks about eating and drinking, and no spiritual interpretation is possible.[22] It makes explicit some of the sacramental interests that John has throughout his work. "Whoever eats my flesh and drinks my blood remains in me and I in him" (6:56). This section is John's strongest statement on the Eucharist.

Other Johannine rituals. A few commentators also see references to other sacraments. Thus, some see Cana with its focus on water and new life as a teaching on baptism. Some see the same episode as a statement on the sacramental nature of Christian marriage. The power to forgive sins, conveyed by Jesus to the disciples, is related by some to a sacrament of penance (20:22-23). None of these suggestions have serious textual support. They are flimsy and evidence too much desire to root what we have in the past rather than looking at the origins to see what is present or absent.

The ritual washing of feet as a gesture of community love and humble service is important enough to appear during the Last Supper. It is presented in a fashion similar to the synoptic ritual of the Last Supper. When Jesus returns to table he says, "I have given you a model to follow, so that as I have done for you, you should also do" (13:15). This injunction sounds very like "Do this in memory of me" (Lk 22:19). Jesus also instructs the participants "you ought to wash one another's feet" (13:14), and he ends with the delightful assurance, "If you understand this, blessed are you if you do it" (13:17).

Washing of feet never became an established ritual in the universal Christian body, even though some small groups did practice it. Generally the footwashing is viewed as a symbolic call to humble, mutual service.[23] John's principal focus is on his high christology and the arrival of a new age of fullness of life. Individual and communal spiritual life flows from this vision in faith. John gives the impression that if he can convince people of this then the rest, including personal and community ethics, will take care of themselves. Nevertheless, there are some traces of community sacramental celebrations of Baptism and Eucharist which are seen as contributing to the community vision of unity in the Lord.

Authority in the Church

Ministerial leadership. Many New Testament writings deal with various forms of Church organization, but John shows little interest in organizational structures. In their recent past his own community had suffered from arrogant religious authorities who had driven some of its members out of the synagogue (9:22; 12:42; 16:2). John's ecclesiology is not based on structures of authority, or official channels of tradition, or established bodies to interpret Jesus' teaching. Moreover, he is writing at a time when other Church leaders, such as the author of the Pastorals and Clement, are centering their attention on structures of Church authority. Although no universally accepted structure existed by the end of the first century, there were already signs of a change from pluralism to standardization of structures. "John combines a deep interest in the apostolic foundation of the church with an indifference toward it as an institution dispensing salvation."[24] When others are establishing distinctive offices John seems uninterested. Admittedly the Johannine letters indicate some concerns for authority and tradition, but they also contain an angry denunciation of attempts to introduce monarchical government into the Johannine communities (3 Jn 9-10).

The unity of the Church, symbolized in Jesus' seamless tunic, and spoken of so frequently in the farewell discourses, is maintained, "If you remain in me and my words remain in you" (15:7). It is fostered by an asceticism of love (15:9-17), and authentic interpretation of Jesus' teaching is fostered by the Paraclete (14:15-16, 26). Jesus and the Spirit animate and guide this community, and if each individual remains united to the vine each one "will bear much fruit" (15:5). The image is not of a body with some members more important than others; it is of a vine that gives abundant life to all the branches which remain united to the vine. John's teaching is presented at a time when the community has lost the Beloved Disciple, yet still insists on spiritual union and its accompanying freedom for this community of love. John has to deal with the death of the Beloved Disciple, with persecution, some factionalism, and the debate with the Great Church; these tensions may have forced the Johannine community to re-examine whether its simple structures could assure permanence.

Besides the Beloved Disciple whose "testimony is true" (21:24), Martha makes the confession which the Synoptics ascribe to Peter (11:27; Mt 16:16; Mk 8:29; Lk 9:20), and Magdalene receives the only individual resurrection appearance and proclaims her faith in the risen Lord (20:18). These are experiences which the Synoptics consider point to authority in the Church. The Fourth Gospel presents a group that claims the authority of experience and authentic interpretation (1:14; 3:11; 21:24). This "we" need not be an apostolic authority, but could be the community that believed it was in continuity with Jesus. There are also references to pastoral office (13:20; 20:21), but the community places its trust first in the charismatic Beloved Disciple, and later in spirit-filled leaders (3:34). In general, John speaks of "disciples," "friends," "brothers"; "titles which imply the 'democratization' of leadership in the community."[25]

The two principal images of Church — the Good Shepherd and the vine — while portraying unity, also speak of the community's efforts to resist false teachings (10:10, 12; 15:2, 6). At the same time believers who remain in union with Jesus "are assured . . . that they will be able to recognize the true revealer and resist the false leaders."[26]

In John's community ministerial leadership is a service of love, rooted in union with Jesus and his Spirit. There are no clearly defined structures and no privileges based on office.

Institutionalized authority. Followers of Jesus are called disciples, friends, or servants. John never uses the ecclesiastical word "apostle" with its presumption of authority, but employs instead the more primitive and universally applicable designation of disciple. Since John continues this practice throughout his letters it would seem to be a deliberate decision. At times the evangelist uses an approximate concept when he applies to disciples the idea of being sent. "As the Father has sent me, so I send you" (20:21; also 17:18). The logic of the statement is typical for John; theology — Father, christology — me, ecclesiology — you. However, there is no suggestion that this is an official delegation of an inner group. Rather, being sent, in John, refers less to authority and more to the concept of union with Jesus, who sends.

John is aware of Jesus' close association with the Twelve. They are mentioned explicitly on only two occasions. First, after some disciples abandon Jesus on the occasion of the Bread of Life discourse, we read: "Jesus then said to the Twelve, 'Do you also want to leave?'" (6:67) Peter, answering for the group, reaffirms their faith. John refers to the Twelve a second time in the post-resurrection appearance to the disciples. "Thomas, . . . one of the Twelve, was not with them when Jesus came" (20:24). Although only mentioning them twice, John conveys the impression that they are around for major experiences such as the farewell discourses. Admittedly he does not explicitly refer to the Twelve, and we are always tempted to read John through the knowledge we have from the Synoptics. Nevertheless, when they are mentioned, they are not given any special introduction. Rather, it is presumed the readers know who they are. Although John nowhere lists the Twelve as the Synoptics do, individual members of the Twelve are referred to: Peter, the sons of Zebedee, Philip, Thomas, Andrew, Judas, and Judas Iscariot.

Jesus started his ministry with five disciples, some of whom appear more actively involved with Jesus in this gospel than in the Synoptics: Andrew, Simon, Philip, Thomas, and Nathaniel. Although mentioning them only twice, John gives no impression of strong opposition to the Twelve as does Mark.[27] It seems that discipleship and ministry are valued in the Johannine church, but ministerial functions and leadership have not yet been institutionalized, not even with the simple equation of the Twelve as the Twelve apostles. The disciples are sent by Jesus (13:20; 15:16; 17:18; 20:21), given power to forgive sins (20:23), and called to witness to Jesus (15:27). The strongest statement about the Twelve is that they remained faithful when others apostasized (6:68-70).

The member of the Twelve who is most frequently mentioned is Peter, but he does not appear as the leader of the group as he does in the Synoptics. Peter was the third disciple called, and from the beginning is referred to with his symbolic name (1:40-44). He expresses the faith of the Twelve after the Bread of Life discourse (6:67-69), appears like his impetuous Synoptic portrayal in the footwashing (13:6-10), and asks the Beloved Disciple to find out from Jesus the identity of the betrayer (13:24). When Peter promises to lay down his life for Jesus, the Lord predicts Peter's denials (13:36-38), which later occur (18:15-18, 25-27). In the garden Peter draws a sword to defend Jesus (18:10-11) and later follows Jesus to the High Priest's house (18:16). After the resurrection Peter is informed of the empty tomb by Magdalene and later visits it himself (20:1-10). In the appendix, which some commentators see as a redactor's attempt to present Peter in more authoritative roles, Peter enthusiastically acknowledges the risen Lord (21:1-14), receives the pastoral commission to watch over the flock (21:15-19), and asks Jesus about the future fate of the Beloved Disciple (21:20-23).

This gospel portrays a close association between Peter and the Beloved Disciple. In fact, a rivalry develops which is not focused on attacking Peter, but rather on defending the authoritative testimony of the Beloved Disciple's teaching for the Johannine community. Thus, both are at the Last Supper, but the Beloved Disciple has a special place of intimate friendship with Jesus, and Peter gets information from Jesus through the Beloved Disciple (13:22-24). Peter denies he is a follower of Jesus (18:17, 25, 27), whereas the Beloved Disciple goes to the cross (19:26). Peter enters the empty tomb, but the Beloved Disciple is the one to express the resurrection faith (20:3-10). Moreover, the mother of Jesus is entrusted to the Beloved Disciple, and Jesus founds the first community on them.

This rivalry is less likely to be an historical development

than the portrayal of the authority clash between the Great Church with Peter and the leaderless Johannine community. After the death of the Beloved Disciple, the latter seeks unity with the Great Church; but does not wish to be forced to abandon its own traditions, which it firmly believes are rooted in a disciple who was loved by Jesus and whose authority in their view was as great as Peter's.

Mary the mother of Jesus. In John's gospel Mary appears on two occasions, Cana and the crucifixion: episodes that include the first and the last signs. Mary is generally referred to with the title of honor, "the mother of Jesus" (2:1, 3, 5, 12). Jesus calls her "woman" which could be acceptable and respectful in every case except that of a son speaking to his mother. Since there is no reason for any disrespect or opposition, we must look for another meaning that John may have intended. "Woman" can mean "Eve" and John here presents Mary as the new Eve.

When we turn to the second episode in which the mother of Jesus appears (19:25-27), she is again referred to as "woman." Besides these two gospel uses, the Book of Revelation (12:1-17) also refers to the "woman" as it portrays the fulfillment of the Old Testament promise that a woman would crush the head of Satan (Genesis 3:15). Here, at Cana and at the cross, John uses inclusion and in both episodes portrays the mother of Jesus as the new Eve. This is not so much an emphasis on Mary as an individual but as the new Eve, a symbol of the Church.[28] As Eve, the powerful mother of all the living, Mary responds to human need at Cana, and is entrusted to John at the cross. The entrusting of Mary to John cannot be understood as a personal request. The solemn moment implies something theologically significant and probably means the entrusting of the Church to the Johannine community.

It would be inaccurate to interpret the episode as presenting a role of influence and authority for Mary as an individual. Clearly she has honor in the community but this cannot be interpreted as institutionalized authority. Like the Beloved Disciple, the mother of Jesus is never named. "The anonymous status makes it probable that the narrator viewed them in their representative character."[29] As in the case of other aspects of John's approach to authority, the structures are not important, individuals do not have privileges. Rather the guides remain Jesus and his Spirit.

Mission in John's Community

Mission and ministry. Before ministering to the blind man Jesus said to his disciples, "We have to do the works of the one who sent me while it is day" (9:4). This invitation to participate in Jesus' ministry should be complemented with the spiritual advice on the style of one's ministry, given after the example of the footwashing (13:12-17), especially the reminder that no messenger is greater than the one who sent him (13:16). Jesus was totally dedicated to his Father's mission for him: "My food is to do the will of the one who sent me and to finish his work" (4:34). Elsewhere Jesus clarifies the nature of his ministry: "My teaching is not my own but is from the one who sent me" (7:16). This concept of ministry, based on John's theology of union, is then extended to disciples. "I gave them your word" (17:14). Jesus gives to the disciples the Father's word. In the last discourse, talking about his own departure, Jesus says to his disciples, "On that day you will realize that I am in my Father and you are in me and I in you" (14:20). Mission and ministry are based on awareness of union, a union maintained if you "have his word remaining in you" (5:38; 8:31; 15:7).

The disciples in their ministry are described in a series of metaphors: they are shepherds to the sheep (21:15-17), harvesters of the grain (4:34-38); fishers of the fish (21:5-11), and branches bearing grapes (15:1-8). John has no commission other than the final sending (20:21), but he is aware of the mission of outreach that Jesus had in mind (4:38; 17:20), realizes Jesus takes the initiative in calling his disciples (15:16), and is aware of those others who must come to Jesus through the community's missionary work (10:16; 17:20). He also anticipates that the disciples' ministry will be fruitful (14:12) and rewarding (4:32-34; 12:26). Above all, disciples need to foster awareness that they share the same vocation of Jesus, "the words you gave to me I have given to them, and they accepted them" (17:8).

Disciples who are sent by Jesus and proclaim his word

must serve him, follow him, and live united to him (12:26; 17:24). This will imply sacrifice, imitation of Jesus' humble service (13:1-11), facing up to persecution (15:18-27) or even death (16:2), and fidelity to the following of the Lord in whatever vocation, life or death, he wills (21:18-23).

Witnessing. The ministry of bearing witness is a key concept in John. The noun "witness" appears three times in Mark, once in Luke, not at all in Matthew, and fourteen times in John. The verb "to witness" appears only once in Matthew and Luke, not at all in Mark, and thirty-three times in John. John's use of these words is concentrated in the Book of Signs where the noun is used twelve times and the verb twenty-six times. This key concept, like others in John, is rooted in his christology. Disciples learn from the Lord how to bear witness. Jesus replies to Pilate: "I came into the world, to testify to the truth" (18:37). On the feast of Tabernacles, Jesus insists "My testimony can be verified, because I know where I came from and where I am going" (8:14). The truth Jesus testifies to is his revelation of his own divine reality (1:17-18; 8:40). This truth "will set you free" (8:32); it is redemptive. "Whoever hears my word and believes in the one who sent me has eternal life" (5:24).

Jesus' witness is his mission from the Father (18:37). There also appears a series of witnesses who testify to who Jesus is. The Baptist bore witness about Jesus to the priests and levites from Jerusalem (1:19-28), and to his own disciples (1:29-37; 3:22-30). The first disciples of Jesus testify to each other that Jesus is teacher, Messiah, the one Moses spoke about, Son of God, and King of Israel (1:40-50).[30]

Throughout his ministry Jesus encountered individuals who often end by testifying to him in a personal confession. The Samaritans proclaimed Jesus as Savior (4:42); the crowd who witnessed the multiplication of loaves said: "This is truly the Prophet, the one who is to come into the world" (6:14); this confession is repeated by the blind man (9:17). After the Bread of Life discourse Peter testified that Jesus is "the Holy One of God" (6:69). In Jerusalem for the feast of Tabernacles, some in the crowd acknowledge Jesus as the Prophet (7:40), others as the Messiah (7:41). Before the raising of Lazarus, Martha bore witness that Jesus is "the Messiah, the Son of

God, the one who is coming into the world" (11:27). After the resurrection Thomas uttered his confession, "My Lord and my God!" (20:28). Sometimes witnesses unknowingly say far more than they appreciate. Thus Caiaphas proclaimed Jesus' vicarious salvific death (11:50-52), Pilate unknowingly acknowledged Jesus' kingship (18:33, 37), and the Sanhedrin ironically testified to Jesus' universal mission (11:47-48).

When Jesus was in Jerusalem for a Sabbath celebration, at which he healed the man in Bethesda, an argument arose regarding his authority to work a healing on the Sabbath. As part of his response Jesus assembled a group of witnesses on his behalf: the Father (5:31-32), the Baptist (5:33-35), the signs he performs (5:36), and the scriptures (5:39). Thus, the Father who expresses the Word, the Baptist in his prophetic word, each sign as an acted word, and scripture as the written word, all bear witness to Jesus' origin from God.[31] In fact, the whole gospel is a prolonged testimony to Jesus (20:30-31); and Jesus announces: "I testify on my behalf and so does the Father who sent me" (8:18). Jesus also claims that after his departure "the Spirit of truth ... will testify to me" (15:26).

During the farewell discourses Jesus makes his wishes very clear to the disciples: "you also testify, because you have been with me from the beginning" (15:27). John despises secret discipleship, like Nicodemus'. Such disciples' faith is inadequate (3:1). They appreciate Jesus but are afraid to go public with their acknowledgement of him (9:22); they refuse to witness to him in order to maintain their comfort and retain "human praise" (12:43).

The many witnesses who courageously testify to Jesus are examples for John's community; the episodes of inadequate faith and stunted witness are there to warn present members with similar tendencies. John does not offer a handbook on witnessing. Rather he expects this aspect of ecclesiology, like all the others, to be drawn out from his christology. "Whoever loves me will keep my word" (14:23).

Jesus reminds disciples "It was not you who chose me, but I who chose you and appointed you to go and bear fruit" (15:16; also 15:8). Disciples go forth with courage, bearing the same message Jesus had from his Father (17:8); and they go with confidence since Jesus has already acknowledged that their witnessing will be fruitful (17:20).

Building unity. This aspect of the mission of the Church is rooted in John's theology of union between the Father and Jesus, a union then shared with disciples (15:9, 12, 17; 17:20-21).

Other gospels deal with the problem of the entry of the Gentiles into the Church, but John's community seems to have already dealt with the issue, and its present appeal is universal (1:9, 29; 3:17; 10:16; 12:32; 17:2), even cosmic (3:16; 6:51; 12:30-32; 16:33). The ongoing ministry of the Church calls the world to God. "I say to you, whoever receives the one I send receives me, and whoever receives me receives the one who sent me" (13:20).

In this universal extension of Christ's revealing and transforming word his followers are responsible for unity. Thus Jesus says: "I pray . . . for those who will believe in me through their word, so that they may all be one, as you, Father, are in me and I in you" (17:20-21). The Church is a communion, a community of love based on the Word and the Spirit.

A practical dimension of building unity arose for the Johannine community after the death of the Beloved Disciple and the call they feel to seek unity with the Great Church. The appendix of the gospel shows the Johannine community's appreciation of the Petrine pastoral ministry (21:15-19). Several decades after the death of Jesus, John's community still existed, with its own independent traditions of Jesus. When efforts toward unity were initiated the community moved to union with love, knowing that Jesus prayed "That they all may be one" (17:21). Nevertheless, they valued their tradition, knowing it was true and reliable (21:24); and above all they were convinced of their understanding of the high Christ, for they could say with confidence "We saw his glory" (1:14).

The gospel evidences some friendly posturing on the part of the Johannine community. They insist on retaining their own tradition while coming into the unity of the Great Church. They are convinced that their Beloved Disciple is at times closer to Jesus than Peter is (13:23-26). While they both run, side by side, to the resurrection, the Beloved Disciple gets there first; both enter, but it is John who first believes in the resurrection of the Lord. Thus, the Beloved

Disciple and his community tell Peter and his Great Church that Jesus is the preexistent Lord (20:8). "This shows that the 'Petrine communities,' the Churches of the 'twelve,' in some way find the full meaning of Jesus in the belief of the Johannine community and its book."[32]

John's community moves to unity but it brings with it its own understanding of Christ as preexistent God and enriches the Great Church with its faith.

John's ecclesiology focuses less on the specifics of the Church's life — structures, disciplines, rituals, and ministries — and more on the theological vision from which Church flows. Speaking of the deep union between himself and his Father, Jesus twice says "Whoever sees me sees the one who sent me" (12:45). In John's theology, Jesus could also have said "he who looks on the ones I send is seeing me." Thus, the nature of the Church flows from who Jesus is; living as Church integrates the life Jesus gave; authority in the Church flows from the life of union; and the mission is to prolong the word of Jesus. John's vision complements the Synoptics' approach and can help us refocus our priorities, rekindle our faith, renew a humble awareness that, without Jesus, we can do nothing in our Church, or for our Church.

A CONCLUDING WORD FROM THE JOHANNINE JESUS

"As the Father loves me,
so I also love you.
Remain in my love.
If you keep my commandments,
you will remain in my love,
just as I have kept my Father's commandments
and remain in his love.
I have told you this so
that my joy might be in you
and your joy might be complete.
This is my commandment:
love one another as I love you.
No one has greater love than this,
to lay down one's life for one's friends.
You are my friends
if you do what I command you.
I no longer call you slaves,
because a slave does not know what his master is doing.
I have called you friends,
because I have told you everything I have heard from my
    Father.
It was not you who chose me,
but I who chose you
and appointed you to go
and bear fruit that will remain,
so that whatever you ask the Father in my name
he may give you.
This I command you:
love one another." (John 15:9-17)

NOTES

Chapter One

[1] See Josephus, *Antiquities of the Jews*, vol. 9 (Cambridge, Mass: Harvard University Press, 1965), 18. 63 and 20. 200.

[2] See Howard Clark Kee, *Jesus in History*, 2nd ed. (New York: Harcourt Brace Jovanovich, Inc., 1970), pp. 48-54.

[3] See Dennis C. Duling, *Jesus Christ Through History* (New York: Harcourt Brace Jovanovich, Inc., 1979), pp. 10-11.

[4] For an overview of Jewish history, see Wilfrid J. Harrington, "An Outline History of Israel," *Key to the Bible*, vol. 1 (New York: Doubleday and Co., Inc., 1976), pp. 83-178.

[5] See Sean Freyne, *The World of the New Testament* (Wilmington, Del: Michael Glazier, Inc., 1980), pp. 99-122.

[6] See A. R. C. Leaney, "The Qumran Writings,"*The Jewish and Christian World: 200 BC to AD 200* (New York: Cambridge University Press, 1984), pp. 171-183.

[7] See Freyne, pp. 22-41.

[8] For a fine overview of historical developments in the first century, see Floyd V. Filson, "The Church Anchored in History," *A New Testament History* (Philadelphia: The Westminster Press, 1966), pp. 293-354.

[9] See Leonard Doohan, *Mark: Visionary of Early Christianity* (Santa Fe: Bear and Co., 1986), pp. 61-66.

[10] See Leonard Doohan, *Matthew: Spirituality for the 80s and 90s* (Santa Fe: Bear and Co., 1985), pp. 113-117.

[11] See Leonard Doohan, *Luke: The Perennial Spirituality*, 2nd ed., (Santa Fe: Bear and Co., 1985), pp. 98-103.

[12] See Helen Doohan, *Leadership in Paul* (Wilmington, Del: Michael Glazier Inc., 1984), pp. 161-167.

[13] See Doohan, *Mark*, pp. 120-122; *Matthew*, pp. 107-113; *Luke*, pp. 103-108.

[14] See C. H. Dodd, *The Interpretation of the Fourth Gospel* (New York: Cambridge University Press, 1968), p. 122.

[15] See Dodd, *Interpretation*, p. 44.

[16] See J. M. Lieu, "Gnosticism and the Gospel of John," *Expository Times*, 90 (1979), pp. 233-237.

[17] See Dodd, *Interpretation*, p. 103.

[18] John Marsh, *Saint John* (Harmondsworth, England: Penguin Books, 1968), p. 33.

[19] See Raymond E. Brown, *The Gospel According to John*, vol. 1. (New York: Doubleday and Co., Inc., 1966), pp. LVI-LVIII.

[20] See the previous section in this chapter: "Hellenistic Setting of Early Christianity," pp. 19-23.

[21] Dodd, *Interpretation*, p. 86.

[22] See Robert Kysar, *The Fourth Evangelist and His Gospel* (Minneapolis: Augsburg Publishing House, 1975), p. 155.

[23] See Kysar, *Fourth Evangelist*, pp. 270, 278.

[24] See Robert Kysar, *John, The Maverick Gospel* (Atlanta: John Knox Press, 1976), p. 19: "The parallels between johannine thought and the literature discovered in the so-called Dead Sea Scrolls are enough to convince us that the evangelist was acquainted with a broad type of Judaism which embraced a great variety of forms and expressions." Raymond E. Brown, "The Qumran Scrolls and the Johannine Gospel and Epistles," *New Testament Essays* (New York: Doubleday and Co., Inc, 1968), p. 169: "First, and of this there should be no question, there remains a tremendous chasm between Qumran thought and Christianity. No matter how impressive the terminological and ideological similarities are, the difference that Jesus Christ makes between the two cannot be minimized."

[25] See Charles H. H. Scobie, "The Origins and Development of Samaritan Christianity," *New Testament Studies*, 19 (1972-73), pp. 390-414; Kysar, *Fourth Evangelist*, p. 160; Edwin D. Freed, "Samaritan Influence in the Gospel of John," *Catholic Biblical Quarterly*, 30 (1968), pp. 580-587; D. Moody Smith, *John: Proclamation Commentaries* (Philadelphia: Fortress Press, 1976), p. 76: "There seems, however, to be a pronounced leaning in the direction of heterodox Judaism, especially an interest in Samaria and the Samaritans. Not by coincidence is the Samaritan woman, whom Jesus encounters by Jacob's well in Samaria, able to understand him better than the learned Nicodemus. If salvation is from the Jews, in the sense that it originates among them, it is received by the Samaritans, while they reject it."

[26] Kysar, *Fourth Evangelist*, p. 145.

[27] Raymond E. Brown, *The Community of the Beloved Disciple* (New York: Paulist Press, 1979), p. 23.

[28] Kysar, *Maverick Gospel*, p. 56: "The Jews are almost always the villains in the Gospel. They persecute Jesus (5:16); they misunderstand him (8:22); they attempt to stone him (8:59); they

are responsible for his arrest and crucifixion (18:12 and 19:12). Most characteristically they are the ones who refuse to believe in him (10:31ff.)."

[29]Brown, *Community*, p. 37.

[30]See Brown, *Community*, pp. 171-182 for his analysis of the views of other authors, and pp. 166-169 for the summary of his own view. For an analysis of Brown's position that leads to rejection of his views, see J. S. King, "R. E. Brown on the History of the Johannine Community," *Scripture Bulletin*, 13 (1983), pp. 26-30.

[31]Kysar, *Maverick Gospel*, p. 64; see also Francis J. Moloney, "Revisiting John," *Scripture Bulletin*, 11 (1980), p. 12: "I am not at all happy with the picture of the Johannine community's developing into a closed inward-looking group, critical of all who would not see Christ and Christian life exactly the way they saw it."

[32]See R. Alan Culpepper, *Anatomy of the Fourth Gospel* (Philadelphia: Fortress Press, 1983), pp. 3-4.

[33]Robert A. Spivey, and D. Moody Smith, *Anatomy of the New Testament*, 3rd. ed (New York: Macmillan Publishing Co., Inc., 1982), p. 168: "Those scholars who do not accept the traditional locus of Ephesus tend to favor a Near-Eastern, especially Syrian, rather than Egyptian origin."

[34]See C. K. Barrett, *The Gospel According to John*, 2nd. ed. (Philadelphia: The Westminster Press, 1978), p. 129; J. J. Gunther, "The Alexandrian Gospel and the Letters of John," *Catholic Biblical Quarterly*, 41 (1979), pp. 581-603.

Chapter Two

[1]Brown, *John*, p. LXXXVIII.

[2]Marsh, p. 25.

[3]Dodd, *Interpretation*, p. 6.

[4]William Barclay, *The Gospel of John*, vol. 1 (Edinburgh: The Saint Andrew Press, 1955), p. xx: "The loaves which the lad brought to Jesus were barley loaves (6:9); when Jesus came to the disciples as they crossed the lake in the storm, they had rowed between three and four miles (6:19); there were six stone waterpots at Cana of Galilee (2:6); it is only John who tells of the crown of thorns (19:5), and the four soldiers gambling for the seamless robe as Jesus died (19:23); he knows the exact weight of the myrrh and aloes which were used to anoint the dead body of Jesus (19:39); he remembers how the perfume of the ointment filled the house at the Anointing at Bethany (11:32)."

[5]This could, of course, speak against the authorship of the son of Zebedee, as Barrett points out, *John*, p.121.

⁶Rudolf Schnackenburg, *The Gospel According to St. John*, vol. 1 (New York: Herder and Herder, 1968), p. 102.
⁷Barrett, *John*, p. 142.
⁸See Dom. Ralph Russell, "St. John," *A New Catholic Commentary on Holy Scripture* (London: Nelson, 1969), p. 1031.
⁹Clement of Rome makes no direct reference to John, but there are some similarities: 43 /// Jn 12:28 and 17:3; 49 /// Jn 14:15 and 6:51; 60 /// Jn 17:17. Ignatius' letters, Philadelphians 7:1 /// Jn 3:8; Philadelphians 9:1 /// Jn 10:7, 9; 14:6; Magnesians 8:2 /// Jn 1:18; 8:29; 7:28; Romans 7:3 /// Jn 6:27, 33, 54. Justin's Dialogue with Trypho, 63 /// Jn 3:3-5; 88 /// Jn 1:13; 91 /// 1:20. Melito of Sardis, Homily 78 /// Jn 11:39-44; Homily 95 /// Jn 19:19; Homilies 5 and 7 refer to the paschal lamb. The epistle of Barnabas 12:7 uses the image of the serpent as does Jn 3:14.
¹⁰See J. N. Sanders and B. A. Mastin, *The Gospel According to St. John* (London: A. & C Black, 1968), p. 39.
¹¹Justin, *Dialogue with Trypho*, LXXXI: 4; see also a disciple of Justin, Tatian, *Oratio ad Graecos*, xiii. I, is a direct quote of Jn 1:5; and xix: 4 of Jn 1:3.
¹²Irenaeus, *Against Heresies*, 3. I, I, quoted by Eusebius, *Church History*, V, viii, 4.
¹³Polycrates quoted by Eusebius, *Church History*, 3, 31 and 5, 24, 3f. See Schnackenburg, *John*, p. 81: "The value of Polycrates testimony is, however, lessened by the fact that this second-century bishop confused the 'evangelist' Philip, one of the seven deacons (cf. Acts 6:5; 8; 21:8), whose two daughters he refers to, with the Apostle Philip ('Philip, one of the twelve Apostles'). He could also have made a mistake about the Apostle John."
¹⁴Smith, *John*, p. 7.
¹⁵Schnackenburg, *John*, p. 192.
¹⁶Papias, quoted by Eusebius, *Church History*, III, 39, 4; *Apostolic Constitution*, VII, 46; Eusebius, *Church History*, III, 39, 6; Dionysius of Alexandria, quoted by Eusebius, *Church History*, VII, 25, 16.
¹⁷C. H. Dodd, *Historical Tradition in the Fourth Gospel* (New York: Cambridge University Press, 1963), p. 12.
¹⁸Barclay, p. xxxvi.
¹⁹See Sanders and Mastin, p. 31.
²⁰According to II Tim 4:11 Mark was in Ephesus; see also Marsh, p. 24; Sanders, pp. 8-10, lists possible resemblances between John and Mark; see also Stephen S. Smalley, *John: Evangelist and Interpreter* (Exeter, England: The Paternoster Press, 1978), p. 77.
²¹Kysar, *Fourth Evangelist*, p. 169; also Culpepper, *Anatomy*, p. 47.
²²See Brown, *Community*, p. 33.
²³Bruce Vawter, "The Gospel According to John," *The Jerome*

Biblical Commentary (Englewood Cliffs, NJ: Prentice Hall, 1968), p. 415.

[24]Dominic Crossan, *The Gospel of Eternal Life* (Milwaukee: The Bruce Publishing Co., 1967), p. 4; Leon Morris, *Studies in the Fourth Gospel* (Grand Rapids, MI: William B. Eerdmans Publishing Co., 1969), p. 278, comments: "It is putting a very great strain on our credulity to ask us to believe that a disciple should write a book about scenes and events in which his teacher figured prominently and should pass him by so completely that he does not so much as once mention his name!"

[25]See, for example, William Grossouw, *Revelation and Redemption* (Westminster, MD: The Newman Press, 1955), p. 126.

[26]Hans Conzelmann, *History of Primitive Christianity* (Nashville: Abingdon Press, 1973), p. 157.

[27]Barrett, *John*, p. 4.

[28]Kysar, *Fourth Evangelist*, p. 169.

[29]See Kysar, *Fourth Evangelist*, p. 92; or Thomas E. Crane, *The Message of Saint John* (New York: Alba House, 1980), p. 5.

[30]See Pheme Perkins, "Koinonia in 1 John 1:3-7: The Social Context of Division in the Johannine Letters," *Catholic Biblical Quarterly*, 45 (1983), p. 637.

[31]See Joseph A. Grassi, "The Role of Jesus' Mother in John's Gospel: a Reappraisal," *Catholic Biblical Quarterly*, 48 (1986), p. 72; also Paul S. Minear, "The Original Functions of John 21," *Journal of Biblical Literature*, 102 (1983), p. 95.

[32]E. C. Hoskyns, *The Fourth Gospel* (London: Faber and Faber Ltd., 1947), p. 19: "He does not intend us to busy ourselves with him as though he were himself the goal of our inquiry. He has, in fact, so burnt himself out of his book that we cannot be certain that we have anywhere located him as a clear, intelligible figure in history."

[33]Pheme Perkins, *The Gospel According to John* (Chicago: Franciscan Herald Press, 1978), p. ix.

[34]See Smalley, *Evangelist and Interpreter*, p. 187.

[35]1:23; 2:17; 6:31, 45; 7:38, 42; 8:17; 10:34; 12:15, 38, 40; 13:18; 15:25; 17:12; 19:24, 28, 36, 37.

[36]For other unanswered questions, see 1:46; 4:12; 6:42, 52; 7:20, 26, 35, 42, 48; 8:22, 53; 9:40; 18:37-38.

[37]For a complete list of explanatory notes, see Culpepper, *Anatomy*, p. 17 and also p. 39; see also E. Richard, "Expressions of Double Meaning and Their Function in the Gospel of John," *New Testament Studies*, 31 (1985), pp. 96-112.

[38]See Urban von Wahlde, "A Redactional Technique in the Fourth Gospel," *Catholic Biblical Quarterly*, 38 (1976), pp. 520-533.

[39] See Russell, p. 1027; Crossan, *Gospel of Eternal Life*, pp. 79 and 122.

[40] Culpepper, *Anatomy*, p. 178.

[41] Crane, p. 169.

[42] Paul-Marie de la Croix, *The Biblical Spirituality of St. John* (Staten Island, NY: Alba House, 1966), p. 39.

[43] Raymond E. Brown, "The Gospel Miracles," *New Testament Essays*, p. 245.

[44] See J. Edgar Bruns, "The Use of Time in the Fourth Gospel," *New Testament Studies*, 13 (1966-67), pp. 285-290.

[45] Crane, p. 7.

[46] Russell, p. 1028.

[47] Perkins, *John*, p. 12.

[48] Culpepper, *Anatomy*, p. 165.

[49] See D. Moody Smith, "The Sources of the Gospel of John: An Assessment of the Present State of the Problem," *New Testament Studies*, 10 (1963-64), pp. 336-351; also Robert T. Fortna, *The Gospel of Signs* (New York: Cambridge University Press, 1970), p. 226.

[50] See D. Moody Smith, "John and the Synoptics: Some Dimensions of the Problem," *New Testament Studies*, 26 (1979-80), p. 426; S.I. Buse, "St. John and the Passion Narratives of St. Matthew and St. Luke," *New Testament Studies*, 7 (1960-61), p. 65.

[51] See F. Lamar Cribbs, "St. Luke and the Johannine Tradition," *Journal of Biblical Literature*, 90 (1971), pp. 422-450.

[52] See Frans Neirynck, "John and the Synoptics: the Empty Tomb Stories," *New Testament Studies*, 30 (1984), pp. 161-187; J. Muddiman, "John's Use of Matthew. A British Exponent of the Theory," *Ephemerides Theologicae Lovaniensis*, 59 (1983), pp. 333-337.

[53] See Smith, "John and the Synoptics," p. 443; see also John A. T. Robinson, "The Relationship of the Prologue to the Gospel of St. John," *Twelve More New Testament Studies* (London: SCM Press, 1984), p. 65, where he quotes Professor Pierson Parker: "If the author of the Fourth Gospel used documentary sources, he wrote them all himself."

[54] Brown, *John*, p. L.

[55] See Kysar's synthesis of opinions, *Fourth Evangelist*, pp. 38-54.

[56] See Kysar, *Fourth Evangelist*, pp. 50-53

[57] Morris, p. 83.

[58] Barclay, p. xxxviii; Kee, p. 216; Smith, *John*, p. 62.

[59] See Smalley, *Evangelist and Interpreter*, p. 69; also D. George Vanderlip, *Christianity According to John* (Philadelphia: The Westminster Press, 1975), p. 28: "The inclusion of the phrase 'urged on by his disciples' supports the suggestion of a group clustered around the author."

⁶⁰For arguments in favor of an early date, see Morris, pp. 288-290, where he lists the following: ignorance of the Synoptic tradition, absence of the virgin birth account, use of "disciples" rather than "apostles", Chapter 5 mentioning that there *is* a pool in Jerusalem, and affinities with Qumran. Although Kysar *Fourth Evangelist*, p. 168, considers an early date a minority opinion, he adds: "a later date for the gospel is no longer as necessary as it once was thought to be."

Chapter Three

¹Clinton D. Morrison, "Mission and Ethic: An Interpretation of John 17," *Interpretation*, 19 (1965), p. 259.

²Morris, p. 119.

³See Smith, *John*, p. 91.

⁴See Culpepper, *Anatomy*, p. 68.

⁵See Ernst Käsemann, *The Testament of Jesus* (Philadelphia: Fortress Press, 1968), p. 36.

⁶See Kysar, *Maverick Gospel*, p. 59.

⁷Morris, p. 70.

⁸Crossan, p. 44.

⁹Käsemann, p. 20.

¹⁰Kysar, *Fourth Evangelist*, p. 207.

¹¹Karl Schelkle, "John's Theology of Man and the World," *A Companion to John*, Michael J. Taylor, ed. (New York: Alba House, 1977), p. 137.

¹²Kysar, *Maverick Gospel*, p. 63.

¹³E. K. Lee, *The Religious Thought of St. John* (London: SPCK, 1962), p. 230.

¹⁴Robert T. Fortna, "From Christology to Soteriology," *Interpretation*, 27 (1973), p. 41.

¹⁵Read the following passages for an appreciation of "seeing" in John: 1:14, 50-51; 3:11, 32; 5:19; 6:40; 9:39; 14:7, 9; 17:24; 19:35; 20:8, 25, 29; for the links between "knowing" and "believing" read: 6:69; 8:31-32; 17:7-8, 21-23; for the links between "knowing" and "seeing" read: 6:69; 14:7, 16-17; 16:30; 17:8.

¹⁶Dodd, *Interpretation*, p. 167.

¹⁷Kysar, *Maverick Gospel*, p. 51.

¹⁸Culpepper, *Anatomy*, p. 124.

¹⁹For the various opinions see: Vanderlip, p. 57; David G. Deeks, "The Prologue of St. John's Gospel," *Biblical Theology Bulletin*, 6 (1976), pp. 62-78; Kysar, *Maverick Gospel*, p. 24; Schnackenburg, *John*, p. 56.

[20]Kysar, *Maverick Gospel*, p. 30.
[21]Brown, *Community*, p. 28.

Chapter Four

[1]See Wilbert F. Howard, *The Fourth Gospel in Recent Criticism and Interpretation*, revised by C. K. Barrett (London: Epworth, 1955); Kysar, *Fourth Evangelist*; Bruce Vawter, "Some Recent Developments in Johannine Theology," *Biblical Theology Bulletin*, 1 (1971), pp. 30-58; D. Moody Smith, "Johannine Christology: Some Reflections on Its Character and Delineation," *New Testament Studies*, 21 (1974-75), pp. 222-248; Robert Kysar, "Community and Gospel: Vectors in Fourth Gospel Criticism," *Interpretation*, 31 (1977), pp. 355-366; "The Gospel of John in Current Research," *Religious Studies Review*, 9 (1983), pp. 314-323; Moloney, "Revisiting John," pp. 9-15; John F. O'Grady, "Recent Developments in Johannine Studies," *Biblical Theology Bulletin*, 12 (1982), pp. 54-58; Margaret Pamment, "Focus in the Fourth Gospel," *Expository Times*, 97 (1985), pp. 71-75; Stephen S. Smalley, "Keeping up with recent studies: XII. St John's Gospel," *Expository Times*, 97 (1986), pp. 102-108.

[2]Kysar, *Fourth Evangelist*, p. 11.
[3]See Kysar, "Vectors," pp. 355-366.
[4]See Crossan, p. 109.
[5]1:4; 3:15-16; 5:24, 26, 29, 39, 40; 6:35, 63; 8:12; 10:10, 28; 11:25; 14:6; 17:2, 3; 20:31.
[6]Fortna, "From Christology to Soteriology," p. 40.
[7]See Alan Culpepper, "The Pivot of John's Prologue," *New Testament Studies*, 27 (1980-81), pp. 1-31.
[8]See Vanderlip, p. 32.
[9]J. Edgar Bruns, *The Art and Thought of John* (New York: Herder and Herder, 1969), p. 97.
[10]T. W. Manson, "The Johannnine Jesus as Logos," *A Companion to John*, Michael J. Taylor, ed., p. 49.
[11]Vanderlip, p. 17.
[12]Morrison, p. 260.
[13]Barclay, p. xxv.
[14]Marsh, p. 67.
[15]Kysar, *Fourth Evangelist*, p. 227; see also Brown, *John*, "Appendix III: Signs and Works," pp. 525-532.
[16]Käsemann, p. 53.
[17]Brown, *John*, vol. 2, p. 1090.
[18]See Brown, *John*, pp. 225-226; Barnabas Lindars, *The Gospel*

of John (London: Oliphants, 1972), pp. 245-246, where he suggests: "the question arises whether a miracle was really involved at all." Sanders and Mastin, p. 183: "If it were not for Mark's story ... no one reading John would suppose that he was describing a miracle." Schnackenburg, *John*, p. 520: "it is better not to include the walking on the waters among the signs."

[19] See Brown, *John*, vol. 2, pp. cxxxix-cxlii; W. D. Davies, "The Johannine 'Signs' of Jesus," *A Companion To John*, Michael J. Taylor, ed., p. 93; Marsh, p. 65.

[20] See Stephen S. Smalley, "The Sign in John XXI," *New Testament Studies*, 20 (1973-74), pp. 275-288.

[21] Grassi, p. 69.

[22] Kysar, *Maverick Gospel*, p. 71.

[23] Kysar, *Fourth Evangelist*, p. 71.

[24] See Smalley, *Evangelist and Interpreter*, p. 177; Dodd, *Historical Tradition*, p. 225.

[25] Smalley, *John*, p. 208.

[26] Dodd, *Interpretation*, p. 386.

[27] Kysar, *Fourth Evangelist*, p. 68.

[28] See H. C. Kee, F. W. Young, K. Froehlich, *Understanding the New Testament*, 3rd. ed. (Englewood Cliffs, NJ: Prentice Hall, 1973), p. 349; Dodd, *Interpretation*, p. 451.

[29] See Brown, *John*, vol. 1, pp. xxxiv-xxxv; Crossan, p. 43.

[30] Kee, Young, Froehlich, p. 364.

[31] We will leave the farewell discourses for consideration in Chapter 5.

Chapter Five

[1] Bruce Vawter, "John's Doctrine of the Spirit; A Summary of His Eschatology," *A Companion to John*, Michael J. Taylor ed., p. 177.

[2] Regarding problems of subordinationism met in the expression "The Father is greater than I," see Perkins, *John*, p. 167.

[3] See Lee, p. 67: "The intimate relation between the Father and the Son is illustrated by the fact that in the Fourth Gospel Jesus never refers to God as 'our Father.' He speaks of 'the Father,' or 'my Father,' or sometimes 'the Father who sent me.'"

[4] See Doohan, *Mark*, chapter 4, and *Luke*, chapter 4.

[5] Marsh, p. 72

[6] Spivey and Smith, *Anatomy*, p. 199.

[7] Rudolf Schnackenburg, *The Moral Teaching of the New Testament* (New York: Herder and Herder, 1965), p. 308. Barclay, p. xxxviii,

recalls that the best description he had heard of John's portrait of Jesus was W. M. Macgregor's "What Jesus becomes to a man who has known Him long."

[8] See Kysar, *Maverick Gospel*, p. 42. In the Old Testament see Psalm 35:3; Proverbs 8:22-31; and Sirach 24:1-34.

[9] Brown, *John*, vol. 1, "Appendix IV: Ego Eimi — 'I AM,' " p. 535.

[10] See Lee, pp. 76-89, where he describes the logos in Greek philosophy and in Philo. See the following Old Testament references: Wisdom 9:1-2; 18:14-15; Hosea 6:5-11; Jeremiah 1:9-10; 23:29; Zechariah 5:1-4; Sirach 42:15; 43:26; Psalm 147:15.

[11] See Kee, *Jesus in History*, pp. 243-244; and Brown, *John*, "Appendix II: The Word," pp. 519-524.

[12] Kysar, *Fourth Evangelist*, p. 197.

[13] See Jeff Staley, "The Structure of John's Prologue: Its Implications for the Gospel's Narrative Structure," *Catholic Biblical Quarterly*, 48 (1986), p. 249.

[14] See J. M. Boise, *Witness and Revelation in the Gospel of John* (Grand Rapids, MI: Zondervan, 1970), p. 40.

[15] Lee, p. 68; Kysar, *Maverick Gospel*, p. 39; Francis J. Moloney, *The Johannine Son of Man* (Rome: LAS., 1976), p. 208: "In John, Jesus speaks of his sonship twenty times (3:16, 17, 18; 5:18 (twice), 20, 21, 22, 23 (twice), 25, 26; 6:40; 8:35-36; 10:36; 11:4; 14:13; 17:1 (twice); four times it is a Johannine comment (3:35, 36 (twice); 20:31); it appears once in the prologue (1:18) and four times on the lips of others (1:34 — John the Baptist; 1:49 — Nathaniel; 11:27 — Martha; 19:7 — the 'Jews')."

[16] Brown, *Community*, p. 26.

[17] Smalley, *Evangelist and Interpreter*, p. 213; Kysar, *Maverick Gospel*, p. 35; Kee, *Jesus in History*, p. 242.

[18] Moloney, *Son of Man*, p. 220; see also p. 21 for his summary of positions regarding the Son of Man passages.

[19] See Kysar, *Maverick Gospel*, p. 7.

[20] See Brown, *John*, vol. 2, pp. 555-558.

[21] See J. Painter, "The Farewell Discourses and the History of Johannine Christianity," *New Testament Studies*, 27 (1980-81), pp. 525-543.

[22] See Fernando F. Segovia, "The Theology and Provenance of John 15:1-17," *Journal of Biblical Literature*, 101 (1982), pp. 115-128; "John 15:18-16:4a: A First Addition to the Original farewell Discourse?" *Catholic Biblical Quarterly*, 45 (1983), pp. 210-230; "The Structure, Tendenz, and Sitz im Leben of John 13:31-14:31," *Journal of Biblical Literature*, 104 (1985), pp. 471-493.

[23] Käsemann, *Testament*, p. 5.

[24] See Dodd, *Tradition*, p. 150: "The evidence of the few passages

which suggest prima facie literary dependence of the Fourth Gospel upon the others in the Passion narrative is not sufficient to prove such dependence. On the contrary there is cumulative evidence that the Johannine version represents an independent strain of the common oral tradition."

[25] Bruns, *Art and Thought*, p. 42.

[26] See David Resberger, "The Politics of John: The Trial of Jesus in the Fourth Gospel," *Journal of Biblical Literature*, 103 (1984), pp. 345-411.

[27] The trial scene develops in nine stages: Introduction 18:28; 1st scene: 18:29-32; 2nd scene 18:33-38a; 3rd scene 18:38b-40; 4th scene 19:1-3; 5th scene 19:4-7; 6th scene 19:8-12; 7th scene 19:13-15; Conclusion 19:16. The scenes alternate between Jesus going out to the darkness of the disbelieving crowd that accuses him as a malefactor, prefers Barabbas, demands the crucifixion; and the revelations of Jesus as truth, king, the one who has power from above.

[28] The scene at Calvary is again arranged chiastically, hinged on 19:25-27: the founding of the first community.

[29] See Kysar, *Fourth Evangelist*, p. 140: "Jesus dies as the priests are preparing the paschal lambs in the temple (19:14); his blood is poured out like the paschal victim's (19:34); no bone in his body is broken in accord with the treatment of the paschal lamb (19:33-36 and Exodus 12:46; Numbers 9:12); and finally the reference to the hyssop (19:29) which is unique to the fourth gospel recalls Exodus 12:22."

[30] See Lindars, p. 602.

[31] Kysar, *Maverick Gospel*, p. 38.

[32] Brown, *John*, vol. 2, pp. 1045-1046.

[33] Vawter, "John's Doctrine of the Spirit," p. 178.

[34] See Brown, *John*, vol. 2, "Appendix V: The Paraclete," pp. 1135-1144.

[35] See Culpepper, *Anatomy*, p. 43; Kysar, *Maverick Gospel*, pp. 95-96.

Chapter Six

[1] See the chapters on discipleship: Doohan, *Luke*, Chapter 6; *Matthew*, Chapter 6; *Mark*, Chapter 5.

[2] Russell, "St. John," p. 1035.

[3] See R. Collins, "Discipleship in John's Gospel," *Emmanuel*, 91 (1985), pp. 248-255.

[4] See Sandra Schneiders, "Women in the Fourth Gospel and the

Role of Women in the Contemporary Church," *Biblical Theology Bulletin*, 12 (1982), pp. 35-45; J. Kopas, "Jesus and Women: John's Gospel," *Theology Today*, 41 (1984), pp. 201-205.

[5]Schneiders, "Women," p. 41.
[6]Schneiders, "Women," p. 41.
[7]See Francis J. Moloney, "John 20: A Journey Completed," *Australian Catholic Record*, 59 (1982), pp. 417-432.
[8]Nathaniel, one of the early disciples, is found under the fig tree, which in rabbinical lore was the tree of Torah study, possibly suggesting John's conviction that true belief in Moses would lead to a recognition of Jesus (1:47-49; 5:46).
[9]See Francis J. Moloney, "From Cana to Cana (Jn 2:1-4:54) and the Fourth Evangelist's Concept of Correct (and Incorrect) Faith," *Salesianum*, 40 (1978), pp. 817-843.
[10]Culpepper, *Anatomy*, p. 135.
[11]See Culpepper, *Anatomy*, pp. 146-148.
[12]Perkins, *John*, p. 23.
[13]Kysar, *Maverick Gospel*, p. 71.
[14]Culpepper, *Anatomy*, p. 147.
[15]Sandra Schneiders, "Reflections on Commitment in the Gospel According to John," *Biblical Theology Bulletin*, 8 (1978), p. 45.
[16]See Kysar, *Maverick Gospel*, p. 80.
[17]Kysar, *Maverick Gospel*, p. 76.
[18]See Dodd, *Interpretation*, p. 186.
[19]See Schnackenburg, *John*, p. 573.
[20]Russell, "St. John," p. 1035.
[21]Morrison, p. 260.
[22]See Thomas Barrosse, "The Johannine Relationship of Love to Faith," *A Companion to John*, Michael J. Taylor, ed., pp. 159-175.
[23]The uses of love are as follows: agape/agapan: Mt 9, Mk 6, Lk 14, Jn 44, 1 Jn 46; philein: Mt 5; Mk 1; Lk 2; Jn 13.
[24]Spivey and Smith, p. 196.

Chapter Seven

[1]See Doohan, *Matthew*, Chapter 5, *Mark*, Chapter 6, and *Luke*, Chapter 5.
[2]Käsemann, p. 27.
[3]Lindars, *John*, p. 195.
[4]Smalley, *Evangelist and Interpreter*, p. 234.
[5]Paul S. Minear, "The Audience of the Fourth Evangelist," *Interpretation*, 31 (1977), p. 353.
[6]See Brown, *Community*, p. 19.

[7] John F. O'Grady, "Individualism and Johannine Ecclesiology," *Biblical Theology Bulletin*, 5 (1975), p. 260.

[8] Joseph Crehan, *The Theology of St. John* (London: Darton, Longman, and Todd, 1965), p. 32; see also Crossan, p. 116, where he gives the following Old Testament references to the vine: Hosea 10:1-2; Isaiah 5:1-7; 27:2-5; Jeremiah 2:21-22; 12:10-11; Ezekiel 15:1-8; 17:1-10; 19:10-14; Psalm 80.

[9] Segovia, "Theology and Provenance of John," p. 126.

[10] See John F. O'Grady, "The Good Shepherd and the Vine and the Branches," *Biblical Theology Bulletin*, 8 (1978), pp. 86-89; Severino Pancaro, "The Relationship of the Church and Israel in the Gospel of St. John," *New Testament Studies*, 21 (1974-75), pp. 396-405.

[11] See Severino Pancaro, "'People of God' in St. John's Gospel?" *New Testament Studies*, 16 (1969-70), pp. 114-129.

[12] Charles H. Giblin, "Confrontations in John 18:1-27," *Biblica*, 65 (1984), p. 230.

[13] See Brown, *John*, pp. 910-913.

[14] Smalley, *Evangelist and Interpreter*, p. 129; Brown, "The Johannine Sacramentary," *New Testament Essays*, pp. 51-75.

[15] See K. Matsunaga, "Is John's Gospel Anti-Sacramental? — A New Solution in Light of the Evangelist's Milieu," *New Testament Studies*, 27 (1980-81), pp. 516-524.

[16] See Francis J. Moloney, "When is John Talking about Sacraments?" *Australian Biblical Review*, 30 (1982), pp. 10-33.

[17] Brown, "The Eucharist and Baptism in John," *New Testament Essays*, p. 128.

[18] Lindars, p. 340.

[19] G. H. C. MacGregor, "The Eucharist in the Fourth Gospel," *New Testament Studies*, 9 (1962-63), p. 112.

[20] MacGregor, p. 117.

[21] See Brown, *John*, p. 248: "Thus, even if we cannot be sure of every detail, the eucharistic coloring of the Johannine account of the multiplication seems beyond doubt."

[22] See MacGregor, p. 118: "The objection, 'How can this man give us his flesh to eat?' is quite incredible in Jesus' own day; but it is exactly the argument met with at the end of the century. Indeed the whole setting belongs to a later age when the Eucharist had become the main target of the Jewish attack on Christianity"; see also James D. G. Dunn, "John VI — A Eucharistic Discourse?" *New Testament Studies*, 17 (1970-71), pp. 328-338.

[23] For some possible connections with the Eucharist see my article, "Eucharist and Group Asceticism," *Sisters Today*, 46 (1975), pp. 586-589.

[24] C. K. Barrett, *The Gospel of John and Judaism* (London: SPCK, 1975), p. 74

[25] Kysar, *Fourth Evangelist*, p. 247.

[26] Kysar, *Fourth Evangelist*, p. 245.

[27] See Doohan, *Mark*, pp. 64-66.

[28] See Brown, *John*, pp. 107-109; Juan Alfaro, "The Mariology of the Fourth Gospel: Mary and the Struggles for Liberation," *Biblical Theology Bulletin*, 10 (1980), pp. 3-16; Grassi, pp. 67-80.

[29] Paul S. Minear, *John: The Martyr's Gospel* (New York: The Pilgrim Press, 1984), p. 145.

[30] Robert Kysar, *John's Story of Jesus* (Philadelphia: Fortress Press, 1984), pp. 19-20.

[31] See Perkins, *John*, p. 74.

[32] Michael J. Taylor, *John: The Different Gospel* (Staten Island, NY: Alba House, 1983), p. 256.

BIBLIOGRAPHY

Alfaro, Juan. "The Mariology of the Fourth Gospel: Mary and the Struggles for Liberation." *Biblical Theology Bulletin*, 10 (1980), pp. 3-16.
Barclay, William. *The Gospel of John.* vol. 1. Edinburgh: The Saint Andrew Press, 1955.
Barrett, C. K. *The Gospel of John and Judaism.* London: SPCK., 1975.
_____ *The Gospel According to St. John*, 2nd. ed. Philadelphia: The Westminster Press, 1978.
Barrosse, Thomas. "The Johannine Relationship of Love to Faith." *A Companion to John.* Michael J. Taylor, ed., pp. 159-175.
Boice, J. M. *Witness and Revelation in the Gospel of John.* Grand Rapids, MI: Zondervan, 1970.
Brown, Raymond E. *The Gospel According to John.* New York: Doubleday and Co., Inc., vol. 1, 1966, vol. 2, 1970.
_____ *New Testament Essays.* New York: Doubleday and Co., Inc., 1968.
_____ *The Community of the Beloved Disciple.* New York: Paulist Press, 1979.
Bruns, Edgar J. "The Use of Time in the Fourth Gospel." *New Testament Studies*, 13 (1966-67), pp. 285-290.
_____ *The Art and Thought of John.* New York: Herder and Herder, 1969.
Buse, S. Ivor. "St. John and the Passion Narratives of St. Matthew and St. Luke." *New Testament Studies*, 7 (1960-61), pp. 65-76.
Collins, R. "Discipleship in John's Gospel." *Emmanuel*, 9 (1985), pp. 248-255.
Conzelmann, Hans. *History of Primitive Christianity.* Nashville: Abingdon Press, 1973.
Crane, Thomas E. *The Message of Saint John.* New York: Alba House, 1980.
Crehan, Joseph. *The Theology of St. John.* London: Darton, Longman, and Todd, 1965.
Cribbs, F. Lamar. "St. Luke and the Johannine Tradition." *Journal of Biblical Literature*, 90 (1971), pp. 422-450.

Crossan, Dominic. *The Gospel of Eternal Life*. Milwaukee: The Bruce Publishing Co., 1967.
Culpepper, Alan R. "The Pivot of John's Prologue." *New Testament Studies*, 27 (1980-81), pp. 1-31.
_____ *Anatomy of the Fourth Gospel*. Philadelphia: Fortress Press, 1983.
Davies, W. D. "The Johannine 'Signs' of Jesus." *A Companion to John*, Michael J. Taylor, ed., pp. 91-115.
Deeks, David G. "The Structure of the Fourth Gospel." *New Testament Studies*, 15 (1968-69), pp. 107-129.
_____ "The Prologue of St. John's Gospel." *Biblical Theology Bulletin*, 6 (1976), pp. 62-78.
De La Croix, Paul-Marie. *The Biblical Spirituality of St. John*. Staten Island, NY: Alba House, 1966.
Dodd, C. H. *Historical Tradition in the Fourth Gospel*. New York: Cambridge University Press, 1963.
_____ *The Interpretation of the Fourth Gospel*. New York: Cambridge University Press, 1968.
Doohan, Helen. *Leadership in Paul*. Wilmington, Del: Michael Glazier, Inc., 1984.
Doohan, Leonard. "Eucharist and Group Ascetism," *Sisters Today*, 46 (1975), pp. 586-589.
_____ *Luke: The Perennial Spirituality*. 2nd. ed. Santa Fe: Bear and Co., 1985.
_____ *Matthew: Spirituality for the 80s and 90s*. Santa Fe: Bear and Co., 1985.
_____ *Mark: Visionary of Early Christianity*. Santa Fe: Bear and Co., 1986.
Duling, Dennis C. *Jesus Christ Through History*. New York: Harcourt Brace Jovanovich, Inc., 1979.
Dunn, James D. G. "John VI — A Eucharistic Discourse?" *New Testament Studies*, 17 (1970-71), pp. 328-338.
Filson, Floyd V. *A New Testament History*. Philadelphia: The Westminster Press, 1966.
Fortna, Robert T. *The Gospel of Signs*. Cambridge: University Press, 1970.
_____ "From Christology to Soteriology." *Interpretation* 27 (1973), pp. 31-47.
Freed, Edwin D. "Samaritan Influence in the Gospel of John." *Catholic Biblical Quarterly*, 30 (1968), pp. 580-587.
Freyne, Sean. *The World of the New Testament*. Wilmington, Del: Michael Glazier, Inc., 1980.
Giblin, Charles Homer. "Confrontations in John 18:1-27." *Biblica*, 65 (1984), pp. 210-232.

Grassi, Joseph A. "The Role of Jesus' Mother in John's Gospel: A Reappraisal." *Catholic Biblical Quarterly*, 48 (1986), pp. 67-80.

Grossouw, William. *Revelation and Redemption.* Westminster, MD: The Newman Press, 1955.

Gunther, J. J. "The Alexandrian Gospel and the Letters of John." *Catholic Biblical Quarterly*, 41 (1979), pp. 581-603.

Harrington, Wilfrid J. *Key to the Bible*, vol. 1. New York: Doubleday and Co., Inc., 1976.

Hoskyns, E. C. *The Fourth Gospel.* London: Faber and Faber, Ltd., 1947.

Howard, W. F. *The Fourth Gospel in Recent Criticism and Interpretation.* Rev. ed. by C. K. Barrett. London: Epworth, 1955.

Käsemann, Ernst. *The Testament of Jesus.* Philadelphia: Fortress Press, 1968.

Kee, Howard Clark. *Jesus in History.* 2nd. ed. New York: Harcourt Brace and Jovanovich, Inc., 1977.

King, J. S. "R. E. Brown on the History of the Johannine Community." *Scripture Bulletin*, 13 (1983), pp. 26-30.

Kopas, J. "Jesus and Women: John's Gospel." *Theology Today*, 41 (1984), pp. 201-205.

Kysar, Robert. *The Fourth Evangelist and His Gospel.* Minneapolis: Augsburg Publ. House, 1975.

———— *John: The Maverick Gospel.* Atlanta: John Knox Press, 1976.

———— "Community and Gospel: Vectors in Fourth Gospel Criticism." *Interpretation*, 31 (1977), pp. 355-366.

———— "The Gospel of John in Current Research." *Religious Studies Review*, 9 (1983), pp. 314-323.

———— *John's Story of Jesus.* Philadelphia: Fortress Press, 1984.

Leaney, A. R. C. *The Jewish and Christian World: 200 BC to AD 200.* New York: Cambridge University Press, 1984.

Lee, E. K. *The Religious Thought of St. John.* London: SPCK., 1962.

Lieu, J. M. "Gnosticism and the Gospel of John." *Expository Times*, 90 (1979), pp. 233-237.

Lindars, Barnabas. *The Gospel of John.* London: Oliphants, 1972.

MacGregor, G. H. C. "The Eucharist in the Fourth Gospel." *New Testament Studies*, 9 (1962-63), pp. 111-119.

Manson, T. W. "The Johannine Jesus as Logos." *A Companion to John.* Michael J. Taylor ed., pp. 33-58

Marsh, John. *Saint John.* Harmondsworth, England: Penguin Books, 1968.

Matsunaga, K. "Is John's Gospel Anti-Sacramental? A New Solution in Light of the Evangelist's Milieu." *New Testament Studies*, 27 (1980-81), pp. 516-524.

Minear, Paul S. "The Audience of the Fourth Evangelist." *Interpretation*, 31 (1977), pp. 339-354.
_____ "The Original Functions of John 21." *Journal of Biblical Literature*, 102 (1983), pp. 85-98.
_____ *The Martyr's Gospel*. New York: Pilgrim Press, 1984.
Moloney, Francis J. *The Johannine Son of Man*. Rome: LAS., 1976.
_____ "From Cana to Cana (Jn 2:1-4:54) and the Fourth Evangelist's Concept of Correct (and Incorrect) Faith." *Salesianum*, 40 (1978), pp. 817-843.
_____ "Revisiting John." *Scripture Bulletin*, 11 (1980), pp. 9-15.
_____ "When is John Talking about Sacraments?" *Australian Biblical Review*, 30 (1982), pp. 10-33.
_____ "John 20: A Journey Completed." *Australian Catholic Record*, 59 (1982), pp. 417-432.
Morris, Leon. *Studies in the Fourth Gospel*. Grand Rapids, MI: William B. Eerdmans Publ. Co., 1969.
Morrison, Clinton D. "Mission and Ethic: An Interpretation of John 17." *Interpretation*, 19 (1965), pp. 259-273.
Muddiman, J. "John's Use of Matthew. A British Exponent of the Theory." *Ephemerides Theologicae Lovaniensis*, 59 (1983), pp. 333-337.
Neirynck, Frans. "John and the Synoptics: the Empty Tomb Stories." *New Testament Studies*, 30 (1983-84), pp. 161-187.
O'Grady, John F. "Individualism and Johannine Ecclesiology." *Biblical Theology Bulletin*, 5 (1975), pp. 227-261.
_____ "The Good Shepherd and the Vine and the Branches." *Biblical Theology Bulletin*, 8 (1978), pp. 86-89.
_____ "Recent Developments in Johannine Studies." *Biblical Theology Bulletin*, 12 (1982), pp. 54-58.
Painter, J. "The Farewell Discourses and the History of Johannine Christianity." *New Testament Studies*, 27 (1980-81), pp. 525-543.
Pamment, Margaret. "Focus in the Fourth Gospel," *Expository Times*, 97 (1985), pp. 71-75.
Pancaro, Severino. " 'People of God' in St. John's Gospel?" *New Testament Studies*, 16 (1969-70), pp. 114-129.
_____ "The Relationship of the Church to Israel in the Gospel of St. John." *New Testament Studies*, 21 (1974-75), pp. 396-405.
Perkins, Pheme. "Koinonia in 1 John 1:3-7: The Social Context of Division in the Johannine Letters." *Catholic Biblical Quarterly*, 45 (1983), pp. 631-641.
_____ *The Gospel According to John*. Chicago: Franciscan Herald Press, 1978.
Resberger, David. "The Politics of John: The Trial of Jesus in the

Fourth Gospel." *Journal of Biblical Literature*, 103 (1984), pp. 395-411.

Richard, E. "Expressions of Double Meaning and Their Function in the Gospel of John." *New Testament Studies*, 31 (1985), pp. 96-112.

Robinson, John A. T. "The Relation of the Prologue to the Gospel of St. John." *Twelve More New Testament Studies*. London: SCM Press, Ltd., 1984, pp. 65-76.

Russell, Ralph. "St. John." *A New Catholic Commentary on Holy Scripture*. London: Nelson, 1969, pp. 1022-1074.

Sanders, J. N. and B. A. Mastin. *The Gospel According to St. John*. London: A & C Black, 1968.

Schelkle, Karl. "John's Theology of Man and the World." *A Companion to John*. Michael J. Taylor, ed. pp. 127-140.

Schnackenburg, Rudolf. *The Moral Teachings of the New Testament*. New York: Herder and Herder, 1965.

_____ *The Gospel According to St. John*. vol. 1. New York: Herder and Herder, 1968.

Schneiders, Sandra. "Reflections on Commitment in the Gospel According to John." *Biblical Theology Bulletin*, 8 (1978), pp. 40-48.

_____ "Women in the Fourth Gospel and the Role of Women in the Contemporary Church." *Biblical Theology Bulletin*, 12 (1982), pp. 35-45.

Scobie, Charles H. H. "The Origins and Development of Samaritan Christianity." *New Testament Studies*, 19 (1972-73), pp. 390-414.

Segovia, Fernando F. "The Theology and Provenance of John 15:1-17." *Journal of Biblical Literature*, 101 (1982), pp. 115-128.

_____ "John 15:18-16:4a: A First Addition to the Original Farewell Discourse?" *Catholic Biblical Quarterly*, 45 (1983), pp. 210-230.

_____ "The Structure, Tendenz, and Sitz im Leben of John 13:31-14:31." *Journal of Biblical Literature*, 104 (1985), pp. 471-493.

Smalley, Stephen S. "The Sign in John XXI." *New Testament Studies*, 20 (1973-74), pp. 275-288.

_____ *John: Evangelist and Interpreter*. Exeter, England: The Paternoster Press, 1978.

_____ "Keeping up with Recent Studies: XII. St. John's Gospel." *Expository Times*, 97 (1986), pp. 102-108.

Smith, D. Moody. "The Sources of the Gospel of John: An Assessment of the Present State of the Problem." *New Testament Studies*, 10 (1963-64), pp. 336-351.

_____ "Johannine Christology: Some Reflections on Its Character and Delineation." *New Testament Studies*, 21 (1974-75), pp. 222-248.

———— *John: Proclamation Commentaries*. Philadelphia: Fortress Press, 1976.

———— "John and the Synoptics: Some Dimensions of the Problem." *New Testament Studies*, 26 (1979-80), pp. 425-444.

Spivey, Robert A., and D. Moody Smith. *Anatomy of the New Testament*. 3rd. ed. New York: Macmillan Publishing Co., Inc., 1982.

Staley, Jeff. "The Structure of John's Prologue: Its Implications for the Gospel's Narrative Structure." *Catholic Biblical Quarterly*, 48 (1986), pp. 241-264.

Taylor, Michael J. ed. *A Companion to John*. New York: Alba House, 1977.

———— *John: The Different Gospel*. Staten Island, NY: Alba House, 1983.

Vanderlip, D. George. *Christianity According to John*. Philadelphia: The Westminster Press, 1975.

Vawter, Bruce. "The Gospel According to John." *The Jerome Biblical Commentary*. Englewood Cliffs, NJ: Prentice Hall, 1968, pp. 414-466.

———— "Some Recent Developments in Johannine Theology." *Biblical Theology Bulletin*, 1 (1971), pp. 30-58.

———— "John's Doctrine of the Spirit; A Summary of His Eschatology." *A Companion to John*. Michael J. Taylor, ed. pp. 177-185.

Von Wahlde, Urban. "A Redactional Technique in the Fourth Gospel." *Catholic Biblical Quarterly*, 38 (1976), pp. 520-533.

INDEX OF SUBJECTS

Alexander the Great 19
AntiChrist 64
Ascension 23, 125
Authority 3, 4, 6, 23, 24, 34, 40, 51, 52, 53, 54, 63, 80, 95, 102, 114, 115, 123, 124, 129, 155, 167, 168, 170, 171, 173, 175
Authorities 11, 25, 117, 166
Baptism 25, 29, 44, 75, 116, 134, 162, 163, 165, 166
Beloved Disciple 2, 3, 33, 34, 37, 38, 39, 40, 41, 51, 52, 53, 54, 62, 99, 125, 126, 129, 144, 146, 160, 167, 169, 170, 174, 175
Call 3, 96, 126
Chiasm 42, 90, 97, 160, 161
Christology 1, 29, 31, 32, 64, 65, 67, 80, 95, 101, 102, 103, 105, 110, 111, 116, 118, 122, 127, 130, 153, 157, 159, 160, 165, 168, 172, 173
Christology, high 10, 14, 30, 80, 110, 125, 127, 130, 138, 166
Church 1, 38, 43, 44, 62, 83, 84, 96, 105, 117, 129, 130, 138, 140, 150, 151, 153, 155, 156, 157, 158, 159, 160, 161, 162, 163, 166, 167, 168, 170, 174, 175
Church, local 4, 6, 25, 54
Community 3, 5, 57, 61, 62, 84, 91, 92, 93, 108, 125, 126, 127, 132, 140, 144, 149, 152, 153, 157, 158, 159, 160, 161, 162, 163, 165, 166, 167, 169, 170
Controversy 55, 83, 84, 121

Conversion 29, 108, 138, 163
Council of Jerusalem 3, 23, 24
Crucifixion 11, 12, 87, 124, 125, 170
Diaspora 22, 29, 30, 31, 40, 55, 80, 81, 83
Disciple(s) 3, 5, 13, 14, 64, 67, 69, 73, 76, 83, 85, 87, 90, 91, 94, 101, 102, 103, 104, 106, 107, 108, 116, 118, 120, 122, 124, 125, 126, 128, 129, 130, 131, 132, 133, 134, 136, 137, 139, 141, 142, 144, 145, 146, 147, 148, 149, 150, 151, 152, 153, 155, 156, 157, 159, 168, 169, 170, 171, 172, 173, 174
Discipleship 1, 3, 6, 10, 38, 110, 126, 131, 132, 133, 135, 137, 139, 140, 142, 147, 153, 162, 168
Discourse(s) 2, 42, 47, 48, 51, 81, 84, 85, 86, 87, 91, 95, 96, 98, 99, 100, 101, 102, 103, 104, 111, 117, 121, 122, 128, 129, 130, 134, 135, 136, 138, 139, 141, 143, 155, 158, 159, 163, 164, 165, 166, 168, 169, 171, 173
Docetism 28, 30, 32, 54, 55, 81, 119
Ecclesiology 31, 82, 84, 156, 158, 159, 160, 161, 166, 168, 173, 175
Eschatology 63, 64, 66, 67, 82
Essenes 18
Eucharist 47, 121, 162, 164, 165, 166
Evangelization 25

Faith 1, 2, 3, 4, 5, 9, 13, 14, 25, 26, 29, 41, 45, 51, 57, 59, 60, 63, 65, 66, 68, 79, 80, 84, 88, 92, 93, 96, 97, 98, 102, 104, 105, 109, 113, 125, 129, 131, 134, 138, 139, 140, 141, 144, 145, 146, 147, 148, 149, 150, 152, 153, 156, 157, 167, 168, 169, 173, 175

Father 2, 13, 34, 43, 64, 69, 70, 72, 73, 86, 88, 89, 90, 91, 92, 94, 97, 99, 102, 103, 105, 106, 107, 108, 109, 110, 111, 112, 113, 114, 115, 118, 119, 122, 124, 125, 127, 128, 129, 130, 135, 136, 137, 141, 143, 144, 147, 148, 149, 150, 151, 152, 153, 155, 156, 158, 159, 164, 168, 171, 173, 174, 175

Feasts 85, 86, 103, 111, 117, 121, 128, 132, 145, 147

Forgiveness 125, 157

Freedom 6, 43, 91, 92, 107, 167

Glory 1, 34, 46, 52, 57, 59, 64, 72, 73, 75, 85, 87, 97, 105, 111, 116, 119, 120, 127, 130, 136, 150, 151, 156, 157, 174

Good Shepherd 57, 68, 89, 101, 103, 108, 112, 116, 133, 159, 160, 167

Gnosticism 27, 28, 31, 32, 36, 55, 56, 67, 73, 80, 81, 119

Great Church — see Mother Church

Hellenists 23, 24

Heresy (ies) 9, 26, 84

Holy Spirit 2, 90, 91, 106, 128, 129, 130, 135, 144, 150, 151, 155, 157, 163

Hour 64, 65, 97, 104, 106, 108, 119, 122

Humanity of Jesus 1, 30, 119

Irony 45, 101, 124, 138

Jerusalem 16, 24, 25, 46, 59, 60, 80, 85, 118, 120, 131, 172

"Jews, the" 29, 44, 56, 83, 123, 124, 138

John the Baptist 10, 18, 29, 47, 59, 60, 74, 75, 85, 89, 111, 116, 117, 120, 127, 137, 142, 145, 161, 172, 173

John the Baptist, anti-baptist 27, 55

John the Baptist, followers of 10, 28, 37, 75, 80, 81, 136

John's community (Johannine community) 2, 3, 10, 26, 28, 29, 30, 31, 39, 41, 52, 54, 56, 61, 74, 75, 77, 79, 80, 81, 82, 88, 99, 102, 116, 121, 122, 124, 125, 129, 130, 134, 136, 137, 138, 139, 153, 161, 162, 165, 166, 167, 170, 173, 174, 175

Judaism 55, 80, 120, 121

Judgment 2, 63, 65, 66, 67, 69, 70, 71, 75, 103, 104, 107, 109, 118, 135, 141, 142

Kingdom of God (of heaven) 42, 46, 63, 64, 67, 69, 70, 75, 90, 92, 115, 118, 123, 127, 128, 134, 148, 153, 155, 156, 163

Last Supper 94, 111, 121, 139, 140, 147, 151, 162, 164, 165

Letters (of John) 30, 53, 54, 64, 81, 168

Life 2, 5, 68, 69, 70, 71, 72,

73, 74, 76, 77, 79, 86, 88, 89, 90, 91, 92, 93, 95, 98, 99, 101, 102, 103, 104, 107, 108, 109, 110, 112, 113, 115, 118, 124, 128, 129, 130, 132, 133, 134, 135, 136, 141, 142, 143, 144, 148, 149, 151, 152, 153, 155, 158, 159, 160, 162, 163, 164, 165, 167, 168, 169, 172, 175

Light 2, 5, 46, 57, 58, 65, 67, 68, 69, 70, 72, 74, 75, 76, 77, 86, 88, 99, 102, 103, 106, 112, 113, 114, 116, 123, 124, 128, 135, 136, 141, 142, 143, 144, 149, 151, 155, 157

Lord's Supper 25, 59

Love 1, 3, 5, 63, 68, 73, 84, 91, 92, 93, 105, 106, 107, 108, 110, 115, 116, 122, 124, 125, 129, 135, 136, 139, 141, 147, 149, 150, 151, 152, 153, 155, 157, 158, 159, 160, 161, 165, 166, 167

Love, God's 71, 88, 91, 113, 150, 162

Mary 37, 38, 44, 119, 139, 145, 160, 170

Messiah 12, 49, 73, 76, 88, 99, 102, 110, 116, 117, 119, 127, 137, 139, 172

Ministry 25, 102, 104, 106, 107, 120, 123, 126, 127, 133, 136, 137, 141, 145, 151, 168, 171, 172, 174

Ministry of Jesus 10, 12, 34, 43, 46, 50, 54, 59, 60, 66, 70, 85, 86, 94, 97, 98, 99, 102, 107, 109, 111, 112, 120, 171

Miracle(s) 45, 93, 94, 95, 96, 147

Missionary expansion 10, 24, 26

Morality 1, 5, 69

Mother Church (Great Church) 3, 6, 9, 14, 30, 32, 54, 63, 80, 84, 122, 125, 126, 167, 170, 175

Orthodoxy 10, 11, 25, 26, 32, 88

Parable(s) 11, 91, 93, 95, 96

Paraclete 47, 122, 128, 129, 130, 144, 157, 167

Parallelism 42, 43, 90, 101, 118

Passion 46, 68, 76, 85, 86, 91, 97, 111, 122, 152, 160

Paul 3, 22, 23, 25, 26, 35, 100, 158

Persecution 23, 24, 31, 66, 142, 167, 172

Peter 4, 24, 35, 37, 40, 46, 49, 59, 66, 87, 88, 90, 96, 118, 121, 123, 125, 126, 132, 133, 137, 139, 140, 144, 146, 167, 168, 169, 170, 172, 174, 175

Pharisees 17, 18, 44, 68, 83, 97, 138, 144

Pontius Pilate 11, 118, 123, 124, 138, 172, 173

Prayer 2, 25, 87, 106, 109, 111, 122, 151, 156

Preexistence 1, 2, 3, 5, 30, 46, 61, 63, 64, 73, 74, 111, 112, 114, 116, 143, 145, 175

Prologue 34, 48, 57, 72, 73, 97, 113, 114, 141

Reign of God 11, 92

Resurrection 12, 13, 63, 64, 65, 87, 89, 91, 92, 93, 97, 98, 99, 104, 111, 125, 127, 137, 140, 142, 157, 167,

169, 173, 174
Revelation (Book of) 53, 54, 55, 117, 170
Savior 3, 27, 116, 172
Sadduccees 16, 17
Samaritans 10, 19, 76, 102, 120, 139, 146, 147, 156, 172
Signs 2, 42, 45, 47, 48, 58, 61, 81, 84, 86, 93, 94, 95, 96, 97, 98, 99, 100, 104, 108, 114, 116, 118, 119, 124, 127, 136, 138, 139, 144, 145, 146, 147, 150, 159, 162, 170, 172, 173
Son of God 2, 60, 65, 85, 110, 116, 137, 139, 172
Son of Man 3, 63, 66, 73, 85, 102, 112, 113, 116, 118, 119, 125, 138, 146, 163
Spirit 2, 63, 65, 69, 70, 71, 72, 77, 90, 106, 113, 115, 124, 125, 127, 128, 129, 130, 134, 139, 151, 161, 162, 163, 167, 171, 173, 174
Structure of the gospel 84, 100
Suffering 117, 149
Symbolism 2, 35, 38, 43, 44, 45, 46, 58, 68, 71, 98, 137, 158, 166
Synagogue 22, 29, 55, 117, 122, 145, 166
Synoptics 1, 2, 26, 34, 35, 40, 42, 45, 46, 48, 49, 50, 54, 58, 60, 62, 64, 73, 80, 81, 88, 90, 93, 95, 96, 100, 106, 110, 115, 116, 118, 119, 120, 121, 122, 127, 131, 134, 136, 137, 138, 141, 145, 152, 162, 167, 168, 169, 175
Tradition(s) 2, 3, 6, 35, 37, 40, 41, 49, 50, 51, 52, 53, 55, 62, 65, 82, 83, 101, 123, 166, 170, 174
Truth 2, 5, 57, 58, 60, 67, 68, 69, 70, 71, 72, 75, 76, 77, 89, 90, 102, 103, 106, 107, 112, 113, 114, 116, 118, 124, 128, 129, 130, 134, 135, 139, 141, 143, 149, 150, 151, 155, 162, 172, 173
Twelve, the 3, 4, 23, 25, 131, 137, 141, 155, 168, 169, 175
Union 4, 69, 91, 97, 99, 109, 114, 115, 119, 125, 131, 135, 136, 141, 149, 151, 152, 158, 159, 161, 167, 168, 171, 174, 175
Unity 3, 10, 20, 25, 26, 33, 49, 50, 51, 84, 92, 93, 95, 115, 122, 135, 151, 152, 153, 157, 161, 166, 167, 174
Vocation 6, 171, 172
Vision 4, 5, 6, 34, 52, 53, 58, 72, 76, 77, 79, 92, 110, 116, 149, 157, 166, 175
Wisdom 72, 82, 111, 113, 129, 132, 164
Witness 5, 45, 74, 84, 95, 106, 112, 127, 137, 140, 169, 172, 173
Women 5, 6, 123, 124, 139, 140
Word 2, 34, 46, 57, 63, 67, 69, 71, 72, 73, 89, 90, 91, 103, 105, 107, 111, 112, 113, 114, 116, 126, 127, 132, 134, 135, 141, 142, 148, 149, 151, 155, 157, 158, 161, 171, 173, 174
World 2, 3, 70, 71, 86, 89, 99, 103, 106, 107, 108,

109, 110, 113, 116, 117, 123, 124, 125, 130, 141, 142, 144, 150, 151, 152, 173, 174

INDEX OF AUTHORS

Bacon, B. W. 83
Barrett, C. K. 51, 81, 83
Barth, K. 34
Borgen P. 82
Brown, R. E. 29, 30, 38, 40, 51, 82, 96, 116, 126, 129, 160, 163
Bultmann, R. 27, 48, 81, 95
Clement of Alexandria 37, 52
Clement of Rome 36, 158
Crossan, D. 39
Cullman, O. 82
Culpepper, R. A. 82, 83, 129
Dionysius of Alexandria 37, 54
Dodd, C. H. 82, 100
Ephrem 55
Eusebius 37
Flavius Josephus 11
Fortna, R. T. 48, 81, 82, 95
Gaius of Rome 36, 54, 55
Ignatius of Antioch 55, 158
Irenaeus 36, 37, 81
Justin 36
Käsemann, E. 82
Kysar, R. 28, 40, 82
Lightfoot, J. B. 83
Lindars, B. 51, 81, 163
Marsh, J. 110
Martyn, J. L. 30, 82
Melito of Sardis 36
Moloney, F. J. 82
Origen 36
Papias 35, 37
Polycrates 36
Ritcher, G. 30
Schnackenberg, R. 38, 82
Schneiders, S. 140
Smalley, S. 97
Smith, D. M. 82
Temple, S. 81

Theophilus of Antioch 36, 55
Tatian 36, 37, 55
van Unnik, W. C. 83
Vawter, B. 39
Wilkens, U. 51

INDEX OF SCRIPTURE REFERENCES

Scripture	page
OLD TESTAMENT	
Genesis	
3:15	170
22:6	124
Exodus	
3:14	112
10:1	98
Numbers	
14:11	98
14:22	98
21:9	44
27:16-17	159
Deuteronomy	
7:19	98
18:15-18	117
30:14	113
2 Samuel	
7:7-9	159
1 Kings	
2:35	17
2 Kings	
2:9-10	129
2:15	129
Psalms	
27:1	68
85:8	125
105:39	68
119:105	68, 113
119:107	113
119:130	113
Proverbs	
8:22-31	111
9:4-6	164

Scripture	page
9:5	165
Wisdom	
8:4-6	111
18:15-16	113
Sirach	
24:21	164
Isaiah	
40:11	159
42:1-4	116, 127
42:6	68
49:1-6	116
50:4-9	116
52:13-53:12	116
53:5	125
53:7	116
55:10-11	113
61:1-3	127
Jeremiah	
1:4	113
31:10	159
Ezekiel	
34	44
34:11-16	159
34:23-24	117
Daniel	
2:22	68
Joel	
2:28-29	127
Zechariah	
9:9	44
NEW TESTAMENT	
Matthew	
3:13	10

Scripture	page	Scripture	page
8:5-13	96	1:7	74
9:37-38	156	1:8	29
14:13-33	96	1:9	71, 174
16:16	167	1:9-10	9
18:12-14	159	1:9-12	43
28:17	132	1:9 - 2:11	73
Mark		1:11	61, 63, 132, 141
1:9	10	1:12	69, 90, 107, 133, 141, 147, 149, 152
2:24	11		
3:22	11		
6:32-51	96		
8:29	167		
8:32	132	1:13	133
Luke		1:14	45, 52, 57, 62, 65, 72, 73, 105, 107, 109, 111, 116, 148, 149, 157, 167, 174
2:41-52	13		
3:23	10, 12		
5:1-11	96, 126		
7:1-10	96		
7:36-50	48		
9:10-17	96		
9:20	167	1:15	29, 73, 74, 111, 116
12:32	159		
15:3-7	159	1:16	45, 52, 62, 63, 92, 150, 152
16:19-31	95		
22:14-38	48		
22:19	165	1:17	42, 57, 150
22:39-53	48	1:17-18	73, 88, 172
23:1-25	49	1:18	107, 109, 112, 113, 114, 115, 137
23:25-56	49		
24	49		
John			
1:1	63, 111, 112, 126	1:19-28	172
		1:20	29, 117
1:1-5	43	1:21	35, 117
1:2-3	74	1:23	74
1:4	69, 89, 113	1:25	117
1:5	68, 75	1:27	74
1:6-8	73	1:28	43, 59

Scripture	page	Scripture	page
John *(continued)*		2:1 - 4:54	144
1:29	60, 65, 73, 74, 75, 107, 116, 142, 174	2:3	170
		2:4	61, 120
		2:5	44, 170
		2:6	59
1:29-37	172	2:11	59, 75, 94, 98, 105, 111, 132
1:29-30	60		
1:30	74, 111, 116		
1:32	59, 127	2:12	170
1:32-33	127	2:13	59
1:33	74	2:13-22	46, 95, 120, 162
1:34	110		
1:35	59, 60, 75	2:16	106
1:35-37	75	2:18	75
1:35-51	60	2:18-22	120
1:36	116	2:19-22	43, 75
1:38	137	2:20	10
1:39	42, 44, 132	2:22	42, 43, 147
1:40	37	2:23	95
1:40-41	59	2:23-25	29, 146
1:40-44	169	2:24	145
1:41	46, 73, 117	2:25	121, 141
1:42	42, 46	3:1	173
1:43	60	3:1-2	138
1:43-45	59	3:1-15	47
1:45	73, 119	3:1-21	45, 145
1:45-51	59	3:2	29, 100, 138, 144, 146
1:46	43, 44		
1:47	29, 137		
1:48-49	59	3:3	43, 63, 69, 75, 92, 134
1:49	73, 118		
1:49-51	42	3:3-8	43
1:50-51	116, 118	3:3-15	115
1:51	42, 73	3:5	92, 102, 127, 134, 163
2:1	59, 60, 98, 170		
2:1-11	43, 61, 139, 145	3:5-6	101
		3:6	72, 153
2:1-12	47, 95, 120	3:8	63, 72

Scripture	page	Scripture	page
John *(continued)*		3:31-34	114
3:9-15	42	3:31-36	145
3:11	75, 113, 114, 134, 157, 167	3:33	106
		3:34	91, 115, 128, 167
3:12	102	3:35	106, 108, 109
3:13	114, 118		
3:14	43, 44, 118, 125	3:36	63, 89, 90, 91, 107, 121, 148, 149
3:14-15	91		
3:16	57, 71, 107, 134, 148, 150, 174	4:4-42	45, 47
		4:6	42, 119
		4:7	119
3:16-17	150	4:7-30	139
3:16-18	42, 147	4:10	43, 108
3:17	66, 75, 107, 174	4:10-15	43, 69, 102
		4:12	43, 44
3:18	65, 121	4:13-14	76
3:18-21	75	4:14	89
3:19	65, 68, 102, 114, 142, 151	4:16-17	111
		4:16-18	102
		4:16-26	102
3:19-20	146	4:18	59
3:19-21	151	4:21	65
3:20	113, 142	4:21-24	162
3:20-21	68	4:22	128
3:21	67, 68, 69, 102, 106, 107, 134, 135	4:23	57, 65, 106, 128
		4:23-24	151
		4:24	106, 128
3:22	47	4:25	35, 76
3:22-30	172	4:25-29	145
3:23	59	4:26	46, 49, 76, 117
3:27	74, 133		
3:28	117	4:27	140
3:29	74, 146, 161	4:27-38	102
3:29-30	74	4:29	117
3:31	71, 106, 115, 141	4:32	69
		4:32-34	171

Scripture	page	Scripture	page
John *(continued)*		5:21-25	66
4:34	109, 115, 171	5:22	67, 107, 109, 115
4:34-38	171	5:24	58, 65, 67, 89, 90, 91, 113, 135, 172
4:35	65, 76, 156		
4:38	171		
4:39-42	156		
4:41	113	5:25	65
4:42	116, 146, 147, 172	5:26	88, 107, 109
		5:26-30	66, 102
4:43-45	46	5:27	66, 107, 109, 115
4:43-54	43, 44, 47, 95		
		5:28-29	42, 64, 65, 91
4:43 - 5:1	120		
4:45	146	5:29	142
4:46-54	98, 145	5:30	114
4:48	94, 98, 126, 146, 147	5:31-32	173
		5:33	74
4:50	113, 147	5:33-35	173
4:52	42	5:35	74
4:53	98	5:36	74, 94, 108, 109, 113, 173
4:54	94		
5:1-15	95		
5:2	59	5:37	106
5:5	59	5:38	113, 131
5:6	111	5:39	42, 63, 90, 173
5:11-12	146		
5:15	115, 141, 146	5:40	90, 142, 147
		5:40-44	151
5:16	123	5:42	150
5:17	106, 115	5:42-43	121
5:17-18	115	5:43	133, 143
5:18	99	5:44	106, 149
5:19	42, 119	5:45	142
5:19-29	42	5:45-47	58
5:19-30	43	5:46	42, 90
5:20	106	5:46-47	47
5:21	65, 71, 106, 108	6:1-15	47, 95
		6:1 - 7:1	48

Scripture	page	Scripture	page
John *(continued)*		6:40	64, 91, 110, 164, 165
6:1 - 7:14	120		
6:3	164	6:41	99
6:4	59, 164	6:42	114, 119
6:4-7	137	6:44	64, 90, 109, 133, 148
6:5-7	59		
6:6	111	6:45	63, 135, 148, 155, 165
6:8-9	59		
6:9	59		
6:11	109, 164	6:46	107, 114
6:14	117, 144, 172	6:47	91, 165
		6:48	103
6:14-15	35, 117	6:50	111
6:15	102, 118	6:51	89, 103, 112, 114, 136, 174
6:16-24	95		
6:20	112		
6:22-24	136	6:51-58	164, 165
6:26	94	6:53	115, 118, 119, 165
6:27	102, 107, 118		
		6:53-55	136
6:29	110, 145, 149	6:54	64, 91, 165
		6:56	91, 136, 165
6:30	58, 94, 146	6:57	89, 107, 115
6:32	42, 106, 111	6:58	102, 111
6:32-35	43	6:60	29, 66, 99, 136, 141
6:33	108, 114		
6:35	58, 88, 89, 102, 103, 112, 164, 165	6:60-66	29
		6:61-64	111
		6:62	111, 119
		6:63	72, 90, 113, 128
6:35-45	147		
6:35-50	164	6:64	71
6:36	148	6:65	109, 133, 148
6:37	106, 109, 136	6:66	136, 141, 146
		6:66-67	120
6:37-40	148	6:67	168
6:38	109, 114	6:67-69	169
6:39	64	6:68	90, 113, 133
		6:68-69	66, 142

Scripture	page	Scripture	page
John *(continued)*		7:43	28
6:68-70	169	7:44	120
6:69	147, 148, 172	7:48	145
		7:51	138
6:70	71, 141	7:52	145
7:2-5	146	7:53 - 8:11	103
7:3-5	29, 148	8:3-11	139
7:5	141	8:7	143
7:6	120	8:11	143
7:6-7	71	8:12	68, 89, 103, 112, 113, 165
7:7	143		
7:8	43, 120		
7:14-36	103	8:12-59	103
7:14 - 8:59	121	8:14	58, 111, 114, 172
7:16	58, 109, 114, 119, 171		
		8:15	62
7:17	114	8:15-16	142
7:19	120	8:16	67
7:23	120	8:18	106, 112, 173
7:24	62, 142		
7:25	120	8:19	120
7:26	117	8:20	120, 122
7:27	70, 117	8:21	69, 72, 143
7:28	114	8:23	70, 111, 112, 115, 141, 151
7:28-29	111		
7:30	120, 122	8:23-24	143
7:31	117, 120, 136, 145	8:24	61, 112, 143, 148
7:33	114	8:26	111
7:35	29	8:27-59	70
7:37	89, 128	8:28	109, 112, 114, 119, 125, 148
7:37-38	90, 147, 163		
7:37-39	125, 127		
7:37-52	103	8:29	115
7:39	43, 72, 163	8:30	147
7:40	117, 145, 172	8:31	148, 149, 171
7:40-44	35	8:31-36	58
7:41-42	117	8:31-38	43

Scripture	page	Scripture	page
John *(continued)*		9:5	68, 99, 103, 112
8:32	69, 113, 143, 172	9:5-7	68
8:33-59	42	9:6	120
8:34	69, 143	9:7	44, 59, 115, 138
8:34-36	92		
8:37	69, 90, 113, 142	9:11	146
		9:13-41	66
8:38	109, 114	9:16	29, 144
8:40	69, 114, 149, 172	9:17	146, 172
		9:22	29, 117, 166, 173
8:40-46	69		
8:41	120	9:24-34	17, 59
8:42	111, 114, 115, 150	9:28	121, 145
		9:31	144
8:42-47	151	9:32	99
8:43	70	9:33	146
8:44	69, 70, 115, 141, 142, 143, 149	9:34	144
		9:34-41	58
		9:35	119, 146
8:44-45	69	9:35-37	149
8:46	143	9:35-38	146
8:47	113, 135, 141	9:39	66, 142
		9:39-41	68, 103
8:48	29	9:40	43
8:49	106	9:40-41	120
8:51	42, 70, 71, 148	9:41	121, 146
		10	68
8:53	44	10:1-18	51, 118, 159
8:54	107, 109	10:3	133, 135
8:56	42, 57	10:4-5	133
8:58	112, 148	10:7	103, 112, 159
8:59	120		
9:1-41	43, 44, 95	10:9	103, 112, 159, 160
9:2	144		
9:3	108, 109, 144	10:10	89, 92, 95, 103, 150, 167
9:4	77, 171		

Scripture	page	Scripture	page
John *(continued)*		10:39	120
10:11	93, 112, 133, 159	10:40	43
		10:41	74
10:11-18	44	11:1-44	47, 71, 95, 139
10:12	167		
10:14	112, 133, 159	11:3	38, 139, 161
		11:4	110
10:14-15	88	11:5	139, 161
10:14-18	126	11:11	139, 161
10:15	108, 109, 133	11:12	134
		11:14	111
10:16	103, 153, 155, 159, 171, 174	11:16	59, 138
		11:22	115
		11:24	42
10:17	89, 106, 133	11:25	89, 133
10:17-18	124	11:25-26	65, 89, 99
10:17-28	103	11:25-29	59
10:18	114, 152	11:26	92
10:19-21	28	11:27	65, 114, 139, 167, 173
10:19-39	50		
10:22	44	11:32	140
10:24	110, 117	11:33	119
10:24-25	121	11:35	119
10:25	94	11:36	139, 161
10:25-26	103	11:38	119
10:26	51, 142	11:38-44	42
10:27	135	11:40	111, 147, 148
10:28	89, 92, 103, 150		
		11:41	109
10:29	119, 148	11:41-42	99, 108, 151
10:30	109, 115	11:45	147
10:32	109	11:45-46	148
10:33	120	11:46	97
10:36	108, 109, 110	11:47	146
		11:47-48	173
10:37	94	11:48	17
10:37-38	94, 104, 109	11:50	108
10:38	62, 94, 115, 147	11:50-52	99, 173

215

Scripture	page	Scripture	page
John *(continued)*		12:35	68, 104, 149
11:52	91, 108, 156, 158, 160	12:36	68, 76
11:54	59	12:37	95, 97, 98, 136, 141
12	70	12:40-41	42
12:1-8	46, 120, 139, 140	12:42	29, 145, 166
		12:42-43	29
12:2-8	48	12:43	149, 151, 173
12:5	59		
12:10-11	123	12:44-50	120
12:11	133	12:45	175
12:12-15	44	12:46	58, 68, 70, 113, 114
12:13	118		
12:16	43	12:46-48	42
12:20-22	156	12:47	149
12:20-32	61	12:48	63, 113, 134
12:20-36	47	12:49	109, 113, 114
12:21	137		
12:22	59	12:49-50	114
12:23	76, 119, 120, 122	12:50	109
		13:1	59, 108, 114, 120, 123, 132, 161
12:23-26	156		
12:24	42, 89, 104		
12:25	92, 134, 139, 151	13:1-7	152
		13:1-11	120, 172
12:25-26	104	13:1-17	160
12:26	64, 107, 134, 171, 172	13:1-20	47, 95
		13:2	71
		13:3	114
12:27	109, 119, 123	13:6-10	169
		13:7	43
12:27-28	151	13:12-17	171
12:28	106	13:14	165
12:30-32	174	13:14-15	142, 160
12:31	71	13:15	165
12:31-32	70, 104	13:16	133, 165, 171
12:32	76, 156, 174		
12:34	35, 117, 119, 125	13:17	133, 149
		13:18	71

Scripture	page	Scripture	page
John *(continued)*		14:12	135, 171
13:19	112, 148, 149	14:13	135
		14:13-14	151, 152
13:20	147, 167, 174	14:15	134, 149, 155
13:21	119	14:15-16	151, 167
13:22-24	169	14:15-17	128, 157
13:23	38, 161	14:16	105
13:23-26	37, 38, 174	14:16-17	129
13:24	169	14:17	69, 71, 128, 129
13:26-30	142		
13:27	71	14:18	158
13:30	44, 71, 141, 142	14:19	89
		14:20	171
13:31	66, 119	14:21	92, 106, 134, 149, 150, 155
13:31-14:31	122		
13:33	29		
13:34	152	14:22	70
13:34-35	152	14:23	91, 105, 134, 135, 137, 149, 151, 173
13:35	152, 153		
13:36-38	169		
14:1	92, 109, 148, 149, 155		
		14:24	109, 113, 114
14:2	106	14:26	43, 90, 106, 128, 129, 130, 155, 157, 167
14:2-3	91		
14:3	64		
14:5	59, 139		
14:6	69, 89, 107, 112	14:27	92, 135, 161
		14:28	107, 109, 114, 119, 151
14:7-9	43		
14:8-9	59, 137	14:29	149
14:9	106, 110, 114, 115, 130, 148, 149	14:30	66, 71
		14:31	51, 107, 114
		15:1	51, 112, 158
		15:1-8	159, 171
14:9-10	61	15:1-17	122, 159
14:10	94, 109, 114	15:1 - 16:4	122, 159
14:11	94, 98, 134	15:2	142, 167

217

Scripture	page	Scripture	page
John *(continued)*		15:25	29
15:3	113, 132	15:26	69, 128, 130, 173
15:4	133, 135		
15:4-5	91, 135	15:26-27	128, 157
15:4-10	137	15:27	135, 149, 150, 169, 173
15:5	58, 112, 167		
15:6	167		
15:6-17	152	16:1-4	142, 149
15:7	135, 137, 148, 151, 166, 171	16:2	29, 65, 166, 172
		16:4	43, 149
15:8	106, 173	16:4-33	122
15:9	106, 135, 150, 153, 155, 161, 174	16:5	114
		16:7	69
		16:7-11	128, 130, 157
15:9-10	131	16:8	71
15:9-17	108, 159, 166	16:8-9	144
		16:11	57, 71
15:10	107, 115	16:12-14	128, 130, 157
15:11	92, 161		
15:12	152, 155, 174	16:12-15	150
		16:13	69, 90, 128
15:12-13	92, 152	16:20	92, 142
15:13	152	16:21	71
15:14-17	92	16:23	106
15:15	132	16:24	92, 152
15:16	106, 134, 137, 152, 169, 171, 173	16:25	65
		16:27	92, 106, 108, 114, 151
15:17	135, 155, 174	16:28	107, 111, 114
		16:30	114
15:18-21	142, 149	16:32	65, 115
15:18-27	71, 108, 172	16:33	57, 142, 174
15:18 - 16:4	122, 159	17:1	120, 123
15:19	141	17:1-2	115
15:22-24	144	17:1-5	122
15:24	94, 97	17:1-19	157

Scripture	page	Scripture	page
John *(continued)*		17:26	134, 150
17:1-26	151	17:29	69
17:2	109, 174	18:1	59
17:3	108, 148	18:1-9	70
17:4	113	18:1-12	48
17:5	61, 111, 115	18:1-27	43
17:6	113, 132, 141	18:5	112
		18:5-6	123
17:6-19	122	18:8-9	108
17:8	70, 109, 113, 148, 171	18:10-11	169
		18:11	108
17:9	71	18:15-16	37
17:9-26	107	18:15-17	49
17:11	92, 106, 136, 149, 152	18:15-18	142, 169
		18:16	169
		18:17	169
17:11-12	109	18:25	142, 169
17:12	42	18:25-27	142, 169
17:12-15	71	18:27	169
17:13	92	18:28	42
17:13-19	149	18:28-40	66
17:14	113, 141, 171	18:28 - 19:16	43
17:15	136, 149	18:29 - 19:16	49
17:17	113, 136	18:31	124
17:18	168, 169, 173	18:33	118, 173
		18:36	64, 70
17:19	150	18:36-37	118
17:20	136, 171, 173	18:37	44, 69, 113, 114, 118, 141, 172, 173
17:20-21	157, 174		
17:20-26	122		
17:21	92, 108, 151, 152, 174	18:38	43
		18:39-40	124
17:22	109	19:5	44, 124
17:23	151	19:6	124
17:24	64, 71, 115, 134, 136, 172	19:14	42, 116
		19:15	118, 124
		19:16	124
17:25	106	19:16-42	160

Scripture	page	Scripture	page
John (continued)		20:22-23	157, 165
19:17-42	43	20:23	169
19:19	118	20:24	168
19:19-20	108	20:24-25	139
19:19-37	43	20:24-28	144
19:19-42	49	20:24-29	59
19:20	42	20:26-28	59
19:21-22	118	20:27	120
19:23	59	20:28	110, 112, 139, 173
19:23-24	124		
19:25	140	20:29	144, 147, 149, 150, 157
19:25-27	37, 124, 139, 170		
19:26	169	20:30	95
19:28	124	20:30-31	59, 79, 126, 144, 173
19:29	116, 120		
19:30	124	20:31	73, 88, 90, 93
19:34	163		
19:35	33, 34, 59	21:1-14	95, 169
19:36	116	21:2	37, 137
19:39	59, 138	21:5-11	171
20	49	21:7	37, 38
20:1-2	139, 140	21:8	59
20:1-10	169	21:11	59
20:1-18	144	21:15-17	118, 151, 171
20:2	37	21:15-19	169, 174
20:3-8	4, 59	21:18-23	172
20:3-10	169	21:20	37
20:8	37, 99, 125, 175	21:20-23	38, 169
		21:22	126
20:9	42	21:24	38, 45, 52, 53, 59, 62, 157, 167, 174
20:11-18	139		
20:17	125		
20:18	140, 167		
20:19	125	21:25	45
20:21	115, 125, 149, 150, 157, 167, 168, 169, 171	Acts	
		1:14	38
		2:32	13
		2:36	13

Scripture	page
Acts *(continued)*	
3:15	13
4:10	13
4:13	40
6:2	23
7:1-54	26
8:1-5	23
8:5	23
8:14	23
8:26-40	23
9:26	23
10:40-43	13
11:27-30	25
11:30	23
12:17	23
13:1-3	25
15:5	24
15:6	23
15:6-29	23, 24
15:22-29	25
19:1-7	55
19:3	29
20:17	25
20:18-38	35
20:28	25
20:28-30	159
21:18	25
21:21	24
Romans	
1:4	12
1:8-15	26
6:9	12
1 Corinthians	
11:17-22	164
15:4	12
15:14	13
16:2	25
16:15	25

Scripture	page
2 Corinthians	
8:1-15	25
Galatians	
1:19	23
2:11-14	24
Ephesians	
1:15-23	26
2:20	25
Philippians	
1:1	25
4:10-20	25
Colossians	
1:15-20	26
4:17	25
1 Thessalonians	
5:12	25
1 Timothy	
3:1	25
Titus	
1:7	25
1 Peter	
2:25	159
1 John	
1:1	103
2 John	
1:1	53
3 John	
1	53
9	55
9-10	166
Revelation	
1:1	53
1:4	53
1:9	53
2:9	55

Scripture	page
Revelation *(continued)*	
3:9	55
4:7	33
5:6-14	117
12:1-17	170
18:20	54
21:14	54
22:8	53

www.ingramcontent.com/pod-product-compliance
Lightning Source LLC
Chambersburg PA
CBHW070250230426
43664CB00014B/2475